'What a great snapshot of eve
knowledge has arrived in Int
– *Iver B. Neumann, Professor of international Relations, London School of
Economics, UK*

'The book treats one of the hottest and coolest issues in IR, the question of identity, in a well-informed, earnest, lively, humorous and entertaining manner. It solves the "big issues" and yet makes pertinent observations on what it means to be a Russian, a Northerner, and most interesting, a Borderlander.'
– *Sergei Medvedev, Professor, Higher School of Economics, Moscow, Russia*

'This book [...] gives a good insight into the way of thinking of the Kola Peninsula's ordinary population and, moreover, in an [...] easily understandable way.'
– *Polar Record*

'Borderland Russians is a good read, and its added value stretches from the local level to the bigger questions dealing with identity-formation and everyday narratives.'
– *The Russian Review*

'Hønneland introduces very interesting, big themes for the wide public.'
– *Nordic Journal of Russian and East European Affairs*

'This book is a valuable source for readers interested in identity constructions.'
– *Europe-Asia Studies*

Palgrave Studies in International Relations Series

General Editors:

Knud Erik Jørgensen, Department of Political Science, University of Aarhus, Denmark

Audie Klotz, Department of Political Science, Maxwell School of Citizenship and Public Affairs, Syracuse University, USA

Palgrave Studies in International Relations, produced in association with the ECPR Standing Group for International Relations, will provide students and scholars with the best theoretically-informed scholarship on the global issues of our time. Edited by Knud Erik Jørgensen and Audie Klotz, this new book series will comprise cutting-edge monographs and edited collections which bridge schools of thought and cross the boundaries of conventional fields of study.

Titles include:

Mathias Albert, Lars-Erik Cederman and Alexander Wendt (*editors*)
NEW SYSTEMS THEORIES OF WORLD POLITICS

Barry Buzan and Ana Gonzalez-Pelaez (*editors*)
INTERNATIONAL SOCIETY AND THE MIDDLE EAST
English School Theory at the Regional Level

Geir Hønneland
BORDERLAND RUSSIANS
Identity, Narrative and International Relations

Oliver Kessler, Rodney Bruce Hall, Cecelia Lynch and Nicholas G. Onuf (*editors*)
ON RULES, POLITICS AND KNOWLEDGE
Friedrich Kratochwil, International Relations, and Domestic Affairs

Cornelia Navari (*editor*)
THEORISING INTERNATIONAL SOCIETY
English School Methods

Dirk Peters
CONSTRAINED BALANCING: THE EU'S SECURITY POLICY

Simon F. Reich
GLOBAL NORMS, AMERICAN SPONSORSHIP AND THE EMERGING PATTERNS OF WORLD POLITICS

Robbie Shilliam
GERMAN THOUGHT AND INTERNATIONAL RELATIONS
The Rise and Fall of a Liberal Project

Rens van Munster
SECURITIZING IMMIGRATION
The Politics of Risk in the EU

Palgrave Studies In International Relations Series
Series Standing Order ISBN 978–0230–20063–0

You can receive future titles in this series as they are published by placing a standing order. Please contact your bookseller or, in case of difficulty, write to us at the address below with your name and address, the title of the series and the ISBN quoted above.

Customer Services Department, Macmillan Distribution Ltd, Houndmills, Basingstoke, Hampshire RG21 6XS, England

---

Borderland Russians

Identity, Narrative and International Relations

Geir Hønneland
Research Director, Fridtjof Nansen Institute, Norway

First published 2010 by
Paperback edition published 2013 by
PALGRAVE MACMILLAN

Palgrave Macmillan in the UK is an imprint of Macmillan Publishers Limited, registered in England, company number 785998, of Houndmills, Basingstoke, Hampshire RG21 6XS.

Palgrave Macmillan in the US is a division of St Martin's Press LLC, 175 Fifth Avenue, New York, NY 10010.

Palgrave Macmillan is the global academic imprint of the above companies and has companies and representatives throughout the world.

Palgrave® and Macmillan® are registered trademarks in the United States, the United Kingdom, Europe and other countries.

ISBN: 978–0–230–25267–7 hardback
ISBN: 978–1–137–29731–0 paperback

This book is printed on paper suitable for recycling and made from fully managed and sustained forest sources. Logging, pulping and manufacturing processes are expected to conform to the environmental regulations of the country of origin.

A catalogue record for this book is available from the British Library.

A catalog record for this book is available from the Library of Congress

10 9 8 7 6 5 4 3 2 1
22 21 20 19 18 17 16 15 14 13

Printed and bound in Great Britain by
CPI Antony Rowe, Chippenham and Eastbourne

For Lavrans

The North is textual per se; it is, in a sense, an *Urtext*, a white field, a blank space, a one-sided sheet of paper, a non-referential sign, a quintessential periphery questioning the dominant narratives of modernity. The North is an abode of schizophrenic solitude and unimpeded creativity. It is all about imagination and invention, a mischievous and playful blizzard, a creative lie.

(Medvedev, 2001, p. 94)

Contents

Illustrations

Maps

Photographs

Foreword

Iver B. Neumann

In the north-western corner of Eurasia, Norway and Russia share a 196 kilometer long state boundary. Before it was drawn up in 1821, Saami (then called by others Lapps) predominated. Finns came here for the fish when harvests failed. With the coming of the railway in the very early 20th century, things began to change on the Russian side. Russia finally had an all-year port open to its west, and people poured in. During the Soviet years (1917–91), the population increased from a few thousands to way over a million. With the Soviet Union gone, the Norwegian–Russian border became one of the steepest standard-of-living gradients in the world. State-to-state and local contacts were facilitated by the establishment of the Barents Euro-Arctic Council. This is the book to read about the state of play in this arena of East–West contacts, and Geir Hønneland was the obvious man to write it. He has been hanging around for the entire post-Soviet period, writing about the fishery industry and oil prospecting, chatting with locals and state officials, reading up on the general political literature about Russian–European relations.

The book is particularly valuable for its quotidian focus. An English-language book has a Western audience as its obvious target, and so Hønneland pays particular importance to how Vanka and Masha – that is, so-called ordinary Russians – experience themselves and others. He finds that they self-identify as competent, calm, cultured and considerate. They are so in comparison to their neighbours to the South, that is, other Russians, and, in a lesser degree, to their Western neighbours, the Nords or Norgs, i.e. the Scandinavians, and particularly the Norwegians. 'Southerners', that is, most Russians, they tend to see as boisterous, unclean and cheesy, whereas Scandinavians are quiet, clean and boring.

Hønneland's point of departure may be the everyday, but it is not the end station. The book is ultimately about the similarity in form, or isomorphsm, between everyday life on the one hand, and general politics on the other. The point is not 'that the president and governor speak as they do because Vanya and Masha in Murmansk do so, or Russia acts as it does because the governor speaks as he does – but the narrative resources available to north-west Russians (or the Russian population) might say something about the governor's (or the president's) room for rhetorical manoeuvre'. All Russians, politicians and population alike, share a language, and even when politicians can step outside of what they take for granted and use it instrumentally, they are still bound by the narratives that make Russians and their world what they are.

To a Western reader, this is pretty depressing stuff. There is, first, apathy towards politics. As was seen in the 1990s, when there was ample opportunity to engage in mass politics, the Russian impulse was not to make parties out of different political groupings, but to find a leader and support him (always him). With Putin in place, this authoritarian pattern repeats itself, and Hønneland reports on one important precondition for how this could be and remain so when he reports on that typical Russian speech genre, the complaint. The typical reaction to political challenges, and economic challenges for that matter, is to complain about it, not to try to do something, for that will not make a difference anyway. Then there is the counterpart to this at the leading political level. When other states, in this case, first and foremost Norway, shows an interest and contributes money towards international cooperation, it must be in order to forward the national interest. When Norway offers to help in environmental programmes to decommission nuclear submarines or store nuclear waste, it cannot be just because Norway has a vested interest in avoiding leaks and radiation. It must be because Norway wants to spy on the military installations and political institutions. When Norway wants to cut the fishing quotas according to scientific advice from a Russian–Norwegian commission, it cannot simply be to save fish stocks; it must also be in order to destroy the Russian fishing industry. And so on, and so forth.

To an International Relations theorist, what we have here is an excellent example of how different theories of international relations appeal to different kinds of people. In Norway, thinking about International Relations overwhelmingly happens in terms of international cooperation; the world is a positive-sum place where everybody may gain from striking a deal. In Russia, thinking about international relations overwhelmingly happens in terms of bald competition; the world is a zero-sum place where one state's meat is another state's poison. Hønneland expertly demonstrates the isomorphism about such abstract differences on the one hand, and the concrete stances taken by the two parties when it comes to political practice on the other.

Russia and Norway differ in their approach to thinking about politics, and they differ in their approach to doing politics. To the International Relations theorist, we have here an excellent example of how what theoretical stance one takes cannot be independent of political practice; theory informs and legitimates practice. To the student of Russian politics, we have here an excellent example of how general social Russian narratives are a precondition for Russian politics, and of why an authoritarian leader like Putin is genuinely popular with many people. He speaks to Russian expectations. On the policy level, that makes for an important reminder: today's Russians are yesterday's Soviets, and that is not going to change any time soon.

Iver B. Neumann,
Montague Burton Professor of International Relations,
London School of Economics, UK

Preface to the Paperback Edition

Borderland Russians – Behind the scenes, before the sequels

> After all, what is the usefulness of people endlessly deploring the fact that dogs don't bark? (Jørgensen, 2010, p. 233)

Borderland Russians was written in 2009, but the idea behind the book had matured for over a decade. I spent much of the 1990s travelling in and around Murmansk – the largest city above the Arctic Circle, located in the northwestern corner of the Russian Federation – on various consultancy and applied research assignments. At the time the Barents Euro-Arctic Region (BEAR) collaboration between Russia and the Nordic states was in its infancy, and several major joint infrastructure and business projects had been started. According to the rhetoric that accompanied these projects, northerners as such were very much alike, and could come together again after 70 years of enforced separation under communist Russia. But it was also a time of political and economic turmoil in Russia, culminating in the financial collapse of August 1998. I couldn't help but notice that the Russians and the Scandinavians didn't seem to be speaking the same language, in more than the literal sense. Scandinavians were clearly keen on 'teaching the Russians democracy' and 'cleaning up the environment', while what the Russians wanted was foreign investment – here and now. And when the Scandinavians flew in humanitarian aid, this was also wrong – the Russians felt humiliated. They could manage very well on their own, they insisted. My knowledge of the Russian language, of Russian history and culture, gave me a way in to understanding *Russian* identity, which now took the form of a more specific interest in the identity of Russian *northerners*. By 1998, I had published an article on identity formation in the BEAR which predicted a conceptual standoff between East and West in the European Arctic – and closed with the now notorious sentence: 'The Russians are tired of Barents bullshit!' (Hønneland, 1998, p. 294). (This was before my stay in the US where I discovered how much worse that last expletive sounds in English than it does in Norwegian. The journal editors accepted it, though.) I also wrote several feature articles for a Norwegian newspaper where I let a fictitious pair of friends, Ivan and Irina, give voice to people's opinions about living in the Russian North. These pieces were subsequently published in Norwegian as *Vårt bilde av russerne* ('Our Image of the Russians') (Hønneland and Jørgensen, 2002). 'I can't stand southerners', Irina once told me, 'they're all lazy – they don't want to work, they just want to do business' (ibid., p. 101). Truly a foretaste of what I would hear from people interviewed for *Borderland Russians*.

The conceptual standoff I had expected to erupt between East and West did indeed come to pass. On the global political scene, NATO was expanding eastwards and invading Kosovo; for many Russians, the West's cosying up to Russia with offers of aid and cooperation was just a foil for continuing the Cold War under a different guise: a Cold Peace. The Russians suspected ulterior motives behind Scandinavian overtures to implement a sustainable region-wide policy on the environment. What they really wanted was to kick the Russians out of the Barents region once and for all.

Working at an institute for applied research, at the time I was intensely occupied with evaluations of joint Norwegian–Russian ventures, for the Norwegian government, businesses and NGOs in fields such as environmental protection, nuclear safety, fisheries management, education, health and social issues. I had access to a unique set of empirical data, not least in the form of interviews, which I hoped to be able to use some day for more theoretical departures. My long-term plan was to write one book about Russian identity, one about discourses at the Norwegian–Russian interface, and one about doing qualitative interviewing in Russia. The second was the first to materialize, *Russia and the West: Environmental Co-operation and Conflict* (Hønneland, 2003). (I had suggested *Environmental Discourse in the European Arctic* as its subtitle, but the publisher wanted something broader.) *Russia and the West* explored the Russian 'Cold Peace discourse' and Norwegian 'Barents euphoria discourse', among others, as they related to fisheries management, nuclear safety and industrial pollution.

My 'identity book' was still some years ahead. On a bright autumn day in 2002, at a Starbucks outlet in New Brunswick, NJ – where I was staying during my sabbatical at Rutgers University – the project became a tangible possibility. I was reading the first proofs of *Russia and the West* when suddenly I started to think about the 'identity book'. '*Borderline Russians* – that's your title!' I thought, adjusting it to *Borderland Russians* a few minutes later. I was on to something that might actually get the ball rolling. Using a Starbucks napkin, I laid out the structure of the book: 1. Introduction; 2. International collaboration in the European Arctic; 3. How to be a northerner: distinguishing North from South; 4. How to be a Russian: distinguishing East from West; 5. Living in the northern environment; 6. Conclusions – all pretty close to the book that was eventually published eight years later. The big leap forward occurred in the winter of 2003–04, when I happened upon Ulrike H. Meinhof's (2002) *Living (with) Borders*. It introduced me to theories of narrative, identity and border studies. It also showed me the art of rendering extended interview extracts. It gave me several intense theoretical 'aha moments' as well as the unalloyed pleasure of reading it. I read it over and over again in the coming years, for its combined pleasure and preparation for my own endeavour. In early spring 2004, I was ready for my first interview. I invited two former interviewees from various evaluation projects, Ivan and Marina, as well as Marina's husband Anton, to dine at the old Soviet-style restaurant in the high-rise Hotel Arktika on Five-corner Square in the very centre of Murmansk. I had briefed them beforehand but was rather nervous. I was planning to ask them three open-ended questions (one for each empirical chapter in the book), and was hoping they weren't expecting a long list of more substantive questions. We were all alone in the big, dark restaurant, which was totally quiet until the band started to play (and we had to start yelling at each other). But my fears were unfounded: Marina talked and talked for hours. Ivan chuckled while offering brief, succinct comments on Marina's stories. Anton provided ad libs. It was a truly memorable evening.

Although I continued interviewing old informants whenever I happened to be in Murmansk over the next couple of years, I decided to add to my own data interviews conducted by Russian researchers. There were two reasons for this. First, I wanted to see if respondents expressed themselves differently when interviewed by another Russian rather than a foreigner. Second, there were practical concerns. I had no funding for my 'identity project'. I'd applied to several sources, but without success. Neither the government nor the business community seemed to consider *identity* sufficiently objective to warrant an applied project, and there were no programmes in the Research Council of Norway suitable for my project. One possibility that did emerge was an internal three-month grant provided by the Fridtjof Nansen Institute (FNI) to members of its research staff to write up applied research material with a view to publication in a peer-reviewed journal. Three months is normally considered far too little to write an entire book, but this was obviously going to be my only chance. Travelling to Murmansk to interview people would be out of the question, of course – every hour would have to be devoted to writing the book and any interviewing would have to be done by others. Natasha Metanovskaya and Sergey Klimashevich were selected for the task. I had met them a few years earlier in connection with various fishery-related projects in Murmansk Oblast. They were now both PhD students at Murmansk State Technical University and had assisted me with interviews in connection with other, more applied research projects. They did a couple of trial interviews and I was convinced they understood what kind of interviews I was after.

Natasha and Sergey's interviews arrived in a big package just a few months later. In the event their package would lie undisturbed in my office for nearly half a decade. Several circumstances prevented me from going ahead with my 'identity project'. New applied projects came my way; I was appointed research director at FNI, with the administrative responsibilities that involved; and there were changes in my personal life too – my head wasn't big enough to tackle a 'non-essential project' like *Borderland Russians*. That state of affairs lasted until late 2008 in fact. In December that year, I spent a month's holiday in Tanzania. I brought a suitcase full of books and articles; I re-read discourse theory near Kilimanjaro, narrative theory and border studies at my sister-in-law's property in Mwanza, and identity in international relations (IR) during the New Year break at Zanzibar. Back in ice-cold Oslo, I was ready to use my allotted three months to write the book – in between other obligations. The inspiration was there, and writing the theoretical introductory chapter was immensely enjoyable even though it took a few weeks. The second chapter – background on the region in question – was boring to write and probably not much fun to read either, but it was in the bag before the summer break, as planned. Finally, in spring 2009, I opened Natasha and Sergey's package. Although a trained translator myself, I decided not to use up valuable time translating the transcripts. I also wanted to take a fresh look at them through my researcher glasses, unaffected by the difficulties that always lie behind a good translation. So my good colleague and dear friend Anne-Kristin Jørgensen agreed to translate the transcripts from Russian to Norwegian, then my excellent language consultant Chris Saunders took them from Norwegian to English. I clearly remember the early summer evening I opened Chris's package on the balcony of my old apartment in Sandvika, overlooking the Oslo Fjord. These interviews had been lying in my office for nearly five years and I hadn't realized what a treasure I was sitting on. Every now and then, I would meet Natasha and Sergey in Murmansk, always excusing myself that I hadn't had time to write the book yet. I was careful not to let on that I hadn't even read their interviews properly. Now I couldn't wait to have them written out, afraid that something might happen to me before the book was ready. The three empirical chapters were written 'at a gallop' during the summer months of 2009, in the middle of which my beautiful daughter Leah was born. While still recovering from the excitement of these two events, I mailed a book proposal and three sample chapters to Commissioning Editor Alexandra Webster at Palgrave Macmillan in September. Within an hour, her assistant Liz Blackmore got back to me. They would be getting one of their consultants to evaluate the proposal as soon as possible. I couldn't help but see this as a good sign. A few weeks later, they duly offered me a publishing contract, based on 'an extremely enthusiastic review'. I finished the concluding chapter and selected the photos. They had been taken by Ruth Helen Thorheim, a visual anthropologist who had done fieldwork in Murmansk. The final manuscript was submitted to Palgrave in early 2010. The proofs were read and copy-editing queries sorted out – with a production company in India! – during my next short break, an enjoyable but nonetheless productive 'summer sabbatical' in northern Denmark with Anne-Kristin and our families.

Borderland Russians was published in October 2010. I have never experienced such a positive response to any book I have written – from students, fellow researchers, even 'the general public'. For the first time (with a possible exception of some of the more general books I have written in Norwegian), I was getting emails from strangers, thanking me for a good read. The book was reviewed widely as well, including in *CHOICE Magazine*. Most reviewers have focused on the book's accessibility to a broader readership than academia, describing it as entertaining, even 'a genuine joy to read' (Berg-Nordlie, 2011, p. 234). Some also commented on its 'personal style'. The first review I picked up was Nikolas Sellheim's (2011, p. 2) in *Polar Record*. He writes,

Due to the very personal style of the book, the writing in first person singular when referring to the author's research, experiences, and the strong focus on interviews, this work can be claimed as a scientific non-science book. This reviewer has not read a book like this before and it took some time to get used to the style, which seems to be a very personal account of the author and rather the call for more research in the field than the end result of a research project.

I agree and disagree. Writing in the first person singular is a common enough ethnographic style, and I don't get half as personal in the book as I do in this preface. I like Sellheim's label 'scientific non-science book', though, and agree with him that the book could well mark the starting point of a research project ('project' conceived in a broader sense of the word). I will return to this below. Tero Mustonen (2012, p. 91), writing in *Nordisk Østforum*, while generally sympathetic to the book, notes a reservation. Kola, he says, 'this always mystical peninsula in the North only occasionally reveals its essential nature in [my] book' (my translation). Contributing to this was clearly beyond the book's epistemological framework.

*   *   *

While reviews of the book have been very positive by and large, it is not without flaws. On the contrary, every time I start reading a review, I wonder whether it will identify any of the book's shortcomings. It expands our empirical knowledge of Russian identity, I think, particularly of Russian *northern* identity, which is so important if foreign actors are to succeed in their practical dealings with the Russian North. This knowledge is useful moreover to the emerging field of border studies. Its starting point is *talk* – the categories that are available to northwest Russians when they speak about themselves as northerners (as opposed to southerners), as Russians (as opposed to Scandinavians) and about the northern environment. In my interview material, I singled out a set of specific narratives on these subjects, often with some kind of stereotype or 'major narrative' which is either reproduced or contested. These narratives, I argue, define how these topics can be talked about; they encircle the topic of conversation, so to speak – and determine which policy options are available. Talk about southerners tended basically to reproduce the narrative portraying northerners as 'better' by far than the others. It was the preferred narrative of most of my interviewees. A minority, though, questioned this widely held premise. Talk of Scandinavians tended in one way or another to oppose material affluence with Russian soulfulness. As Meinhof (2002) and many other theorists suggest (see Chapter 1), in addition to reflecting identity these narratives take part in its constitution. Although I do not make claims regarding the project's generalizability (obviously not part of my epistemology), I believe nonetheless that I have grasped something of central importance about northwest Russian identity, not least since my findings corresponded in the main with what limited research had already been done on the subject (Razumova, 2007). I wasn't looking for the 'essential nature' of people living in the Kola Peninsula; indeed, the aim of narrative analysis is precisely to pinpoint talking practices, no more, no less. I think my most interesting finding is what Tuomas Forsberg (2011, p. 549) in his review of the book in *Russian Review* refers to as the 'many incongruent, almost schizophrenic, elements in this identity construction' – what I call 'narrative juggling', a practice of both my interviewees and political actors in Russia.

So far, so good. The weakest part of *Borderland Russians*, given the bold move to introduce 'international relations' into the book's subtitle, is arguably the rather sporadic evidence and discussion of Russia's foreign relations. In Chapter 2, I provide anecdotal accounts of Russian foreign policy with respect to the Scandinavian countries. I mentioned here what I had discovered during my research for *Russia and the West*, that Russia suspects the West's concern for the environment of being a front, and constructs foreign policies apparently with a view to 'not doing as the West tells us'. As for regional BEAR collaboration and the various regional nuclear safety initiatives for the Kola Peninsula, enthusiasm alternates with derision in the Russian discourse. In practical politics, the Russians sometimes reject a Western policy measure outright, something they did in effect to plans to extend Norwegian participation in the Arctic Military Environmental Cooperation, AMEC, regime. So although they accept a Western presence in northwest Russia, they also take the West to task. Now, is it possible to claim that these foreign policies were determined by identity? For one thing, I do not examine other possible explanations in any detail. What about explanations proposed by realism and other positivist-inclined IR theories, power and interest? What about structural IR theory, like neo-realism, which is happy not to explain states' foreign policy, only their mutual interaction? On this account, Russia's status as a great power is said to ensure stability – Norway wouldn't dare to challenge Russia seriously anyway. And Russia stands to gain financially from Western governments' support of environmental projects. The deeper we engage with this matter, however, the harder it is to defend strictly power- or interest-based explanations. In a recently published book on *Making Fishery Agreements Work* I provide evidence showing that Norway consistently since the end of the Cold War set the agenda and more often than not determined the outcome of matters brought before the bilateral Norwegian–Russian management regime for the Barents Sea fisheries (Hønneland, 2012). Even when decisions patently went against their declared interest, Russia accepted Norway's lead, with or without protest. This, I believe, has to do with the (overt or tacit) modus operandi of the Joint Norwegian–Russian Fisheries Commission, the hands-on approach to reaching agreement at the lower levels of the Commission and between the two heads of delegation. This is simply the way things are done 'around here', and has been for nearly four decades. But I could easily have homed in on the narrative practice of the Commission instead.

Another possible objection to my emphasis on narrative and identity is 'how much do they actually account for?', a question often asked by IR hardliners. The answer is simple, and eloquently expressed by Neumann (2008, p. 62) ('discourse' can easily be replaced by the slightly narrower concept of 'narrative'):

> Because discourse maintains a degree of regularity in social relations, it produces preconditions for action. It constrains how the stuff that the world consists of is ordered, and so how people categorize and think about the world. It constrains what is thought of at all, what is thought of as possible, and what is thought of as the 'natural thing' to do in a given situation. But discourse cannot determine action completely. There will always be more than one possible outcome. Discourse analysis aims at specifying the bandwidth of possible outcomes.

In the international forums on the European Arctic, the Russians elect to 'stay put', while at the same time regaling these very arrangements as a threat to Russian security. The strong narrative undercurrents according to which the Scandinavian countries are up to no good in the Russian North do not actually determine Russian foreign policy in the area, or at least they haven't so far. But they do explain why Russia frequently advises the West not to take Russia's cooperative stance for granted. Russia could well decide one day to take a tougher line. They might also have some impact on Russian domestic policies, as demonstrated in Chapters 2 and 6: when long-serving Murmansk Governor Yevgeniy Yevdokimov was sacked in 2009 it was because his relations with the region's Scandinavian neighbours were too close. (At least that was the official explanation, which goes to show that prevailing narratives can be used by the political elite whenever it suits them.) But northwest Russians have an alternative, more benign narrative about the West, as a good ally in environmental affairs and guardian of law, order and humanitarianism. Can this also help explain why the Russians 'stay put'? My narrative study circles in 'the bandwidth of possible outcomes', but that's about as far as it goes. Like other IR theories, narrative analysis and identity theory do not claim to explain it all. Structural theorists such as neorealists, Jørgensen (2010, p. 84) suggests in his 'new introduction to international relations', are content to explain a few but important things and happy to leave 'what they regard as the nitty-gritty analysis of other issues in international politics' to others. Theories of identity and discourse analysis, which Jørgensen (2010) categorizes as distinct *theories* in the post-positivist *tradition* – and we could add narrative analysis as a sub-domain of discourse analysis, closely related to theories of identity – are in the same manner not intended to take over the whole field, just to enrich it, fill in the nooks and crannies overlooked by the 'grand theories' – and perhaps occasionally modify the conclusions of adherents of other research traditions. More than anything, however, they aim to contribute discussion of how political actors are constituted. As noted by Browning (2008, p. 35), '[W]hilst brute material forces do place physical limits on the policies and actions of states, what they do not tell us is why any state would want to attack another in the first place.'

Jørgensen preaches eclecticism: we should see research traditions, he maintains, at least in part as complementary (p. 217). (The epigraph to this chapter refers to what at times is reminiscent of trench warfare between research traditions.) Wider traditions and practical tools of various denominations appeal to different individuals. He cites (p. 214) Robert O. Keohane's (1989, p. 29) reasons for abandoning game theory to illustrate this: 'I was intellectually unequipped and temperamentally unsuited to making a contribution toward that enterprise.' I read realism-inspired accounts of world politics with great interest, but can't really seem get a handle on things when I try to do the same myself. I bear overall responsibility for research at an institute whose main theoretical input is in the field of regime theory, but experience has taught me that I am 'temperamentally unsuited' to contributing to it myself. It is only when I shine the torch at the nooks and crannies of lower-level political practices and discourses that I get fired up, so to speak.

As I note in Chapter 6, as far as the IR aspect of my research is concerned, I have sought to reflect over the relationship between borderland identities and cross-border political practices. IR identity research, I also mention, is dominated by theoretical reflection and empirical study at the macro level, particularly in studies of young independent states in the Third World and post-Soviet area. I would have liked to have seen more research 'taken down' to the micro level of day-to-day political practices – and talk. As for my own *Borderland Russians* endeavour, a sequel is clearly warranted. Which narratives inform the mindset of the wider northwest Russian public, including the media and politicians? What characterizes Russian *Arctic talk*?

*   *   *

I didn't write a preface for the first edition of *Borderland Russians*. To make up for that omission I would like to take this opportunity to thank helpers already mentioned in this Preface: Natasha and Sergey for their wonderful interviews, Anne-Kristin and Chris for their translations – and Chris for his magnificent work on my English. I would also like to thank other colleagues at the Fridtjof Nansen Institute, in particular Pål Skedsmo for his comments on the draft manuscript and great conversations on the road in Russia and the Caucasus; Leif Christian Jensen for our discussions on theoretical matters in offices and bars; Arild Moe for mentorship and sound advice over the years; Lars Rowe for our intense conversations about Russian identity and everything else between heaven and earth – and to all of them for their friendship. Jørgen Holten Jørgensen belongs to the group, though he is no longer with the institute. Our talks in the office have morphed instead into evenings out on the town, though *the Russians* are an ever-returning topic of conversation. I owe a debt of thanks to Iver B. Neumann for his constant support from the 'sidelines' so to speak – years sometimes pass between each time we meet – and for agreeing to write a foreword to the paperback edition. Similarly, I thank Sergei Medvedev for allowing me to use the marvellous quote in his Glenn Gould article as an epigraph for the book, and for writing such a fabulous endorsement for the back cover. I also need to express my gratitude to other sources of inspiration, Ulrike H. Meinhof, Nancy Ries, Svetlana Boym and Erik Ringmar – whom I have never actually met in person – and to Martin Müller, with whom I got in touch while writing the book and who later invited me to give a lecture in St. Gallen, to what probably is the liveliest group of students I've ever met. My own students at the University of Tromsø aren't bad either, of course, and *Borderland Russians* continues to spur interesting discussions in class. Many have personal experiences that add to my study; teaching them is always a pleasure. Thanks to the participants of the master class organized by Iver and Patrick Thaddeus Jackson at the Norwegian Institute of International Affairs in December 2009. The discussions prompted important last-minute adjustments to my theoretical approach. Staff at Palgrave Macmillan deserve an accolade as well, in particular Julia Willan and Harriet Barker in Palgrave's present politics team for useful advice and enthusiasm for the paperback edition. Finally, thanks go to my family: Kristin, Lavrans, Alva and Leah.

I have published more than a dozen books, but I have never dedicated a book to anyone before. I want to dedicate this book to my son Lavrans, who has been with me as long as *Borderland Russians* matured in my head. He has been a shining light and the most constant point in my life; he will soon be ready to go out in the world on his own so a dedication is long overdue.

The third 'surplus book' of my long-term plan hasn't materialized yet, the one on doing qualitative interviews in Russia. I scribbled down the table of contents under the magic northern Jutland light two summers ago, though. Given the past rate of progress, that should indicate another six or so years to go.

Geir Hønneland

References

M. Berg-Nordlie (2011) 'Borderland Russians: Identity, Narrative and International Relations (book review)', *Arctic Review on Law and Politics*, 2: 229–34.

C.S. Browning (2008) *Constructivism, Narrative and Foreign Policy Analysis: A Case Study of Finland*, Oxford: Peter Lang.

T. Forsberg (2011) 'Borderland Russians: Identity, Narrative and International Relations (book review)', *Russian Review*, 70: 548–9.

G. Hønneland (1998) 'Identity Formation in the Barents Euro-Arctic Region', *Cooperation and Conflict*, 33: 277–97.

G. Hønneland (2003) *Russia and the West: Environmental Co-operation and Conflict* (London and New York: Routledge).

G. Hønneland (2012) *Making Fishery Agreements Work: Post-Agreement Bargaining in the Barents Sea* (Cheltenham and Northampton, MA: Edward Elgar).

G. Hønneland and A-K. Jørgensen (2002) *Vårt bilde av russerne: 25 debattinnlegg om samarbeidet i nord* (Kristiansand: Høyskoleforlaget).

K.E. Jørgensen (2010) *International Relations Theory: A New Introduction* (Basingstoke and New York: Palgrave Macmillan).

R.O. Keohane (1989) *International Institutions and State Power: Essays in International Relations Theory* (Boulder, CO and London: Westview).

U.H. Meinhof (ed.) (2002) *Living (with) Borders: Identity Discourses on East–West Borders in Europe* (Aldershot and Burlington, VT: Ashgate).

T. Mustonen (2012) 'Borderland Russians: Identity, Narrative and International Relations (book review)', *Nordisk Østforum*, 26: 88–91.

I.B. Neumann (2008) 'Discourse Analysis' in A. Klotz and D. Prakash (eds) *Methods in International Relations: A Pluralist Guide* (Basingstoke and New York: Palgrave Macmillan).

I. Razumova (2007) 'Sotsialisticheskiy gorod v pamyati zhiteley' in N. Baschmakoff, P. Fryer and M. Ristolainen (eds) *Texts and Communities: Soviet and Post-Soviet Life in Discourse and Practice*, Aleksanteri Series 4/2007 (Helsinki: Aleksanteri Institute), pp. 145–58.

N. Sellheim (2011) 'Borderland Russians: Identity, Narrative and International Relations (book review)', *Polar Record*, Online FirstView article, available on CJO 2011 doi:10.1017/S0032247410000707.

1
Introduction

They're completely normal people. But they should visit us more often and let their hair down. There they sit, turning sour. They need to add a bit of zest to their lives. We're always ready to help, right?[1]

Introduction

This book touches on some of the big questions in contemporary social science: What is identity? How is it narrated by subjects? Can identities help explain events in international relations? But in addition it addresses some of the 'smaller' questions in more specialized fields of the social sciences: How does living close to a border affect people? Are borderland people different from other people? Above all, we ask a few empirical questions about identities in a specific geographic location: What does it mean to be Russian? What does it mean to be a northerner? How do people in Russia's north-western corner define themselves in relation to their Scandinavian neighbours and their southern relatives? This is a book about what it means to be a borderland Russian – living in the high north, hailing from the south, with Western neighbours within throwing distance across an increasingly permeable border.

The Kola Peninsula is the north-western outpost of the Russian Federation, for centuries located at the periphery of the Russian empire, but for several decades now the centre of attention of world politics. Home to the country's Northern Fleet, during the Cold War the peninsula was generally regarded as the world's most heavily militarized area. Indeed, the region was literally built during the Soviet era, its population rising from around two thousand before the revolution to well beyond a million in the late 1980s. With the fall of the Iron Curtain, the Kola Peninsula became infamous in the West for the Soviet Union's environmental legacy: heavily polluted areas around the nickel works at Pechenga and Monchegorsk and stockpiles of radioactive waste from the Northern Fleet and civilian ice-breakers under woefully inadequate and badly maintained storage or dumped in the waters of the Barents and Kara Seas. The 1990s were, more widely, a troubled decade for the Kola Peninsula, as indeed for the rest of Russia: The economy slumped, there was social unrest and the region's population fell by a third. But underneath the gloom, a new Russian borderland was emerging, with the Kola Peninsula becoming Russia's gateway to Scandinavia and EU (or possibly the other way around). The number of people crossing the borders between Russia, Norway and Finland rose dramatically from the early 1990s, and all three countries now host diasporas of varying sizes from the other side. Political collaboration between Russia and the Nordic countries began with the establishment of the Barents Euro-Arctic Region (BEAR),[2] set up in 1993 on a Norwegian initiative, followed by several other bilateral and multilateral institutional arrangements. Multinational cooperation is particularly extensive in environmental protection and nuclear safety. Since the turn of the millennium, the likelihood of a major oil and gas industry being put in place to utilize the resources beneath the Barents Sea has created new optimism in the region. If it materializes, the Shtokman gas condensate field off the coast of the Kola Peninsula will be the largest operative offshore gas field in the world. Russian gas giant Gazprom, French Total and Norwegian Statoil started a feasibility project in 2007. The Prirazlomnoye oil field, a bit further east, is closer to completion. The Kola Peninsula may be set to become Europe's next big oil playground.[3]

I found inspiration in writing this book from, among others, Ulrike H. Meinhof's (2002) study of identity discourses on East–West borders in Europe. Like her, I am mainly preoccupied with 'ordinary people's cultural identities and how they are constructed and confirmed through every-day conversations and narratives' (Meinhof et al., 2002, p. 6). Like her, I focus on a region that was divided by the Iron Curtain during the Cold War, using ethnographic fieldwork and in-depth interviews, with the aim to subject the interview data to 'detailed, finely-tuned methods of linguistic discourse analysis' (ibid., p. 7). Again like her, I search for key narratives through which people construct their identities, assuming that 'narratives are constitutive of the self rather than the reflective action of an already constituted individual' (Armbruster and Meinhof, 2002, p. 18). Unlike Meinhof, however, I look at my observational and interview data through the eyes of a political scientist. Sympathetic to the view that identities form a legitimate unit in political analysis, I use the stories of my interviewees – ungeneralizable as they may be – as a point of departure for reflection on the political processes underway in northern Europe. Without pretending that the personal narratives of a few dozen ordinary people can explain the big picture in international politics, it is worth investigating, nonetheless, whether they might at least shed some light on events at the interstate level.[4] This is in line with recent developments in international relations (IR) theory that not only embrace the concept of identity but also view the construction of identities 'as not being the exclusive domain of intellectuals of statecraft at the centres of state power or in high politics, but as taking place just as much in the everyday lives of ordinary people' (Müller, 2008, p. 6). More than anything, however, I approach the issue from a background in area studies, as a specialist on Russian politics and north-west Russian society.[5] My endeavour is, above all, a study of Russian identity – and of Russian talk.[6] In addition to the interviews with small groups of Kola residents, organized for the purpose of this study, I draw on extensive observation from several years of fieldwork in the Kola Peninsula. Murmansk has been my 'second home' for fifteen years all told. In that sense, this book is in no small part also a personal account.

Other sources of inspiration are recorded below. Drawing on fields as diverse as linguistics, sociology, human geography and international relations – not to speak of the cross-disciplinary area studies of Russia and of the North – I attempt to get at general trends and interrelations, rather than dropping names or delving deeper theoretically than necessary for the present study. Before discussing the questions motivating the research and methodology, I review the theoretical and empirical background. While it is sometimes difficult to draw a fine line between theory and empirical discussion, I spend some time in the first part of the chapter examining some of the more recent studies of border regions, the role of identities in the IR literature and of narrative in identity formation. The second part introduces the reader to studies of Russianness and northernness, on how writers have compared Russian and Western identities and why the concept of the North often looms large in discussions about Russianness.

Borderlands, identity, narrative

Boundaries, borders, frontiers and borderlands are known as edge concepts in geography and indicate dividing lines or zones between geographical areas, especially states. Boundaries are the lines that demarcate where one state ends and another begins. Border usually refers to the restricted sections of the boundary where crossings take place. A frontier traditionally refers to the transition zone between two states where the boundary is not fixed. Today we use it for the zone in one state that leads up to the boundary of another state. The borderland is the entire area around the border, boundary and frontiers on both sides.[7] Their primary features are revealed in the dialectic between boundaries as political demarcations and regions as geographical entities that resist the artificial divisions imposed by political borders.[8] As Konrad and Nicol (2008, p. 31) note,

> The boundary fades to a degree, and the cross-border region gains in substance to a degree. The result is a spatial construct which has extent or area beyond the substance of the borderline. There exists an area in which people have characteristics of land and life in common across the nation-state boundary.[9]

Since the 1980s, border studies have grown from relative obscurity as a speciality of geography to engage a widening circle of social scientists and humanists. Again to quote Konrad and Nicol (2008, p. 21), 'Boundaries, borders, borderlands and other geopolitical edge concepts have emerged from loosely defined terms in the public discourse, and over-defined concepts in the traditional geographical literature, to become more precise and carefully defined elements in global analysis.' As a result of the globalization process, borders are taking on new meanings. Where they once divided almost everything between the two adjacent states, they now differentiate only the essential elements of sovereignty that define the core identity of each country; they act increasingly as transition zones enabling the flow of cultural, political and economic influences in both directions. The modern 'permeable border' is an arena of 'cultural-symbolic borrowing rather than cross-border othering', and when both processes are at work, the result is 'a complex and richly layered archaeology of separation and integration at the border' (ibid., p. 22).[10] Houtum et al. (2005, pp. 2–3) remind us of Latour's (1993) metaphor that a key can transform a door into a border for some, but a pass-through for others. And further: '[...] a territorial b/*order* is a normative idea, a belief in the existence and continuity of a territorially binding and differentiated power that only becomes concrete, objectified and real in our own everyday social practices' (Houtum et al., 2005, p. 3).[11]

If we accept borderlands as areas for 'separation and integration at the border', we obviously need to ask whether borders actually promote integration or maintain separation. And if people perceive them as gateways for cross-border contact, would it affect their sense of belonging to the region and to their nation state? Do people feel a spirit of community with their neighbours on the other side? Does the proximity to the border make them identify less with their own nation state? We are approaching the complex question of identity, discussed in all areas of the social sciences, to capture the essence of what constitutes people's self-conception. Both human geography and international relations have seen an upsurge in interest in identity since the end of the Cold War.[12] As the maps of Eastern Europe and Central Asia were redrawn – at the same time as globalization took off and the European Union was effectively dismantling national borders in Western Europe – it was no longer possible to view identity as unitary, fixed and given by an individual's nationality. Identity has come to be viewed as a relation rather than a possession, a quality conditional to individuals in different situations rather than categorical pertaining to individuals as such. Identities are 'emergent and constructed (rather than fixed and natural), contested and polymorphic (rather than unitary and singular), and interactive and process-like (rather than static and essence-like)' (Lapid, 1996, p. 8). Goff and Dunn (2004b) do not take such claims for granted, but set out to study empirically whether identities are in fact constructed (as opposed to given by belonging to, e.g. race, ethnic group or political entity), multiple (as opposed to singular), fluid (as opposed to static) and relational (as opposed to autonomously defined). Not unexpectedly, their conclusions are not unequivocal. Identities are fluid, but not constantly changing. Identities are relational, but the effect of the process of othering differs according to the situation. Likewise, the propensity of individuals to move back and forth between multiple identities varies with the context. And finally, 'Even though identity is a social construction, it is not whatever we want it to be. A limited reserve of discursive resources constrains the ways in which identities evolve [...]' (Goff and Dunn, 2004c, p. 244).[13]

This resonates with theories on the narrative constitution of identity. In a seminal article from 1994, Margaret R. Somers argues for reconfiguring the study of identity formation through the concept of narrative.[14] Leaning on recent criticism of the traditional conception of narrative as simply a mode of representation, she claims 'it is through narrativity that we come to know, understand, and make sense of the social world, and it is through narratives and narrativity that we constitute our social identities' (Somers, 1994, p. 606). And further, '[We] come to *be* who we *are* (however ephemeral, multiple, and changing) by being located or locating ourselves (usually unconsciously) in social narratives *rarely of our own making*' (ibid., p. 606; emphasis in the original). There are two important claims here. First, narratives – that is, the stories people tell[15] – are not just reflections about the world, but rather constitutive of the self. Hence, narratives acquire an ontological dimension in addition to their traditional epistemological one. They not only give expression to the outside world about who people are, but they also contribute to *making* people who they are. Second, narratives are 'rarely of our own making'. Gergen (2001, p. 249) claims that '[people] do not author their own lives'; instead 'stories serve as communal resources' that people avail themselves of when they construct their life stories. Ambruster and Meinhof (2002, pp. 18ff) refer to Taylor's (1989) concept of 'webs of interlocution' – the social frame within which individuals define their self-identification – and to Benhabib's (1999) concept of 'webs of narrative', understood not only as a shared language but also as more or less endurable stories about the big things in life (e.g. race, gender and God), as well as the smaller ones: 'These narratives may be micro-scale stories within a family or macro-scale myths about the nation; they are retold, nourished and transformed by various "defining communities" and, quite importantly, people are born into them' (Armbruster and Meinhof, 2002, p. 19). Or in Benhabib's (1999, p. 344) words, 'We become who we are by learning to be a conversation partner in these narratives', and she goes on, '[Our] agency consists in our capacity to weave out of those narratives and fragments of narratives a life story that makes sense for us, as unique individual selves' (ibid., p. 344).[16] In Gergen's (2001, p. 253) words:

> By using these narrative conventions we generate a sense of coherence and direction in our lives. They acquire meaning, and what happens is suffused with significance. Certain forms of narrative are broadly shared within the culture; they are frequently used, easily identified, and highly functional. In a sense, they constitute a syllabary of possible selves.[17]

Somers (1994, pp. 617ff) identifies four dimensions of narrative: ontological, public, conceptual and meta-narratives. Ontological narratives are the stories that individuals use to make sense of their lives; they 'process events into episodes' (ibid., p. 618). Public narratives are – similar to

Taylor's (1989) 'webs of interlocution' – the intersubjective frames that sustain and transform narrative over time.

> Public narratives are those narratives attached to cultural and institutional formations larger than the single individual, to intersubjective networks or institutions, however local or grand, micro- or macrostories about American social mobility, the 'freeborn Englishman', the working-class hero, and so on. Public narratives range from the narratives of one's family, to those of the workplace (organizational myths), church, government, and nation. Like all narratives, these stories have drama, plot, explanation, and selective criteria. Families, for example, selectively appropriate events to construct stories about their descent into poverty. The mainstream media arrange and connect events to create a 'mainstream plot' about the origin of social disorders. The seventeenth-century church explains the theological reasons for a national famine. Government agencies tell us 'expert' stories about unemployment. Taylor emphasizes the centrality of public to ontological narrative when he states: 'We may sharply shift the balance in our definition of identity, dethrone the given, historical community as a pole of identity, and relate only to the community defined by adherence to the good (or the saved, or the true believers, or the wise). But this doesn't sever our dependence on webs of interlocution. It only changes the webs, and the nature of our dependence.' [Taylor, 1989, p. 39] (Somers, 1994, p. 19)

The third dimension of narrativity refers to the 'master narratives' in which we are embedded as contemporary actors in history and as social scientists. Somers (ibid., p. 619) mentions epic dramas such as Capitalism vs. Communism, the Individual vs. Society, the Emergence of Western Civilization and the Rise of Nationalism or Islam as examples. Finally, conceptual narratives are the concepts and explanations that we construct as social researchers. The challenge, according so Somers (1994, p. 620), is 'to develop a social analytic vocabulary that can accommodate the contention that social life, social organizations, social action, and social identities are narratively, that is, temporally and relationally, constructed through both ontological and public narratives'.[18]

While identity claimed a place in international relations theory during the 1990s (see above), the concept of narrative is more recently doing so. Suganami (2008), for instance, provides an epistemological quest for bridging the gap between international relations and international history through the use of narrative explanation. In their study of Russian politics towards NATO during the 1990s, Williams and Neumann (2000) stress the role of narrative structures in the construction of identities, drawing on the new institutionalist concept of a 'logic of appropriateness', '[t]he narrative resources available to a given actor are neither infinite nor unstructured; they are historically and socially constructed and confined' (ibid., p. 363).[19] Joenniemi (2008) argues that narratives represent a form of layered social and symbolic power, which 'bolster efforts of claiming particular identities and impact the granting or denying them to others' (ibid., p. 121). He pays particular attention to the narrative resources of states, asking 'Which are the narratives carrying the day and why are others doomed to remain at the fringes with little if any constitutive impact?' (ibid., p. 121). Just like Williams and Neumann (2000), his empirical examples are from Russia. As noted also by Müller (2008) – in his quest for the relevance for identity research in IR of studying social practice at micro level – it is particularly in connection with Russian studies that IR scholars have been eager to embrace identity as a fruitful concept.[20]

Russianness, Northernness

Just as much as books about identity declare 'Identity is back!', books about Russian identity (or politics) ask questions like 'What is Russia?[21] What is "Russianness"? Who are Russians?' (Franklin and Widdis, 2004a, p. xi). Or append a quotation by a famous figure commenting on the 'strangeness' of Russia, like Winston Churchill and his characterization of Russia as 'a riddle, wrapped in a mystery inside an enigma' or nineteenth-century poet Fyodor Tyuchev's 'Russia is a thing of which / the intellect cannot conceive. / Hers is no common yardstick. / You measure her uniquely: / in Russia you [can only] believe!' (Brunstad et al., 2004, p. 6). Or how about this one, 'Russia is big. Very big indeed' (Smith, 1999, p. 7)? And one for which I am partly responsible myself: 'Ask any non-Russian what he or she associates with "Russia". The answer is likely to include reference to snow, long winters, and the seemingly endless Siberian forests' (Blakkisrud and Hønneland, 2006a, p. 1). Keywords are 'strangeness' (difficult to comprehend for outsiders, like foreign politicians, and insiders, like the Russian poet), 'otherness' (something different from the Western world), space ('very big indeed') and 'northenness' (snow, winters, Siberia). Each will be investigated in turn in the following.

Students of Russia's cultural history identify two major influences on Russian identity and on Western ideas of the Russian enigma: Orthodox

Christianity and the Tartar invasion and ensuing dominion of Russia (1224–1480).[22] Russia (i.e. 'Land of the *Rus*", with Kiev as the capital) was Christianized by the Eastern Orthodox Church of Constantinople in 988. According to the Nestor chronicle, envoys from Kiev were despatched to different foreign lands to find out which faith suited the Russian mentality best. The Greek Church was preferred to Western Catholicism and the Islam of the Volga Bulgars, allegedly due to the former's emphasis on beauty in the worship. Russians found this aesthetic aspect of the Eastern Church more to their liking than the elaborate doctrines of the West Europeans. In this semi-anecdotal depiction of Russia's acquisition of its religious faith, a cultural identity is staked out. Beauty as a sign of the desirable reflects a synthetic world view, as opposed to the more analytical conception of Christianity, rationality and reality found in the West. Where the Western Church has generally encouraged active participation in worldly affairs, Russian Orthodoxy somehow dissociates the individual from his earthly surroundings. In preaching the possibility of merging with divinity here on earth, it encourages people to indulge in God-seeking contemplation and apocalyptic reflection, largely unknown in Western Christianity.

In 1054, diverging interpretations of the nature of the Holy Spirit forced a split between the Eastern and Western Roman churches. While the Western branch of the church, wishing to accentuate the divinity of Christ above that of the Holy Spirit, added *filioque* ('and the Son') to the creed, the Eastern Church refused to let humans reinterpret the nature of the deity. The Russian theologian Vladimir Losskiy (1972) sees reflected in this controversy the fundamental differences between East and West European identities. From the theological point of view, the West accentuates the human nature of divinity by bringing Christ to the fore in the creed, while the East gives prominence to the spiritual and somewhat mystical aspects of Christianity. More widely, the dispute mirrors different ideas on the limits of knowledge. While the Western Church tends to engage in an intellectual exploration of religious questions, the Eastern Church keeps a respectful distance. The West seeks to challenge the limits of rational thinking, whereas the East maintains that the innermost nature of divinity must always remain a mystery to humans. The heavenly powers can be felt emotionally, but should not be understood intellectually.

Moscow became first city of the Russian Orthodox Church – proclaiming itself 'the third Rome' – after the capture of Byzantium by the Turks in 1453. Before that, other dramatic events influenced the destiny of Russia. In 1224, one of Genghis Khan's grandsons attacked and conquered Russia. The Mongolian Yoke, as the Russians call the period, lasted more than two and a half centuries and affected Russia for years to come. According to Waage (1990), the Mongolian Yoke undermined the status of the individual in Russia. The relatively humane administration of justice in pre-Mongolian times was replaced by torture and other cruel methods of punishment. This misanthropy persisted well into modern times in Russia: while slavery was abandoned in Western Europe in the 13th century,[23] it took hold in Russia only after the withdrawal of the Tartars. People were still being sold at slave markets in Russia in the early 19th century.

The period of Mongolian supremacy had a profound effect on Russian society. Moscow's willingness to collaborate with the Tartars promoted a climate for growth and expansion. When the old capital of Kiev was levelled to the ground at the outset of the Mongolian conquest, Moscow turned out to be the most cooperative town of any importance. It grew rapidly, adopting many Mongolian customs and attitudes. When the Tartars were finally overthrown in the late 15th century, Moscow emerged as the natural centre of the Russian empire. While a separate secular society and culture emerged in Western Europe lodged between church and state, Russia – influenced by its Mongolian heritage and untouched by the Renaissance – embarked on a road towards autocracy and absolutism.

These accounts of early Russian history underscore the 'differentness' of Russia to the West; but by the early 19th century Europe had arguably emerged as the defining 'constituting other' of Russian identity.[24] The process gained momentum from Peter the Great's (1682–1725), and to some extent Catherine the Great's (1762–1796) efforts to westernize Russia and Napoleon's assault on Russia in 1812. In the aftermath of the war, the Decembrist uprising of 1825 sprang from the debate about the country's relationship to Europe. The army officers who staged it were opposed to the *ancien régime* and wanted the feudal system removed. They were also aggravated by Nicholas I's assumption to the throne, the latter event sparking the actual uprising. This is where Neumann (1996) starts his account of 'Russia and the idea of Europe'. He identifies three positions on Europe in early 19th-century Russia. The first was the state's 'conservative nationalist' approach, eager to preserve the *ancien régime* and sceptical of processes in Europe away from enlightened despotism. The second was the Romantic nationalist position. Influenced by German Romanticism, it was anti-modern and protective of ancient Russian culture, including the organic tie between tsar and people, as the hallmark of Russianness. Finally, there was the constitutionalist position, urging Russia to adopt European political and economic models and adapt them to Russian conditions (ibid., p. 13). Some commentators laid the blame for the constitutionalist uprising on the proponents of Europeanism. They had obviously led some of Russia's best and brightest astray. The country needed urgently to do something about its subservient attitude to Europe. This paved the way for a new form of Russian Messianism, a recycling of the old idea of Russia as the embodiment of high moral values with a special mission in the world (ibid., p. 20). Another group, which still held Europe to be superior to Russia, were concerned the two were drifting even further apart. A third group engineered the construction of the doctrine of 'official nationality'. To them the Decembrists were 'a fifth column'. Official Russia, they proclaimed, should be defined by the three pillars of autocracy, Orthodoxy and 'nation-mindedness' (*narodnost*'). By the 1840s, the various groups were becoming increasingly polarized. The Romantic nationalists gathered under the banner of 'Slavophilism', and those who looked to Europe for political and economic guidance came to be known as 'Westernizers'. Slavophilism was a radicalization of the Romantic nationalist position. Europe was decadent, even rotten: 'Some saw redemption for Europe if it could only go to school with Russia; others held that Russia should turn its back and hold its nose while the cadaver that was Europe slowly putrefied' (ibid., p. 38). The aborted 1848 revolutions in Europe were a further confirmation that this was not the way to go, and the Russian state offered a conciliatory hand to the Romantic nationalists, embracing, for instance, the idea of 'Holy Russia'. With Russia's defeat in the Crimean War (1853–1856), however, the state became more preoccupied with economic and military capabilities and made several approaches in the direction of Westernism (ibid., p. 40). Tsar Alexander II abolished serfdom in 1861 and introduced new bodies of local government, the *zemstva*, in 1864. Slavophilism, which had promoted introspectiveness and detachment from Europe, gave way to pan-Slavism, which urged expansive relations with the West. The Westernizers, for their part, dismayed by the half-hearted reforms, adopted a more radical stance. Reflecting the situation in many European countries, liberals and socialists were divided in Russia as well. Further divisions emerged between adherents of a specifically Russian form of socialism (one of their offshoots was a populist movement), and internationalists. The reform tsar was killed in 1881, in an assassination staged by the populists. His successors stifled public debate even further, before war and revolution eventually put a halt to the old rule.

We end our quick trip through Russian history here,[25] noting the triangle between Romantic nationalism, Westernism and variants of 'official nationality' as it continued to influence politics in both the Soviet Union and Russian Federation.[26] For now, we will move from 'Russia in time' to 'Russia as space'. Widdis (2004, p. 33) explores the different ways in which space acts as a metaphor for and expression of Russianness, claiming that '[the concept of] *neob"iatnyi prostor* (boundless territory) offers a powerful symbol of Russian national identity'. Investigating 18th- and 19th-century texts and Soviet films, she notes a tendency to depict Russia in terms of limitless open space, 'a land with no end and no edge [...], a flatness which seems to curve *around* the horizon, which seems to deny the very existence of an edge to the space – of the horizon' (ibid., p. 39). Russia, hence, escapes definition, or its definition lies precisely in its emptiness. 'Thus the lack of definition becomes a form of definition in itself. Like the space, Russia itself is characterised by open-ness, which becomes a symbol of freedom, bravery and open-ness of heart' (ibid., p. 41).

Along the same lines, Hellberg-Hirn (1999, p. 56) notes, 'Russian self-stereotypes promote an idealized image of the national soul as being wide-open: *shirokaja dusha* ["wide soul"], full of passionate feelings, generosity, open-mindedness, hospitality, unlimited kindness, and recklessness verging on anarchy in the constant need for a break-out.'[27] Medvedev (1999, p. 32), for his part, speaks of the 'inherent Russian desire to move along the plain' and, at state level, of the 'inclinations of spread and settlement' (ibid., p. 33). Slezkine (1993, p. 5) claims that 'Siberia as the metaphor for untamed nature offered the ultimate test on the way toward timelessness'. After the Cossack Ermak Timofeevich conquered the Siberian Khanate, one of the last fragments of the Golden Horde, in the 16th century, Siberia became both a symbol of freedom for fugitive peasants, slaves, Old Believers[28] and other settlers, and a forced exile for political prisoners. 'Siberia set forth a popular (and populist) patriotic self-image of Russia as an epitome of unlimited freedom, a treasury of possible riches, an El Dorado for the self-made man, the adventurer, the entrepreneur, the explorer, the "virgin-lander"' (Hellberg-Hirn, 1999, p. 54). Gibson (1993, pp. 68ff) argues that while the upper classes often regarded the untamed wilderness of Siberia with horror, the lower classes 'viewed it positively as a kind of Belovod'e, the mythical Promised Land of abundance and freedom' (ibid., pp. 68–9). At the same time, it was a 'territory of terror' for those sent there against their will – it was 'heaven and hell' (Diment and Slezkine, 1993).

Boele (1996) provides an intriguing account of how the North has been a symbol of national identity in Russian Romantic literature. He takes as his point of departure the historical prominence of the opposition between East and West in Russian world view, where East has signalled 'own', 'clean' and even 'holy', and the West something 'alien', 'unclean' and 'heretical' (ibid., p. 251). At the beginning of the 18th century, however, the importance of the East as a symbol of national identity diminished. In the world view of the ever more westernized upper class, the North took precedence over the East as Russia's spatial-ideological point of reference.

As a symbol of Russia's new, European identity, the North initially gives voice to the belief that the Russians have caught up with the West, or have even surpassed it. In eighteenth century panegyric poetry this miraculous leap forward is often visualised by the image of the paradisiac garden, the 'northern Eden', which has replaced the chaos of 'old' Russia. Northern 'imagery' (snow, ice, barren swamps) almost exclusively represents that state of non-existence from which the 'new' Russia is believed to have emerged. (ibid., p. 251)[29]

Reacting to the supposedly slavish imitation by the Russian aristocracy of Western customs, Russian Romantic literature of the 18th century employed the North increasingly as a symbol of a distinctly authentic Russianness. French culture was ridiculed for its affectation, artificiality and effeminacy, diametrically opposed to the Russian winter and the simple folk of the Russian countryside. 'Once turned into a vehicle for expressing a supposedly manly and northern national character, winter comes to be increasingly regarded as the most "Russian" time of the year' (ibid., p. 252). These sentiments intensified, naturally enough, when Napoleon's forces succumbed to the Russian winter in 1812. To Russians he was the Antichrist, and the providential part played by the Russian winter in the outcome of the war acquired a truly apocalyptic dimension. Winter and northernness were increasingly internalized as symbols of Russianness.

However, whereas [the] antithesis was projected on the East–West axis in the days before Peter the Great, Russia now continues to identify itself with the North, as opposed to the West or even the South (both referring to Europe). Thus the ideological significance of the North as the 'national point of the compass' has been completely reversed: in the middle of the eighteenth century it signified Russia's European character, now it embodies its cultural and religious 'otherness'. The spirit of this 'northern' messianism is captured by Maksin Nevzorov in the line: 'From the North comes God himself.' (Ibid., p. 252)

The interest of Russian writers and intellectuals in the North was not limited to Romantics. During the Soviet era, the North became important politically and economically.[30] From 1920 onwards, Soviet efforts to explore and develop the Arctic represented an unceasing endeavour, the results of which are still felt today. The zenith of the campaign came during the 1930s, when the Soviet Union launched the most systematic and all-compassing sequence of Arctic expeditions in the history of polar exploration (McCannon, 1998, p. 4). Along followed the cultivation of the Arctic in propaganda and popular culture, what McCannon (ibid.) refers to as the 'Arctic myth':

> The Arctic myth was a product of social realism, the hegemonic cultural framework of the Stalin period. "Social realism" in this sense refers not merely to the literary formula of the same name but to the overarching aesthetic that held sway over fact and fiction, fantasy and reality, and official doctrine and public attitudes from the beginning of the 1930s. Socialist realism's principal motifs are well known: the cults of Lenin and Stalin, a keen sense of patriotism, a great emphasis on technological and industrial prowess, and, above all, heroism. The Arctic culture of the high-Stalinist period embraced all of these themes and combined them with two other symbols of great potency: the North Pole, whose enigmatic mystique was age old, and aviation, perhaps the twentieth century's most triumphant expression of modernity. This blend was an extraordinarily successful one, and the Arctic became one of the most visible and appealing elements in a cultural environment already saturated with attempts to make every deed seem grand and epic. (Ibid., p. 9)

The Soviet policy of 'conquering the North' (*osvoenie severa*) changed the patterns of settlement and industry of the Russian North fundamentally (see, e.g., Blakkisrud and Hønneland 2006a, pp. 11ff). The population of the territory divided between the 16 federal subjects that account for what the Russians conceive of as the North, numbered less than 2 million in the late 1920s. By the end of the Soviet period, it was nearly 10 million. The new post-Soviet Russian rulers were not inclined to pay what it cost to maintain the elaborate northern infrastructure. In the ensuing debate, 'Romantic' (or social realist?) views of the North were frequently voiced. The Russian North, a leading Russian specialist of the high North, for instance, declares in the title of an article in a Western geographical journal, is at 'a dangerous crossroads' (Agranat, 1998, p. 268). He speaks of the 'destructive breakdown of the old North' (ibid., p. 268) and refers a former governor of Alaska who compared his state with a child requiring long years of 'highly subsidized' care, but who, however, will 'yield a return', if not to his 'parents', then at least to society (ibid., p. 270). He cites his experience of other Arctic states, saying that provided state protection is forthcoming, the result of investing in the Arctic regions could be highly significant to society as a whole. The reason Finns own so many personal computers and mobile telephones is because of the country's 'northernness', Agranat suggests. 'Is this phenomenon not confirmed by the principle, long ago revealed by Soviet specialists, namely that the most progressive, latest technology, will go to the North, or, at least, should go there?' (ibid., p. 274), echoing old Romantic myths and Soviet slogans about the North as the land of the future.

Is the question of Russian identity, then, only approached in terms of time and space, based on history books, archival material, poems and cultural artefacts? True enough, passages through Orthodoxy, Slavophilism/Westernism and Siberia seem to be obligatory exercises for any student of Russian identity (myself obviously included). The concept of identity is frequently used in analyses of nationalism in the former Soviet republics and of relations between them. But some studies have a more contemporary focus and smaller units of analysis than Russia itself, and make use of a more diverse pool of empirical data than old texts. To mention just a few, Petersson (2001) discusses national self-images on the basis of in-depth interviews with regional politicians in St Petersburg, Volgograd, Khabarovsk and Perm, as well as parliamentarians in Moscow. One of his findings is that the national self-image rests mainly on past events (particularly the Great Patriotic War[31] and the accomplishments of Peter the Great),[32] while regional belonging was becoming more important in the 1990s. Further, 'othering' largely takes place *within* Russia. It is, in particular, Moscow that is being 'othered': 'It is the centre that is scapegoated and blamed for all ills that have befallen the country and the regions, and it is the centre that is seen as continuously scheming to worsen the situation even more' (ibid., p. 187). White (2004), for her part, studies identities and livelihood strategies in three small towns in Central Russia based on interviews with members of the local intelligentsias. One of her main findings is that in the Russian *glubinka*, that is, the country's provincial depths, people became increasingly parochial during the 1990s. As opposed to the 'new Russians', mainly found in Moscow and other large cities, the lower classes had experienced a decline in social and geographical mobility, and lost interest in and respect for Moscow. Their consciousness of being Russian was supplemented and partly overshadowed by local patriotism (ibid., p. 187). Based on ethnographic fieldwork at Moscow State Institute of International Relations (MGIMO), Müller (2008) focuses particularly on the distinction between 'Westernness' and Europeanness for MGIMO students. Many students at the institute, he argues, explicitly address their lifestyle as European, and not Western. While a Western lifestyle in general is understood rather pejoratively, the European signifier signals a more open, two-way relationship between Europeanness and Russianness. Identifying with Europe in this way does not mean imitating Europe or wanting to leave Russia for Europe, but to engage selectively with European attributes. 'Here the European signifier is rather used as a marker of positive distinction from "ordinary" Russianness' (ibid., p. 17). Less empirical, but all the more fascinating is Kelly's (2004) discussion of identity and everyday life in Russia.[33] Taking the untranslatable Russian word *byt* as her point of departure, she reflects upon the Russian disdain for plain, everyday life.[34] ('Everyday life' is the common lexical translation of *byt*, but the word has a strong connotation of dullness to it.) It is preoccupation with the *big* questions in life – art, philosophy, religion – that constitute being a Russian; the *byt* is just a troublesome by-product of being. ' "Life without daily life" would sound absurd in English; *zhizn' bez byta* makes perfect sense' (ibid., p. 167).[35] Finally, there is Ries's (1997) acclaimed study of Russian talk. She argues that 'spontaneous conversational discourses are a primary mechanism by which ideologies and cultural stances are shaped and maintained' (ibid., p. 3), and that the stories she heard 'implicitly or explicitly addressed the structures and practices of power in Russian (Soviet) society' (ibid., p. 5).[36] Her main theoretical contribution is arguably on the identity-constituting role of litanies in Russian talk:

> Litanies were those passages in conversation where a speaker would enunciate a series of complaints, grievances, or worries about problems, troubles, afflictions, tribulations, or losses, and then often comment on these enumerations with a poignant rhetorical question ('Why is everything so bad with us?'), a sweeping, fatalistic lament about the hopelessness of the situation, or an expressive Russian sigh of disappointment and resignation. (Ibid., p. 84)

Research questions and methodology

In the beginning of this chapter, I asked what it means to be a borderland Russian, living in the high north, but with roots in the south (as practically all Kola inhabitants have; see next chapter) – and with Western neighbours just across the fence. Simply put, how do people in Russia's north-western region – one and a half decades or so after 'the border was opened'[37] – narratively[38] differentiate themselves from their southern relatives and Scandinavian[39] neighbours? With my theoretical sources of inspiration in mind, I have devised the following four sets of questions, each containing both theoretical and empirical dimensions:

* Which narratives do north-west Russians use to contrast themselves with southerners and westerners?
* Is there evidence in the ethnographic material that the 'opening of the border' between Russia and the Nordic countries has changed the character of the Kola Peninsula as a borderland?[40]
* Do the people of Kola exhibit 'multiple identities'?[41] That is, in addition to their national identity as Russians do they also speak of themselves as northerners, or even as inhabitants of a transnational Barents Euro-Arctic Region?
* Do the personal narratives in my ethnographic material resonate with political rhetoric about cross-border collaboration in the region? Will my investigation provide further evidence of the need to take identity (and narratives?) into account when studying international relations?

I conducted some twenty-five in-depth interviews with small groups of inhabitants of the Kola Peninsula between 2004 and 2006. Each group consisted of two to four persons in addition to one or two interviewers. My colleague Anne-Kristin Jørgensen took part in some of the interviews I did myself. Around two-thirds of the interviews were carried out by Natalya Metanovskaya and Sergey Klimashevich, both studying at the time for their PhDs at Murmansk State Technical University. In line with the qualitative research tradition, no attempt was made to randomize the sample.[42] However, we did take care to make the sample as representative as possible – within practical limits. For one thing, most interviewees come from Murmansk, the biggest city on the peninsula and 'capital' of the administrative entity of Murmansk Oblast.[43] A few live in other towns, including the closed, military towns of the region (see Chapter 2). We wanted both sexes represented more or less equally and a certain diversification in age, education and professional background. Hence, the age of my interviewees ranges from the early twenties to the late fifties, with a majority in their thirties and forties. Slightly more than half of them are professionals, some with education at university level. Among others, there are economists, teachers, dentists, psychologists, artists, naval officers, engineers, shop attendants, housewives and taxi drivers in the sample, and also a few students. Those that I interviewed myself were largely people I had interviewed before and maintained professional contact with in connection with other research projects. Most of them are therefore involved in various projects with Norwegian partners. Natasha and Sergey, for their part, deliberately sought people from as varied positions in society as possible. However, we lack people in the upper and lower echelons of society: neither the political nor the financial elite of the region is represented, nor the struggling lower class. The interviewees were not asked about their ethnicity, nor was the difference between being a *russkiy* (ethnic Russian) and a *rossiyanin* (citizen of the Russian Federation) an issue in the interviews. On a few occasions, ethnicity became a topic. Several interviewees talked about themselves as 'from the Ukraine', which appeared to mean that one of the parents was Ukrainian or that the interviewees had grown up in the Ukraine, but had Russian as their first language. One interviewee defined herself as Jewish, 'despite being Russian as well, strictly speaking'. Of those I asked, none admitted to being proficient in any of the other 'post-Soviet' languages, nor in the indigenous language of the region, Sámi (see Chapter 2).

I wanted the interviews to be more like an informal conversation rather than just a question–answer session. The interviewers were instructed to indicate themes for the conversation – how do people on the Kola Peninsula distinguish themselves from southerners and Scandinavians, and what's it like living in the northern environment[44] – and let the conversation run as freely as possible, only changing the subject when they felt the current theme was exhausted. Most interviews took place at the homes of the interviewees or in public places like coffee bars and restaurants. A few were done at the interviewees' workplace after working hours. A typical interview lasted a couple of hours, though some went on for three to four hours. Tape recorders were not used, but we took care to note down in writing what was said as accurately as possible.[45] Being two interviewers in most of the interviews allowed us to compare notes, which probably enhanced the accuracy of our interview transcripts. It should be noted, nevertheless, that the extracts presented below are not verbatim renditions of what was actually said. One thing is the omission of small nuances (at best) because the interviewers were unable to keep up with the flow of words. Another is the fact that the interviews were conducted in Russian, translated into Norwegian and then into English.[46] My interview transcripts would not satisfy the requirements either of pure linguistic analysis, nor for several other variants of discourse analysis, including conversation analysis (CA). That said, I was not interested in analysis of talks for the sake of it, noting, for example, when interviewees paused or hesitated, which particles of speech were used, and the order of turn-taking. While I do maintain an interest in 'how people talk' (and the concepts they use), I am more interested in what they say and in discussing this in relation to a wider context: the utterances of others, the findings of other researchers, social and political background.[47]

As mentioned in the introduction to this chapter, this study is informed more broadly by one and a half decades of studying politics and society on the Kola Peninsula. Although my ethnographic fieldwork has never extended over many weeks at a time, I have visited the area frequently – on average four or five times a year – to conduct interviews for other research projects.[48] So while this study concerns mainly the interviews set out above, I do sporadically refer to other interviews – and indeed to other written records, including the Russian media.

The rest of the book

This introductory chapter is followed by a background chapter on the Kola Peninsula. In addition to a brief history of the region, the chapter provides an overview of political, economic and social life there and describes how the region was drawn into a comprehensive network of international cooperation after the end of the Cold War. Chapters 3–5 present the results of my empirical investigation, focusing on how north-west Russians distinguish themselves from Russian southerners on the one hand (Chapter 3) and Scandinavians (Chapter 4) on the other, and their perceptions of living in the northern environment (Chapter 5). Each chapter starts out with three relatively extensive interview extracts, which are each commented on in turn. Then follows a more general discussion where also other interviews, observations and literature are taken into consideration. Focus is on which narratives are at work and how the changing role of the East–West border has affected narrative and identity. Chapter 6 recapitulates and discusses the theoretical contributions on the narrative constitution of identities in borderlands and international relations.

2
The Kola Peninsula: Politics, Society, International Networks

What resources! What a country! And it was all given to Vanya and Masha.[1] Imagine if all this had been given to a France or an Italy, they would have created a mighty empire (*derzhava*)! But no. God knows how to divide things up and share them out.[2]

Introduction

Murmansk Oblast, which covers the geographical area of the Kola Peninsula, is a prime example of the Soviet industrial and military adventure. While permanent settlements had been established in the sixteenth century, the Kola Peninsula was inhabited by only a few thousand people when World War I started. By the end of the Cold War, its population had reached well beyond one million, it had the world's largest stockpiles of nuclear warheads, it was the country's most developed fish-processing region – and had gained notoriety in the West for the state of its environment. Panning forwards two decades, the region is considered by many to be one of the world's most promising new energy provinces.

In this chapter, I shall introduce the reader to the region, recount the history of the Russian north-west in general, and the Kola Peninsula in particular, from the point of view of habitation, industrialization and militarization. I include here sections on civil–military relations and a discussion of the likely growth of a an oil and gas industry based on the resources under the Barents Sea. I shall focus on the region's broader demographic, resource-related and economic trends, rather than go into details. I outline post-Cold War relations between north-western Russia and the Nordic countries in the Barents Euro-Arctic Region (BEAR) (see Map 2.1) and examine the various bilateral arrangements. I concentrate

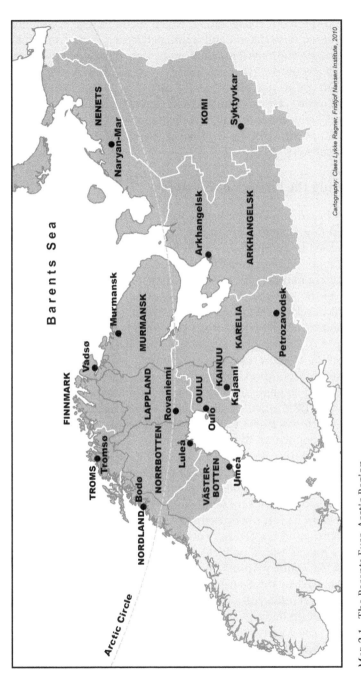

Map 2.1   The Barents Euro-Arctic Region

mainly on the BEAR collaboration, which spans a range of functional fields, and various bilateral and multilateral partnerships to promote nuclear safety and environmental protection more widely. I discuss Russian perceptions of these cooperative arenas, drawing on material gathered in connection with several evaluations of the Nordic–Russian interface in the European North. This chapter also includes some of the interviews I have made during my ongoing investigation of borderland identities, not primarily for the sake of theorizing, but to add flair to the political story.

Populating the Russian north-west[3]

Russians began the exploration of the north during the ascendancy of Kievan Rus' (c. 880–1250). Monks looking for peace and quiet were accompanied by industrious people hunting for furs, precious stones and salt followed the rivers to the White Sea and northern Urals. An abundance of natural resources coupled with the risk of military incursions from the south and west were the push and pull factors behind the rapid development of the southern parts of today's Arkhangelsk Oblast and the republics of Karelia and Komi in the sixteenth century (see Map 2.1). Arkhangelsk was founded in 1584 to serve as the main seaport of the Moscow state. The future capital of the Republic of Komi, Syktyvkar, was founded two years later. Arkhangelsk was Russia's leading naval and shipbuilding city, and a centre for the region's lumber industry. By 1719, when the first Russian census was undertaken, the Russian north was home to some 400,000 people, or 2.5 per cent of the Russian population. When restrictions on the movement of Russian peasants came into effect, and the Russian government re-assessed its strategic options, the colonization of the Russian north slowed down. By the beginning of the nineteenth century, about 550,000 people lived in the north, or 1.8 per cent of the Russian population.

World War I had clearly demonstrated the geopolitical importance of the far north, and the region's natural resources attracted the interest of Soviet leaders whose political goals included the rapid industrialization of the country. In the late 1920s and early 1930s, a number of towns emerged in the Soviet north-west to service the extraction of various natural resources, among them oil in Komi, coal in the Pechora river basin in Arkhangelsk and apatite deposits in Khibiny on the Kola Peninsula. The forest industry reached new heights, and large mining centres were founded at Kirovsk, Apatity and Monchegorsk in the mid-1930s.

Around 1.4 mill. people (1.5 per cent of the Russian population) resided in the European Russian north in 1926. During the 1930s, a deliberate policy was adopted to increase the population by persuasion, resettlement and by force: thousands of prisoners were dispatched to labour camps in the region. By 1939, the population had risen to 2.2 mill. people, or 2 per cent of the Russian population. From the end of the 1950s, the main form of resettlement to the north was individual migration, though the Communist youth or labour brigades ran recruitment campaigns, which accounted for part of the more organized effort. In the 1950s, migration slowed down as development of the virgin lands in Kazakhstan was given priority. Interest in the north rose again in the early 1960s with the development of oil and gas fields in the Timan-Pechora basin, divided between the Komi Republic and Arkhangelsk Oblast (Nenets Autonomous Okrug). At the same time, the pulp and paper mills in Arkhangelsk and Komi and the military-industrial complex in Severomorsk (Murmansk), Severodvinsk and Plesetsk (both Arkhangelsk) were expanding rapidly.

In the 1970s and 1980s, growth was supported by significant investment and an active migration policy to attract people to the north. People living in particularly harsh climatic areas, such as the Russian north, were paid more, enjoyed higher pensions, earlier retirement, extra holidays and were assured a better supply and wider assortment of goods in the shops. Soviet migration policy was largely based on the principle of rotation: after working several years in the north, migrants were expected to return to 'the big land' and let young migrants take over. In the 1970s, policies were changed. The authorities were now urging people to stay in the north, creating similar living conditions as those in traditionally populated areas of the country. According to the 1989 census, the percentages of those who were either born in the region or had lived there twenty years or more amounted to 67 per cent for Arkhangelsk and Karelia, 57 per cent for Komi, 56 per cent for Murmansk and 52 per cent for Nenets (the average for Russian regions was 70 per cent). By then, the population of the area had reached 4.8 mill., or 3.2 per cent of the Russian population.

To illustrate these changes from the vantage point of individuals living in the region, I want to present the first of my interviews – actually a monologue by a woman in her late thirties telling the story of how her parents arrived at the Kola Peninsula in the 1950s. The reader should pay attention not only to the chain of events that resulted in her parents and relatives ending up in the area – labour camps and economic incentives play a part – but also to how she herself spent much of her childhood with her grandparents in Moscow while her parents were working up north.

– Perhaps I ought to start by filling in the background, how my parents got to Kola in the first place. I'll start with my mother. You'll see how her story coincides with my dad's. My mother, she was born in Smolensk, in western Russia, in the country. There were twelve children altogether. Their father was killed by gypsies when my mother was just a year old. He'd been the foreman of a collective farm. My mother's 15-year-older sister got tired of looking after all the kids. She left home and started living with a woman. Anyway, she apparently shoved this woman down a well, where she drowned. [My aunt] was convicted and sent to prison; that would have been in the '40s, either during the war or soon after. When she got out she headed for Kirovsk. Why, I don't know. Probably to earn a livelihood. Then she was joined by some of her brothers and sisters, including my mum, who was nineteen by then.

– My dad's from Kiev originally. A Ukrainian. Babushka was half-Polish, a communist too, but my biological grandpa was 'grey' (seryy) – a member of different party. They were divorced and she met another man, from Leningrad. He was lying low to avoid paying maintenance. They travelled the whole country. Babushka, she was arrested under article 57 for political agitation. But they didn't arrest her husband. Dad lived alone for a spell before joining the army at seventeen. He'd been born in 1927 and was the first generation not to see active war service. To make up, though, they kept them in the army longer after the war. Seven years, in Armenia. Instead of receiving a prison sentence, Babushka was sent off to build the BAM [Baikal-Amur Mainline]. What they taught us at school about it being built by young communists isn't true. Prisoners built it. Well, that was where she met her third husband. An Armenian. He was doing time for political agitation too. He'd had a senior position in Moscow. They sentenced Babushka to seven years in the gulag, ded ['granddad'] got ten. In 1950 or 51 they arrived in Kirovsk, or Twenty-Fifth Kilometre [a real place name: Dvadtsat' Pyatyy Kilometr]. Moscow was out of bounds. Why they went to Twenty-Fifth Kilometre I don't really know. After he was demobbed, my dad started looking for his own mother. He found her. He had taught himself Armenian and could talk to his step-father in his native language. Babushka started applying for permission to travel to Moscow again. Ded was rehabilitated in 1964, just before I was born. They went to Moscow, ded worked at the main statistics bureau. He was very well educated. Babushka only had four years of school. She was a bit eccentric. Light-headed. Never worked, and never got a pension either. Ded died in 1986, babushka in 1987. I don't know how old they were; you didn't always know that sort of thing in the country.

– Between the ages of one and seven I lived with babushka and ded in Moscow nine months in every year. I was only at home in Twenty-Fifth Kilometre in the winter. After I'd started school, it was just three months a year. I lived in Moscow because my parents did shift work. Me living in Moscow made it easier. Babushka didn't work, and they had more food in Moscow too. Ded tried persuading me to stay with them, but I wanted to go to a school near my own parents. Don't really remember much of the northern part of my childhood. I can't recall liking one place any more

than the other. It made me feel a bit special, exotic in Moscow, though – people wanted to know whether I lived north of the Polar Circle. I didn't know whether we did or didn't. Did we have a banya [sauna] at home, were there shops there, did we have polar bears? People in St Petersburg and Moscow have always looked down their nose at everyone else, 'here they come and empty our shelves' etc. 'What's up north for pity's sake?' [chto sever?] they'd say [shrugs her shoulders]. As far as I was concerned, it was the other way round. I felt proud of being from Murmansk when I was in Moscow or even further south, like Sochi. Why? Because it was so far away. It wasn't Novgorod or anything. It was Murmansk. Now that's really far off...

Murmansk Oblast: Population, economy, environment

Until World War I, the vast territory of the Kola Peninsula was inhabited by a few thousand people and of practically no significance, militarily or otherwise, to the Russian empire. The Terskii Coast (the eastern part of the peninsula) came under the control of the republic of Novgorod in the thirteenth century, but there are no records of permanent Novgorodian settlement on the peninsula until the first half of the fifteenth century. Following the collapse of the Novgorodian state in 1487, the area became a relatively neglected northern outpost of the Muscovite principality. Almost a century later, permanent settlements were established along the northern coast at Kola and Pechenga, the first centred around a new fortification, the latter around a monastery.

In 1708, Kola Uyezd ('district') was incorporated into the new Arkhangelsk Gubernia. In 1883, however, the uyezd was re-established within the gubernia and subsequently renamed Aleksandrovsk Uyezd in 1899 after the young town of Aleksandrovsk, which today is the closed military town of Polyarnyy (see below). Although the strategic potential of the ice-free Murman Coast had been recognized at least a half-century earlier, the Russian authorities did nothing to exploit this gift of nature until forced to act by World War I.

The lack of ice-free ports in European Russia, excepting those in the Black and Baltic Seas where narrow straits made it relatively easy for an enemy to blockade the Russian fleets, prompted the construction of the Murman Railway, which reached the Kola Fjord in 1916. At the end of the line, a supply port was built, called Romanov-na-Murmane, but renamed Murmansk the very next year, 1917. The development of fisheries was a main priority from the outset. Towards the end of the Soviet era, Murmansk had the largest fish-processing plant in the Soviet Union; some 80,000 people were working in the region's fishing industry; and the region's fishing fleet plied the oceans of the world.

The Soviet Northern Fleet came into being in 1933. For more than two decades, it remained the smallest of the Soviet Navy's four fleets. In the 1950s, as the Soviet Union struggled to achieve nuclear parity with the US, more resources were poured into expanding the fleet. 1958 saw the launch of the country's first nuclear-powered submarine; it was stationed at Zapadnaya Litsa on the Kola Peninsula. Over the ensuing decade, many more nuclear-powered submarines joined the Northern Fleet. By the late 1960s, the Northern Fleet was greater and more important than any of the other Soviet naval fleets.

The civilian sector of the post-war economy in the oblast came to be dominated by heavy industry. Entire towns were built from scratch around large mining, metallurgical and chemical enterprises. The Murman Railway linked many of these industrial centres, and it still constitutes the infrastructure backbone of the Kola Peninsula. Nonferrous mining and metallurgy (primarily nickel and copper) and fertilizer production from mined phosphates are particularly important.

The government needed to move enormous numbers of people to the Kola Peninsula during the years of industrial expansion, mainly from the rest of Russia, but also from the other Soviet republics, especially Ukraine and Belarus. By the end of the Soviet period, the population of Murmansk Oblast had reached nearly 1.2 mill. As noted above, incentives included higher wages, lower retirement age (45 for women and 50 for men in heavy industry) and subsidized holidays at Black Sea resorts. Although the standard of living was well above the Soviet average (but not as high as Moscow's; see interview extract above), many still regarded it as a temporary arrangement, returning to their native towns upon retirement. The fisheries and military sector were particularly prone to high personnel turnover rates.

Much changed with the break-up of the Soviet Union and ensuing economic reforms. Steep inflation in the early 1990s decimated the value of people's savings, making it impossible for many to buy a home to retire to in more temperate areas of Russia. Most of the economic and material incentives for working in the North disappeared. The birth rate dropped, and younger people left the region in droves. The population of Murmansk Oblast fell below one million around the turn of the millennium. In the 2002 census, it was 892,534, down 24 per cent from the last Soviet census in 1989 (the sharpest drop of any of the north-west Russian federal subjects). In 2008, the population was down to 842,500. Murmansk is the largest city, counting 311,200 souls in 2007 (336,137 in the 2002 census and 468,039 in the 1989 census). The closed city of Severomorsk (see below) was the peninsula's second largest city until the

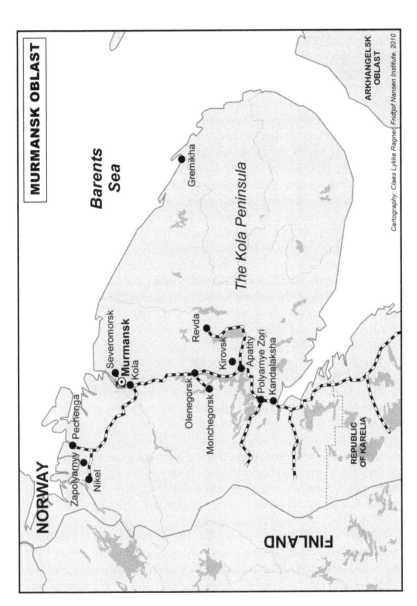

Map 2.2   The Kola Peninsula/Murmansk Oblast

mid-2000s, with a population of around 75,400 in the 2002 census. By 2008, it had fallen to 53,500, leaving Apatity as the region's second city, with 61,600 people. Then follow Severomorsk and Monchegorsk, the latter with a population of 48,100. Russians constitute 85.25 per cent of the population, Ukrainians 6.37 per cent, Belarusians 2.28 per cent, Tatars 0.89 per cent and the indigenous population of the region – the Sámi – 0.2 per cent. Both federal and regional authorities have tried various programmes to help people to leave the Russian North, but they have generally been underfinanced. And many people have no option but to stay in the North because they have nowhere to move to and can't afford to buy a place to live in the south; see interview extract below.

Most sectors of the economy changed radically during the 1990s. Russian fishermen started delivering catches abroad, crippling most of the land-based processing industry in Murmansk by the mid-1990s. Total catches also declined by more than 50 per cent since Russian shipowners could not afford to fund fishing in the waters off Africa and South America any more. In the military sector, the number of vessels in the Northern Fleet more than halved during the 1990s, largely as a result of international disarmament obligations and economic hardships. Further, budget cutbacks affected routine maintenance, causing problems for the region's four large naval shipyards. Strikes and social unrest in the shipyard towns became a recurrent theme in regional media in the late 1990s.

Much attention has been given to the environmental problems of Murmansk Oblast since the break-up of the Soviet Union. The sulphur dioxide (SO_2) spewed out of the nickel smelters in Nikel and Monchegorsk cause acid rain to fall within the Kola Peninsula and in neighbouring Nordic countries. The Northern Fleet and Murmansk Shipping Company, the owner of the nuclear-powered ice-breakers stationed at Murmansk, had been suffering storage capacity problems since the 1960s, and radioactive waste and spent nuclear fuel were dumped in the Barents and Kara Seas until 1992. Growing numbers of decommissioned naval vessels increased the problem from the late 1980s. There are several reasons for this situation. First, there is only enough infrastructure in place for the de-fuelling of a handful submarines a year. Second, because intermediate storage facilities for spent nuclear fuel and for liquid and solid waste were filled to capacity many years ago, much of the spent nuclear fuel and radioactive waste is stored under unsatisfactory conditions. Third, it has been impossible to transport much of the spent nuclear fuel to processing plants because of inadequate transport facilities. Finally, the Kola nuclear power plant, located in Polyarnye Zori in the southern parts of the Kola Peninsula, is considered the most hazardous industry in the European North. Several operational incidents have taken place since the plant was put into operation in 1972, among them a loss-of-cooling incident in 1993, which might have resulted in a meltdown incident in the oldest reactor. The International Atomic Energy Agency (IAEA) has calculated the probability of a serious meltdown in the oldest reactors to be 25 per cent over a period of twenty-three years (Bergman and Baklanov, 1998). Such an accident would not have Chernobyl dimensions, since the reactors are of a different and less dangerous design. Nevertheless, the local effects would be grave, and deposits of radioactive matter in parts of Russia and neighbouring countries would probably be high enough to influence both cancer statistics and patterns of food consumption.

Russia's economic recovery since the crisis of 1998 has improved social and economic conditions in Murmansk Oblast as well. Population is still in decline and the environmental problems are far from solved, but the future looks more promising, not least with the prospect of an oil and gas industry, which we will return to below. First, however, a brief extract from my interview with Tamara and Konstantin, a married couple in their mid-fifties. The interview extract illustrates the situation of many pensioners on the Kola Peninsula in the post-Soviet period.

Interviewer: Is it safe living in the north, d'you think, thinking of nuclear safety for instance?
Tamara: It's a very difficult question. We try obviously not to dwell on it too much, we've got to live here anyway.
Interviewer: What do you mean by got to live here? Is there anywhere else you'd like to live?
Tamara: The northern climate, it suits me down to the ground. I couldn't live in the south, not in that heat, you know. Petrozavodsk – that's where I draw the line [Petrozavodsk, the capital of the Republic of Karelia, is about 62° North].
Konstantin: Agree, and anyway, moving in this country is so unbelievably complicated. Moving south, for us, would be like moving to a foreign country. If we did move to Ukraine, there would be so many problems not many would want to take the risk. That is, if it's people of our age you're thinking about. Travelling abroad is something that appeals more to the young.
Tamara: The extra pension they gave us here in the north will soon be history too. Pensioners will find it harder to cope, though how it could be worse than it is at the moment is a moot point. But if we wanted to relocate to Ukraine, the pension we've earned here in the north wouldn't be enough to stop us dying of hunger.
Interviewer: What makes you say that?

> Konstantin: Because, well, when people moved north, we all shared a united, fantastic country. We all thought we'd be here for a certain time, doing our bit for the country; then we'd move back to our homes in the south again. But today, Ukraine doesn't want an influx of 'northern' pensioners – they've more than enough trouble with their own. The pension they give to people who've come back is 100 griven [about 20 USD]. People have to make do as best they can.

Civil–military relations

During the Soviet era, there was little interaction between the military and civilian sectors of Murmansk Oblast.[4] The two structures relied on separate communication infrastructures, and the majority of the servicemen and their families were housed in military towns, settlements built to serve the naval or air bases, or within the garrison precincts where they served. For all practical purposes, the military was 'a state within the state'. But are relations between civil society and the military more relaxed in the post-Soviet period?

One of the most striking features of the military presence on the Kola Peninsula is the six 'closed towns'. In 1992, the Law on Closed Administrative-Territorial Formations was introduced to regulate the status of some forty formerly secret cities in the Russian Federation. These cities were 'opened' or 'civilianized' in the sense that their existence was officially admitted, they could be found on ordinary maps and they were known by proper names rather than a numerical code. A closed administrative-territorial formation, a *ZATO* in its Russian abbreviation (*zakrytoe administrativno-territorial'noe obrazovanie*), differs from ordinary military bases inasmuch as it is a political and administrative entity (at the local level) in its own right, with its own civilian authorities. On the other hand, it is not under the control of the federal subject in which it is located, but the Ministry of Defence.[5] Further, ZATOs keep their tax revenues for their own use, and the inhabitants enjoy special social privileges.[6]

With six ZATOs, Murmansk Oblast has more than any other Russian federal subject.[7] They provide housing for the navy and workers at the region's naval shipyards. Zaozyorsk (formerly Murmansk-150) is located southeast of the Rybachiy Peninsula, close to the Norwegian border. Gadzhievo (formerly Murmansk-130 or Skalistyy), Snezhnogorsk (formerly Murmansk-60), Polyarnyy and Vidyaevo are on the western side and Severomorsk on the eastern side of the Kola Fjord, all just north of Murmansk City. Combined population was

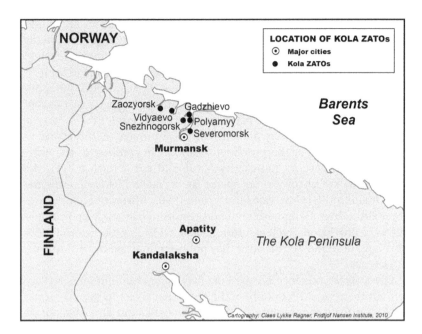

Map 2.3   The Kola ZATOs

about 150,000 in the mid-2000s, with Severomorsk accounting for about one half of this total.

So despite some moves towards increased civil–military integration, the old division is still intact. Physical distance limits contact between civilians and the military settlements located in the vicinity of Murmansk, that is, Severomorsk and, to some extent, Polyarnyy, Snezhnogorsk, Vidyaevo and Gadzhievo. Here it should be noted that ZATO status is related mainly to financial, not security factors. Severomorsk, Polyarnyy and Vidyaevo did not become ZATOs until some years after the ZATO system was established. They had petitioned the national authorities for ZATO status and were backed by regional authorities because they wanted the Ministry of Defence to take financial responsibility for these largely military settlements. While ZATO status is generally perceived as a form of financial security for the towns, the inhabitants of the ZATOs on the Kola Peninsula suffered considerable hardship in the late 1990s due to the strained economy of the Northern Fleet and naval shipyards in the region.

Military units became increasingly reliant on material support offered by local or regional authorities and civilian organizations during the

1990s. A striking illustration is the way civilian institutions and enterprises literally sponsor military units, 'adopting' them to all intents and purposes. The idea received public endorsement in 1997, when Governor Yuriy Yevdokimov invited all the regions of Russia to sponsor a submarine of the Northern Fleet. Renaming the vessel after the sponsoring region and manning it with draftees from that particular part of Russia strengthened the ties between region and vessel.

The military sector has proven more of a burden than blessing to Murmansk Oblast in the post-Soviet period.[8] In addition to the environmental damage by radioactive waste and spent nuclear fuel, the region's civilian sector was not spared the social problems affecting the ZATOs and military garrisons in the late 1990s. Although regional and local authorities along with civilian organizations took it upon themselves to provide material assistance, the ZATOs' situation would probably have been much worse had they not been financed by the Ministry of Defence.

The military presence on the Kola Peninsula also represents a problem for the regional economy in the sense that access to military zones or ZATOs for non-residents, especially foreigners but also Russians, is more difficult. A recurrent obstacle in the joint Norwegian–Russian nuclear safety collaboration (see below) has been the refusal of Russian authorities to grant Norwegians access to nuclear waste storage sites on ZATO territory or in even more restricted zones.[9] Joint projects between the Norwegian fishing industry and the small fishing community of Teriberka on the northern coast of the Kola Peninsula have also been hampered, as the village lies within the administrative area of the Severomorsk ZATO. Likewise, joint fishery studies in the Russian zone of the Barents Sea – a tradition dating back several decades, and central to the management of the Barents Sea fisheries – came to a halt in the late 1990s when the Northern Fleet raised objections.[10]

Big oil playground?[11]

In north-western Russia, only onshore oil and gas resources are currently exploited. The field lies in the Timan-Pechora basin, which straddles the Komi Republic and Nenets Autonomous Okrug (see Map 2.1). Since the early 2000s, oil from Timan-Pechora (and to some extent also from Western Siberia, which is Russia's main petroleum province) is increasingly transported to the West by tankers from Murmansk. North-western Russia has several oil export terminals, but the only port able to accommodate tankers over 100,000 tonnes – and even up to 350,000 tonnes – is the deep harbour at Murmansk. Since the Kola Fjord is never entirely frozen, tankers can sail to and from Murmansk all year-round. The region's main export is crude oil from Nenets and oil products brought to Murmansk by rail and small tankers, and transferred to larger ships for destinations mostly in Europe. Such relatively complicated export routes are economically feasible thanks to increasing production rates, a stagnant domestic demand and bottlenecks in other outlets. Exports via Murmansk increased vastly after 2002, creating a lucrative spinoff market in the region.[12]

The real oil and gas potential of the Kola Peninsula lies offshore. While offshore reserve estimates are highly uncertain, geologists put recoverable oil and gas resources in the Russian part of the Barents and Pechora Seas at around 24 billion tonnes of oil equivalent. Even if these figures turn out to be much smaller in practice, Russians expect to find sizeable deposits. Most is believed to be gas, especially in the western part of the region (in the Barents Sea), while the Pechora Sea seems likely to contain significant amounts of both oil and gas. The Prirazlomnoe oil field will start up first. Located at 57 km from the Nenets shoreline at a water depth of 20 meters, it is currently controlled by two state-owned companies in partnership, Gazprom and Rosneft. The largest offshore gas field so far discovered on the Barents Sea shelf is the Shtokmanovskoe (or Shtokman) gas and condensate field. Located 650 km north-east of Murmansk, it is one of the largest offshore gas fields in the world. As with many offshore structures in the region, the technical hurdles are immense. It lies 550 km from land, the water depth varies between 280 and 380 meters, and it is subject to drifting ice and high waves. The plan is to land Shtokman gas at a spot east of Murmansk, from which it could either be exported through a new pipeline to Europe or as liquefied natural gas (LNG) by ship. There have also been discussions about a two-phase development of the field, the first as an LNG project for the US market and the second to serve the European market through a new gas pipeline. Until 2003, Gazprom continued to insist that 2007 would be Shokman's start-up date. Since then, statements have been less certain. The field is officially slated for production in 2013, but few believe it will be possible to stay within this timeframe or even near it. Taking European and Russian demand into account, Gazprom may not actually need Shtokman gas until around 2020.

The Shtokman project was originally allocated to Rosshelf, a consortium of Gazprom, local naval shipyards and defence-industry design bureaus seeking to convert production to equipment for offshore oil production. A group of foreign companies (Conoco, Fortum, Norsk

Hydro and Total) worked with Gazprom to improve geological data, advise on development solutions and perform market evaluations. In 2002, Rosshelf was pushed aside and the license for Shtokman transferred to a new Gazprom vehicle called Sermorneftegas, owned jointly with Rosneft. The next year, Gazprom invited foreign companies to take part in the establishment of a consortium for extraction of gas, production of LNG, transport and marketing of gas, with a view to start up in 2011. This was supposed to be the first of three steps in the development of Shtokman and involve the production of some 20 bill. cubic metres of gas annually. Most large international companies showed interest, and in 2005 Gazprom announced a short list of five companies: Chevron, ConocoPhillips, Hydro, Statoil and Total, among which Gazprom would choose its consortium partners. They would own a 49 per cent stake in the venture. The final decision was postponed several times, without any clear reason. In autumn 2006, Gazprom abandoned the idea of an international consortium, along with plans to produce LNG for the US market. Instead, Gazprom had decided to go it alone, and send Shtokman gas through a pipeline to the European market. One year later, however, the Norwegian company StatoilHydro (formerly Statoil and Hydro; since November 2009: again Statoil) and the French Total were invited by Gazprom to become partners in a new project. So-called front end engineering design on the project will be finished in the second half of 2009, allowing a final investment decision to be made. The first phase of the project provides for a yield of nearly 24 bill. cubic metres of gas per year, pipeline deliveries commence in 2013 and LNG in 2014.

Brunstad et al. (2004) provide three scenarios for the economic, political and social development of Barents Russia (understood as the Russian part of the BEAR) towards 2015, taking oil and gas developments as their point of departure.[13] In the scenario *Big Oil Playground*, the oil-rich Russian north-west has been captured by the oil and gas majors, both Russian and foreign (mainly US), while the forestry industry has come to dominate the south of the region. Much of the business is centred on the new petroleum hub of Murmansk. Shtokman gas is processed and liquefied at a huge LNG installation, operated mainly by fly-in-fly-out workers. Oil export on supertankers has multiplied thanks to the new oil export pipeline from Western Siberia and shuttle tankers from the Prirazlomnoe field in the Pechora Sea. The Kremlin's focus is on short-term economic growth, and the oil companies are given increasingly free reins at the regional level, as long as they stay out of federal politics and a sufficient part of their windfall ends up in the Federal Treasury.

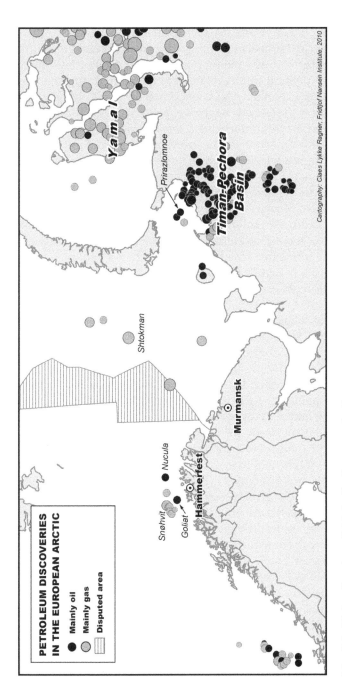

Map 2.4   Main oil and gas fields in the European Arctic

Investment-promoting reforms, such as allowing increased international participation in the Russian economy, take precedence over direct control in this scenario. Heavy industry and nuclear lobbies lose influence. Wealth and political influence are very unevenly distributed. Russian and multinational commercial actors, especially in the oil and gas sector, control most of the elected members of political bodies. Social inequality has increased sharply, influencing access to health and education.

Russian Bear Preserve tells the story of a Barents Russia that is re-securitized and under the tight control of Moscow. Russian politics takes a nationalist turn, and oil and gas resources are cards in efforts to promote national interests in global affairs. Strategic control over petroleum resources becomes a priority, and foreign companies can only participate as distinctly junior partners. The Russian authorities continue to support economic and military presence in the region, eager not to turn it into a resource base for the West. The oil and gas industry in Barents Russia is significant both onshore and offshore. The development of the Shtokman field is postponed, but other big projects have gone forward. Arkhangelsk is the region's 'oil capital'. Heavy industry and nuclear lobbies are strong, and energy reforms are only partial. Democracy is 'governed' from the centre, and local and regional news media are tightly controlled. The state has a relatively active role in the economy, while the influence of business elites and oligarchs in regional affairs is restrained by selective use of the law against the most politically ambitious. Lack of public information hampers international cooperation and work on health and the environment.

In *European Periphery*, we learn about a Barents Russia where the expected oil and gas bonanza does not happen – or at least is delayed beyond 2015. Northern Barents Russia, in particular the Kola Peninsula, loses people and business. Energy price reforms reduce domestic gas demand growth, and high costs and technical challenges put offshore Barents Sea fields last in the line for new field developments. Faced with competition from a new and more profitable Far Eastern pipeline built to serve the growing Chinese market, construction of the planned pipeline from Western Siberia to the Barents Sea coast is put on hold. Russian politics focuses on reforming and diversifying the economy to enable long-term sustainable growth, but sacrifices have to be made in the short term. Much heavy industry in Barents Russia that used to rely on cheap power is closed down, while the forestry and fishing industries are revived. The BEAR collaboration, which is now part of the EU Northern Dimension (see below), the Arctic Council and other cross-border cooperative arrangements, are important to Barents Russia.

But they are mainly involved in environmental projects and social programmes for the underprivileged. The environmental situation and health conditions are better than a decade earlier, due to better air and water quality and lifestyle changes. We are now at the half-way mark between the publication of the scenarios and the time they envisage. Which is most likely to describe the situation in 2015? First, the 'big oil playground' in Brunstad et al.'s (2004) terms does not seem very likely. US oil companies were removed from the Shtokman equation in 2006, with invitations going to companies from small power Norway and middle power France when Gazprom decided a year later not to develop the project alone after all. Plans for a pipeline from Western Siberia to the Kola Peninsula have also been discarded. Second, Barents Russia appears to be turning into a 'Russian bear preserve', following re-securitization, strengthening of federal control of the regions, 'governed democracy' and a general nationalist turn in Russian politics. Restrictions on collaborating with international companies are not as paralyzing as described in this scenario, though. International environmental and health projects still prosper (see below), and it might be possible to view Norwegian and French presence in the Shtokman project as more than a junior partnership. From an international relations point of view, then, the situation in 2009 is more reminiscent of the *European Periphery* scenario. The oil and gas bonanza is not likely to happen before 2015, and the pipeline from Western Siberia will, as mentioned, probably not be built at all. On the other hand, the traditional heavy industry in the region is not dead, contrary to the assumptions of this scenario.

International networks

Since the end of the Cold War, a flourishing network of collaboration has grown up between public and private sector on the Kola Peninsula and neighbouring Nordic countries. The Barents Euro-Arctic Region (BEAR) was established in 1993 by several North European states and regional administrative entities in Norway, Sweden, Finland and Russia.[14] Its aim is to promote relations across the old East–West divide in the European North, and enable joint projects in a number of areas, including trade and industry, student exchange and indigenous issues.[15] In addition, Russia and the Nordic countries are pursuing various bilateral schemes focused on a particular problem or challenge in the North. One of them is the Joint Norwegian–Russian Fisheries Commission, which manages the valuable fish resources in the Barents Sea.[16] In various bilateral and

Figure 2.1 Murmansk dwelling area

multilateral partnerships, Western states are working to address the environmental problems on the Kola Peninsula.

The idea of a Barents region was first ventilated by Thorvald Stoltenberg in April 1992; he was Norwegian Minister of Foreign Affairs at the time. After consulting with Russia and the other Nordic states, BEAR was established by the Kirkenes Declaration of January 1993, whereby Norway, Sweden, Finland and Russia pledged to work together at both the regional and national levels. At the regional level, BEAR initially included the three northernmost counties of Norway, Norrbotten in Sweden, Lapland in Finland, Murmansk and Arkhangelsk Oblasts and the Republic of Karelia in Russia (see Map 2.1). They were joined in 1997 by Nenets Autonomous Okrug, located within Arkhangelsk Oblast, which became a member in its own right, and later by Västerbotten (Sweden), Oulu and Kainuu (Finland), and the Republic of Komi (Russia). All these regional entities are represented on the Regional Council of BEAR, as are the indigenous peoples of the region. The Barents Euro-Arctic Council (BEAC), on which Denmark, Iceland and the European Commission sit in addition to the four core states, was created to promote and facilitate intergovernmental cooperation. The following countries have observer status: Canada, France, Germany, Italy, Japan, the Netherlands, Poland, the UK and the US.

The BEAR was designed to promote stability and prosperity in the area. Its purpose is enshrined in the concepts of normalization, stabilization and regionalization. It works, for example, at reducing the military tension, allaying the environmental threat and narrowing the East–West gap in standards of living in the region. It is also involved in the regionalization process underway in Europe as well as in the Arctic, turning previously peripheral border areas into places where governments can meet in a transnational forum serving a diversity of interests. Areas of particular concern are environmental protection, regional infrastructure, economic cooperation, science and technology, culture, tourism, health care, and the indigenous peoples of region (especially the Sámi, who are found in all four countries of the Barents region).

One of the most striking features of East–West relations of the European North since the end of the Cold War is the massive flow of people in both directions across country borders, some of whom decide to settle for good in the new country. Annual crossings between Norway and Russia increased from 3,000 plus in the early 1990s to nearly 110,000 by the mid-2000s.[17] East–West tourism is thriving; political and business delegations frequently visit partners on the other side of the border; students visit for longer or shorter periods; and finally, most of the towns on the Nordic side of the border are home to Russian communities of various sizes. Many Russians have married Scandinavians and become eligible for a permanent residence permit; other newcomers are the result of numerous exchange programmes run by BEAR, obtaining temporary residence and work permits on account of their special qualifications.

As a political project, BEAR has had its ups and downs. While ambitions were high during the formative years, creating viable cross-border business partnerships in the Barents region turned out to be more difficult than anticipated. Ostensible successes ended in failure. In some notorious cases, the Russians simply forced their Western counterparts out when the joint company started to make a profit.[18] As a result, BEAR downgraded business cooperation as a priority in the late 1990s, devoting its energy instead to people-to-people cooperation: student exchange, cultural projects and other ventures bringing Russians and nationals of the Nordic countries together. BEAR set up a Barents Health Programme in 1999, focusing primarily on communicable diseases such as tuberculosis. Both people-to-people cooperation and the Barents Health Programme are generally judged to be successful, and cooperation between small businesses is also growing.[19]

A Joint Norwegian–Soviet Commission on Environmental Protection was established in 1988. The year before, Soviet leader Mikhail

Gorbachev had held his famous 'Murmansk speech', where he urged the 'civilization' of the militarized European Arctic in general, and wider international cooperation on environmental protection in particular.[20] The Soviet Pechenganikel nickel smelter had already ravaged the countryside on the Kola Peninsula (with visible damage also on the Norwegian side); the Joint Norwegian–Soviet Commission on Environmental Protection made it a top priority during the first few years of its existence to modernize Pechenganikel and reduce SO_2 emissions. By the early 1990s, nuclear safety was the new priority. By then, it was public knowledge that the Soviets had been dumping radioactive waste in the Barents and Kara Seas because they were overwhelmed by an ever-growing stockpile of spent nuclear fuel and radioactive waste on the Kola Peninsula. Norway launched a Plan of Action on nuclear safety in north-western Russia in 1995, and three years later a separate Joint Norwegian–Russian Commission on Nuclear Safety was established. Norway spent around USD 150 mill. on nuclear safety projects on the Kola Peninsula over the next ten years. The Plan of Action was intended to protect public health, the environment and business from radioactive contamination and pollution from chemical weapons. It addressed four defined areas: i) safety measures at nuclear facilities; ii) management, storage and disposal of radioactive waste and spent nuclear fuel; iii) research and monitoring of radioactive pollution; and iv) arms-related environmental hazards. The immediate priority was to make the Kola nuclear power plant safe, to investigate and report on pollution in northern ocean areas and to hasten the construction of storage and effluent treatment facilities for radioactive waste and spent nuclear fuel.[21] Since the turn of the millennium, emphasis has been on preparing removal of nuclear waste from the Northern Fleet's old storage facility in Andreeva Bay, replacing the old radioisotope thermoelectric generators used in navigation buoys with environmentally friendly solar cells, and finally enabling Russians to maintain progress dismantling nuclear submarines at the naval shipyard of the Kola Peninsula.

Along with bilateral cooperation with Russia, the Norwegian government invited other Western countries to join a multilateral nuclear safety scheme for north-western Russia. In 2002, the G8 countries pledged up to USD 20 billion for a Global Partnership Against the Spread of Weapons and Materials of Mass Destruction. Among the G8 priorities were the dismantlement of decommissioned nuclear submarines, particularly on the Kola Peninsula. The signing of the framework agreement on a Multilateral Nuclear Environmental Programme in the Russian Federation (MNEPR) in May 2003, covering *inter alia* taxation and liability issues, further enhanced international nuclear remedial cooperation in the region. Another major multilateral cooperation structure, initiated by Norway in 1996, is the Arctic Military Environmental Cooperation (AMEC) between Norway, Russia, the UK (since 2003) and the US. The initiative is directed towards military-related environmental issues in the Arctic, primarily at the decommissioning of nuclear submarines on the Kola Peninsula.[22] The EU Northern Dimension Environmental Partnership (NDEP), launched in 2001, mainly concentrates on environmental problems in north-western Russia. The NDEP fund supports activities in two areas, nuclear safety and more traditional non-nuclear environmental protection, for example, water quality, waste management and energy efficiency. Some 250 mill. euro have so far been pledged to the fund – the hope is to raise 2 bill. euro – two-thirds of which are earmarked for nuclear safety projects. The flagship project in the non-nuclear sector aims to upgrade the St Petersburg water supply and wastewater management system, while the decommissioning of the old storage vessel for radioactive waste for the north-west Russian nuclear icebreaker fleet, the *Lepse*, currently moored in Murmansk, is the largest nuclear safety project. Much of the waste on board is classified as damaged fuel stemming mainly

Figure 2.2 Alyosha statue, erected on a hill overlooking Murmansk to commemorate the victims of World War II

from the nuclear-powered icebreaker Lenin, which suffered a reactor incident in 1966. The damaged fuel has to be removed by specialized remote-controlled equipment. The vessel itself is also contaminated by radioactivity, and parts of it must be stored as radioactive waste. The project will involve moving the vessel to the Nerpa shipyard on the Kola Peninsula, removing the spent fuel and dismantling the ship. Project costs are estimated at 43 mill. euro.[23]

While nuclear safety absorbed most of the money earmarked for the environment under the bilateral environmental agreement between Norway and Russia, the Joint Norwegian–Russian Commission on Environmental Protection was promoting institutional cooperation between the two countries in areas such as pollution control, biodiversity and the protection of cultural heritage. *Institutional* cooperation became the hallmark of the Commission around the mid-1990s. Emphasizing not only solutions to urgent environmental problems, the Commission also tried to build a workable system of cooperation between Norwegian and Russian environmental institutions. Norway was eager to help Russia strengthen its environmental bureaucracy, not least in the area of specialist competence. The single largest project was the Cleaner Production Programme, where engineers at Russian enterprises were trained in saving resources and reducing waste. Since 2002–2003, protecting the marine environment of the Barents Sea has been the main objective of the Commission.[24] Its initial main priority, the modernization of the Pechenganikel combine, has not materialized. Norway pledged NOK 300 mill. (at the time some US$ 50 mill.) in 1990, but after years of planning the project was shelved in 1997. A Finnish initiative was also stillborn. The Norwegian project was revived in 2001, when the Norwegian Minister of the Environment and the Russian Minister of Economy signed an agreement on a modernization project that would involve a 90 per cent reduction in emissions of SO_2 and heavy metals within ten years. Again the outcome is uncertain, to say the least. The owner of the now privatized smelter, Norilsk Nikel, has little incentive to invest more in improving environmental performance, and Russian environmental authorities cannot force the company to do so.

Russian perceptions of the international collaboration

Moscow's priorities of the international cooperation initiatives involving north-western Russia have varied between the functional sectors and over time. BEAR has not been a major concern of the Russian foreign policy leadership. This is not to say that Russia has not supported the initiative, but project funding has tended to come from the Nordic side.[25] Cooperation on environmental protection has clearly also been supported by Moscow, but progress has been hampered by the lower status of the Russian environmental bureaucracy since the turn of the millennium.[26] Regional authorities have been cooperative and open to Western initiatives, especially as long as project funding is included in the package. Looking at policy statements and public sentiment, however, there is evidence of a change between the early 1990s and late 2000s.

I have earlier characterized the first few years of post-Cold War international collaboration in the European North in terms of 'Barents euphoria' (Hønneland, 2003, pp. 100–1, 121–3). There was a pervading sense of optimism in both East and West: the Cold War was over, the Iron Curtain gone, and the Russian northerners could – with a little help from their Nordic friends – again be included in the 'natural' brotherhood of the European Arctic peoples. Political positions in Russia were to a large extent filled by 'Westernizers' (see Chapter 1); the country was in dire economic straits; and the Nordic governments queued up at the border loaded with money to help Russia renew itself (hopefully, perhaps, on a Scandinavian model). The Russians gladly accepted support from the West to strengthen democracy and civil society and reform the economy under the BEAR agreement. Assistance of Western governments through a variety of international environmental regimes aimed at helping Russia get rid of aging nuclear submarines, secure nuclear installations and handle nuclear waste, was also welcomed. Indeed, the partnerships with the Nordic countries were generally well received, particularly by the professional classes. Extracts from a couple of the interviews that we made during our evaluation of the Norwegian Plan of Action for Nuclear Safety in North-western Russia (Hønneland and Moe, 2000) are illustrative.

What I like about working with Norway – and I've been involved in partnerships with many countries – is their broad approach. Rather than embracing the first and best institution they come across in Russia, they go and get the information before reaching a decision. If the decision isn't always completely on target, it's at least not far off.[27]

Our co-operation with Norway also strengthens our own position in Russia. It's good that Norway plays the role of international organizer. [...] It really helps us. [Have you nothing critical to say about co-operation with Norway?] I'm sorry, but I really don't. Our co-operation is very fruitful indeed. We often come to the meetings with diverging views, but we always end up agreeing.[28]

The winds changed towards the end of the 1990s. The Russians were no longer willing to accept any solution proposed by the West. For the Norwegians, it was particularly evident in the joint management of the fisheries. The fishing quotas on the most important fish stocks in the Barents Sea are based on the recommendations issued each year by the International Council for the Exploration of the Sea (ICES), of which both Norwegian and Russian scientists are members. When the Council called for a lower than ever ceiling for cod for the year 2000, that is, 110,000 tonnes, down from 480,000 tonnes in 1999, quota talks in the autumn of 1999 were particularly difficult and involved a breakdown that lasted for several days. When the Joint Norwegian–Russian Fisheries Commission did agree, they set the ceiling for 2000 at 390,000 tonnes, that is, almost four times higher than scientists had recommended.

Whereas the Norwegian discourse focused on short vs. long-term interests of different types of vessels and regions, the Russian discourse saw the establishment of quotas for the Barents Sea cod as a battle between the two states. Norway, it was assumed, had 'instructed' its Western allies in ICES to lower the Barents Sea cod quota in order to harm Russia, which was already facing an economic downturn. Norway was seen as a strictly rational actor, capable of calculating the value of its own interests precisely and minutely (because it knew exactly what its best interests were). The interests of the two states were considered to be completely at odds and quota setting a zero-sum game in which one party can only win what the other party loses. According to this view, states are always seeking to destroy rivals and maximize their own chances of success. As expressed by Murmansk Oblast Governor Yuriy Yedvokimov, 'It is always like this: when one state is temporarily weakened, its neighbours will try to take an advantage.'[29] A Russian fisheries newspaper commented, 'There is nothing special about this – every country defends its own interest with the means available to it.'[30] Or, as expressed by a Russian fisheries researcher in an interview, pinpointing the Russian perception of the quota establishment exercise as a zero-sum game: 'Of course, it's in Norway's interest to ruin Russia. This is simple economic theory.'[31]

The Russian discourses on marine living resources in the Barents Sea during the 1990s form part of a general Russian discourse on the country's relations with the West: what I have earlier labelled the 'Cold Peace discourse' (Hønneland, 2003, pp. 74–7, 108–9). The term refers to the mounting sense of disappointment in the West felt by many Russians from the early and mid-1990s, as it became increasingly clear that the political and economic reforms were not bringing the results many had hoped for.

Combined with a sense of resentment against NATO expansion eastwards, and the 1999 NATO intervention in Kosovo, many Russians became convinced that the cooperative attitude of the West at the end of the 1980s and the beginning of the 1990s was false, a way to press reforms on Russia that it was known would not work in the Russian setting in any event. The motive of Western powers was allegedly to weaken Russia even further while, at the same time, taking the advantage to boost own military and economic power. The process was conducted under 'positive' slogans such as 'democratization' and 'introduction of market reforms', but many Russians came to see it as little more than a continuation of the Cold War East–West struggle, a situation that gave rise to the term 'Cold Peace'.[32] By the end of the decade, many had become disillusioned with the West and instead sought answers in 'traditional' patriotic values. As expressed by the leader of the Murmansk regional Duma commission on patriotic upbringing in 1999:

> After some years of liberal reform [...], the concept [of patriotism] is again attracting lively interest. To an increasing extent, the ranks of patriots are swelled by those who only recently were indifferent to the national interests of the state, trying instead to convince us of the importance of certain abstract universal human values.[33]

Suspicion of Western motives was also evident in discussions over nuclear safety cooperation and environmental issues more widely, especially where Western NGOs were involved. A former Northern Fleet officer, Aleksandr Nikitin, was arrested in February 1996 on a charge of spying while assembling data for a report on the nuclear risk on behalf of the Norwegian environmental NGO Bellona.[34] There was a notion that the West utilizes environmental collaboration with Russia (often channelled through NGOs) for intelligence purposes, cf. the following news bulletin from Radio Free Europe/Radio Liberty under the heading 'Murmansk – a Hotbed of Foreign Spies':

> Foreign intelligence services have targeted Murmansk Oblast as a 'priority' area for their activities, Nikolai Zharkov, head of the Federal Security Service (FSB) directorate in Murmansk Oblast, told Interfax

North-West on 28 December [...] Zharkov also revealed that foreign governments frequently 'pursue their own interests' under the cover of environmental organizations (RFE/RL Newsline, 30 December 2000).

As noted above, Russians appear to approach international politics as a zero-sum-game between states – this at least is what my studies of East–West interaction in the European North have led me to believe. What one state wins, other states lose. It will always be in a state's interest to harm other states, even without the prospect of actually gaining much from the exercise. Attending an international conference on nuclear safety issues in Russia I found myself together with one of the highest ranking officials in the Russian nuclear sector during a break. At the conference he had joined in the politically correct chorus about international collaboration to solve Russia's environmental problems. But now, during the break, he looked me in the eyes and said: 'You and I don't have to pretend. We both know why Norway and the US are doing this. You want to destroy Russia.' In an interview for an evaluation of Western health initiatives in north-western Russia, an elderly Russian doctor wondered about the motives of Western governments: 'Why are they so interested in us? What is their hidden agenda?' He indicated the direction of his suspicions: 'Every country's Ministry of Foreign Affairs is a legal intelligence agency'.[35] Nordic governments were therefore invading yet another sector to exploit Russian expertise and pressure Russia to make reforms. And there's an anecdote about a Norwegian minister of fisheries who, in the early 2000s, met his Russian counterpart. The Russian allegedly said to the Norwegian: 'You do everything you can to destroy the Russian fishing industry. And I respect you for that.' Again, it is the simple duty of a politician to work against the interests of other states, because this is always for the good of one's own.[36]

International relations were also an issue when Yuriy Yevdokimov was ousted in spring 2009, well into his fourth period as governor of Murmansk Oblast. While the Kremlin probably wanted to get rid of him for internal political or possibly financial reasons, it was arguably easier to explain the move to the public by evoking xenophobic sentiments.[37] As referred by *BarentsObserver*:

> Yury Yevdokimov [suffered a setback] in the recent election campaign for new Murmansk city mayor. After having expressed support to independent candidate Sergey Subbotin and negatively commented on United Russia's election methods, criticism from Moscow mounted on the governor. Much of that criticism was aimed at the international

focus of the governor. As BarentsObserver reported, President Dmitry Medvedev gave Governor Yury Yevdokimov 'one last warning' and told him to concentrate on solving domestic problems instead of 'fooling around abroad'. That warning came just few days after the governor had been in Norway to sign a cooperation agreement with the Norwegian county of Troms. After that, First Deputy Head of the United Russia's Executive Committee Valery Galchenko told journalists that Governor Yevdokimov was 'betraying Russian interests' in the Arctic and that he wanted to 'detach the region from Russia and give it to Scandinavians and Americans who are fighting for their interests in the Arctic'. (*BarentsObserver*, 21 March 2009)

Region building, identity politics

The concept of 'region building' has evolved in the IR literature as an alternative to defining regions as 'inside-out' or 'outside-in' and discussing what constitutes a 'natural' region (Neumann, 1994). Whereas the 'inside-out' approach explains the existence of a region mainly in terms of linguistic, cultural, and social similarities within a specific geographical area, underlining the internal, 'centripetal forces' of the area, the 'outside-in' approach views the emergence of transnational regions largely as the outcomes of the preferences of hegemonic states. The inside-out / outside-in approaches converge, however, in their focus on regions as given entities (with some kind of common identity – in the former case – or superior international power structures – in the latter). They aspire to explain the existence of regions *a priori*, ignoring the capacity of individual and collective actors to define them from other vantage points.

Criticizing these older approaches for lack of self-reflection, region-building theorists claim that political actors are capable of deciding for themselves the terms on which what is inside or outside a region should be specified. Drawing on nation-building literature, they claim that politicians, bureaucrats, researchers, artists and others can contribute to defining and developing regional entities. According to this view, regions are not given by either cultural similarities or international power structures, but have to be actively formed through a region-building process similar to earlier European nation-building projects. In Neumann's (1994, p. 58) words,

When an elite has formulated a political programme which hinges on the existence of a nation, it is [always] possible, to construct for it a prehistory which will embody it in time as well as in space. This is done by identifying, and thus making relevant to the identity of the human collective in question, a host of political ties, cultural similarities, economic transactional patterns etc. Of course, such a political process will always be imposed on a geographical area which is already, in a number of respects, heterogeneous. The point made here is simply that these similarities and dissimilarities are processed politically by nation-builders, and it is *these political actors* who decide which similarities should be considered politically relevant, and which should not.

Political actors will likewise invoke historical events to bolster the construction of a notion of community within an area. Regions may therefore be taken as 'imagined communities' (Anderson, 1983), cognitive outcomes of deliberate political ambitions. In other words, they are 'talked and written into existence' (Neumann, 1994, p. 59).

Several authors have noted how well-suited the North was for region building in post-Cold War Europe.[38] In an article addressing the 'state of northernness' shared by Finland and Russia, as well as the establishment of BEAR, Medvedev (2001, p. 92) claims that 'whereas the East, West and South have more or less fixed meanings, and are interpreted as relatively populated and explored, the North appears as a mythological domain, a semiotic project, a constructed identity.' A more prosaic claim would probably be that the geographical category of the North could be cultivated to deconstruct the established East–West divide in Europe that had been reinforced during the Cold War. As noted by Aalto et al. (2003, pp. 5–6),

The 'modern' identities are reminiscent of the modernity of the Cold War and its rigid division into the 'Western' and the 'Eastern/ Soviet' spheres of influence that critical geopolitics writers, among many others, have attempted to eradicate. These identities are often responsible for producing the 'westernising' and 'europeanising' geopolitical visions and codes, being interested in sovereignty, strictly defined boundaries, and sovereignty support for small northern states that nowadays comes in the form of trying to ally with greater powers and regional blocs such as the US, NATO and the EU. The sovereignty consequences of such transnational and supranational associations are, of course, complex, but the very modern desire for certainty, predictability and order is surely not absent in these progressive openings for organising and transforming political space, geopolitical practices and boundaries. They connote an interest in issues such as regionality, social learning, diversity and common identity. What is particularly remarkable for our purposes, is that in the case of the Nordic countries, the 'postmodern' identities have managed to obtain good access to the policy process, as 'postmodern' or sympathetically disposed scholars have often served as advisors for Nordic foreign ministries and other governmental bodies.

As Browning (2003) notes, two sets of representational practices can be identified in discourses underlying region building in the European North. On the one hand, region-building attempts such as BEAR, CBSS and the EU Northern Dimension move the European North towards a more variegated politics by breaking down discursive structures of self and otherness regarding Russia. On the other hand, this integrative move is challenged and marginalized by a more traditional discourse:

> Whilst the region builders of the 1990s took on board the postmodern understanding of the constructed nature of social reality as a liberating moment to reconstitute their own regional environment, they have been less observant of the way in which the representational practices they have utilised in order to promote change have, in many respects, only served to re-inscribe the very world they have sought to transform. Thus, whilst aims to construct an egalitarian relationship with Russia in order to break down traditional negative self-other depictions are clearly to be welcomed, Russia, in fact, often continues to occupy negative positions in the underlying discourses of region-building projects that serve to re-inscribe Russia's difference from the 'West' European 'us' in negative terms. In short, and to the detriment of its stated objectives, the new region building often resonates badly with a 'West' European legacy that constitutes Europe as a unified civilisational empire. This offers Russia the option, either of being imperialised within its folds, or alternatively of remaining marginalised on the periphery of Europe. In particular, in this discourse Russia remains construed as the object to be acted upon, the diseased that needs to be cured. (Ibid., p. 48)

And further,

> In the new region building, the West, and the EU–Europe more particularly, is therefore emplotted as playing a historically important

role in the new Europe as a guide and teacher of wisdom to Russia. However, there is a danger that Russia, as the recipient of aid, is reduced to the position of the passive object to be acted upon, the body upon which the West (EU–Europe) can actualise its self-endowed role of civilising the barbarian learner, or European apprentice, not quite fully European but on the way to getting there – as long as it attends the lessons and does its homework. (Ibid., p. 58)

3
How to Be a Northerner: Distinguishing North from South

To understand how narratives must be structured within the culture is to press against the edges of identity's envelope – to discover the limits of identifying oneself as a human agent in good standing; it is also to determine what forms must be maintained in order to acquire credibility as a teller of truth. The structure of proper storytelling precedes the events about which 'truth is told'; to go beyond the conventions is to engage in an idiot's tale. If the narrative fails to approximate conventional forms, the telling becomes nonsensical. Thus, rather than being driven by facts truth telling is largely governed by a forestructure of narrative conventions. (Gergen, 2001, pp. 249–50)

Introduction

This chapter discusses how Kola inhabitants talk about themselves as northerners, distinguishing themselves from people in the south of Russia. I start with three rather extensive quotes from the interviews made in connection with this study, each of which I comment on in turn.[1] There follows a more general discussion, illustrated by other interviews, observations and the scholarly literature.[2] Among the questions I raise are what characterizes prevailing stereotypes about northerners and southerners. How is narrative used to shape the northern identity, and to what extent does proximity to the Nordic countries affect perceptions of northernness in the north-western corner of Russia? Does northernness serve to strengthen a sense of Russianness, or is it rather the other way round, a means of distancing oneself from what is typically Russian? If the latter is the case, is there evidence that the opening of the borders with Scandinavia has accelerated this process? All important in this respect is the vocabulary available to north-west Russians to express their perception of themselves as northerners. How must narratives about Russian northernness be structured in order to make sense?[3]

Extract 1: 'When I told them how I lived, they went all misty-eyed'

This interview takes place over a long evening dinner at a Soviet-style restaurant where husband and wife Anton and Marina are joined by a young man, Ivan, and myself, the interviewer. The interviewees are in their early to late thirties. Anton is an officer in the Northern Fleet and lives with his wife in one of the closed towns on the Kola Peninsula. Marina commutes to Murmansk where she works for a private business. Ivan, who holds an advanced university degree, is a civil servant. Although Anton and Marina had met Ivan before, they are only vaguely acquainted. Both Ivan and Marina have visited Scandinavia – Ivan for several longer periods, Marina just briefly. Marina's is clearly the leading voice of this interview. Her father was an army officer and she has lived 'all over the USSR', though she spent her teens in Ukraine, where her parents still live. As an adult, she has always lived in military towns on the Kola Peninsula. Anton is also from the south; Ivan claims to be a 'real northerner'.

> *Marina: I remember exactly what it was like moving north. I was struck by people's friendliness, civility and general unflappable nature, ready to help you at the drop of a hat. If you needed to get somewhere, someone would drive you. No one snaps at you in the shops. It was incredible [diko] to start with. And in the streets, if the traffic light's red, people don't cross the road. Why is it like this? Personally, I think it's [got something to do with] the harsh climate. People are more considerate. It's the dramatic changes [in the weather], that's the explanation. I don't know, but it's what I think.*
>
> *Anton: I was totally amazed! The sun's out all day and all night!...but as soon as darkness sets in again, we all get depressed.*
>
> *Marina: And the children, they're really sensible. They read a lot, maybe because it's too cold to be outside. I don't know if it's true in Murmansk, but it's like that in Severomorsk. But it's also because people are so well educated here. Masses of qualified people move here. My son, for example, he started learning English when he was four! The education system's really something round here.*
>
> *Anton: Indeed it is. An excellent scientific potential.*
>
> *Marina: Whenever I visit my parents in Ukraine...I've got so used to living up north, it sort of gives me a shock whenever I'm in the south. I shouldn't react like that, I suppose, but the things that go on there, awful things. People steal and swindle...don't you agree, Ivan?*

Ivan: I've never been there. I've been more or less everywhere in Norway, but never made it to the south of Russia. [chuckles]
Marina: I think it's a bit like when foreigners visit Russia. They're really shocked with the chaos everywhere. That's what it's like when we travel south. You have to watch your step in the traffic. There's so much rudeness [grubost']. People are evil. Here, where we are now, people are more cultured … And another thing, people are older in the south. Most people round here are young, and the old people complain and moan about everything … Lots of people's parents travel south, stay down there from May to September. But something pulls them back – they can never cut the ties with the north completely. Before, everyone in the military towns travelled to the south. You wouldn't get them to do it today. Depends on what you can afford. The pensions up here are better, and you can keep working longer too. Lots of people have been allocated a flat down south, but they stay put up here. They give their children a hand, and the pension's better … In my opinion, if you want to get away, you've got to do it before you're 40. [If you wait] any longer it'll be too late. You won't want to make the move any more. The old people often say the weather's not good for your health here in the northern parts.
Anton: For eyesight and what have you …
Marina: But there's a movie on at the moment about the navy … The soldiers wanted to go to Severomorsk rather than stay in Ukraine.
Interviewer: D'you feel Ukrainian?
Marina: No. Not at all … I was there on a visit not long ago, a school reunion, twenty years it was, and when I compared myself to the others … well, no, comparison's out of the question. My life would have been totally inconceivable there. I have two sets of qualifications, and I have two children: both would be completely inconceivable for my classmates. What do they have to look forward to? A job at the market and a bit of trading on the side. And a second child … when I told them how I lived, they went all misty-eyed, wishing it were them. The buildings are dreadful. There's no street lighting. Anton's father was here last autumn for a couple of months, helping us redo our flat. We combined two flats into one, so we have three bedrooms and two bathrooms. He was amazed at how clean and spick-and-span it was here. I had the same feeling when I got back after the holidays: everything's so lovely and clean! And at that reunion we talked about children, and I told them about Barents Plus [an exchange programme for schoolchildren under the aegis of the Barents Programme], they simply couldn't believe it, that the kids could travel to Norway and Finland as exchange students …
Ivan: Not too long ago, I was at a party in connection with work, and everyone stood up and the toasts went on forever. When it got to my turn, I just said 'skål' ['cheers' in Norwegian] [laughs].
Interviewer: What do you think about Scandinavians?
[protracted silence]
Marina: Most people have heard about the Norwegian tourists … we've heard it's quiet, clean but, you know, a bit boring perhaps [skuchnovato]. Well, that's what they say, that Norway's boring [skuchno].
Ivan: Ah! We need scandals! [laughs]

Marina: [mentions a story in which Norwegians figure as 'our four-footed friends', i.e. as drunkards] But Norwegians further south might be a bit more civilized ... They would be, of course, because of the capital. Moscow's a capital, too, naturally.

Ivan: I like Piter [St Petersburg]. People there are more enlightened. Everybody takes a book to read on the underground, even if some of them do hold the book upside down and stare at the same page for forty minutes, they've still got their book [laughs]. We take our cues from St Petersburg. It's a tonic. We're well organized, and that's thanks to Piter. Before, we were an insignificant district [uyezd], then came Apatity etc., etc.

Anton: Yeah, in the 60s ...

Ivan: No, it was in the 30s. We've always relied on Piter. All the geologists came from Piter.

Marina: Yes, them and the military.

Ivan: Yes, Apatity was built by people from Piter ... Even our dialect is Piterish, not Muscovite, taakaayaa [laughs]. No, we speak Piter. We speak good, normal, human Russian. I was in Ukraine once and went to get a haircut. Don't stop talking, they said, it's so interesting and amusing the way you talk. Ukrainian is OK if it's spoken well, but what peeves me is the mess the Soviet Union left behind after mixing all the dialects together.

Marina: I know a Russian girl who's married to a Norwegian. They met through a personal ad or the Internet or something; it wasn't face to face anyway [zaochno]. She didn't like the idea of moving to Norway. They had planned to move, but she changed her mind. She said she wanted her children to go to a normal kindergarten, where they could learn something. Norwegian schools produce subnormal [degenerirovannye] children. So they live here; he's one week here and the other in Norway. And the health service there! I wouldn't trust the medical service in Norway if you paid me! You know what they say, it's not very reliable and it's not very good. Our hospitals may not be great as far as building standards go, but we have the best specialists. Lots of Norwegians come here for the sake of our dentists, by the way. Cheaper and better than the Norwegian dentists. But back to the Norwegian schools: everybody will tell you that the Russian education system, from the kindergarten up, is much, much more serious. That's just how it is. [Talks at length about standards of geography teaching before concluding:] In Russia, it's elementary, but not in Norway.

Ivan: But it was better here before. Everybody had to learn at least four languages, two dead, like Latin or Greek, and two living languages.

Interviewer: What about the environment here?

[lengthy pause]

Marina: It's a bit on the negative side ... the climate you know. It's a shame for the children. Anton grew up by the sea, in a yachting club. There's nowhere for the children to go outside. They spend a lot of time in front of the computer screen. But we can afford to pay for transport and send the children off to after-school activities, and we've got good, fresh air, though we could have done with a bit more sun. We've got good swimming baths, and the children learn to swim, but they're not outside as much, I've noticed that. There are probably more things for them to do, and people can afford them, but they don't have the time! Obviously, for some it's the other way round, but it's quite common nowadays ... and I was

> *always ill when I lived in the south. When I moved up here I felt much better. It's filthy in the south – but they're used to it.*
> Interviewer: *What sort of future do you see for the north?*
> Ivan: *Geir, you're never going to get us to move away from here! [laughs]*
> Interviewer: *Why not?*
> Ivan: *We've got the sea, the harbour ... it's just the way it is, how it should be. We've annexed Norway as part of Murmansk Oblast, the ninetieth federal subject! [laughs] The prices here are more or less the same as in the south, but you just can't compare wage levels.*
> Marina: *The birth rate rocketed in Severomorsk last year. It was the only town in Russia, I read, where births exceeded deaths. There are lots of parents and children in Severomorsk. It's really very nice. The children are healthier here I think. When I moved here, my parents were so worried about me, how I'd tackle the climate ... And it's true, I did miss the fruit and vegetables when I came here, missed the big fresh tomatoes, but today, things are completely different, you can get everything. People used to bring suitcases full of fruit and veg back whenever they'd been on holidays in the south, but that's a thing of the past. Unnecessary today.*

Marina and Anton, both hailing from the south, recall their stunning first impressions of the north. Anton was amazed by the midnight sun, and Marina – who remembers exactly what it was like moving north – was struck by people's friendliness. It was incredible (*diko*, literally: 'wild'), she remarked, to find that people didn't snap at her in the shops or for jaywalking, and were 'ready to help at the drop of a hat'. Her explanation (which she admits is only a guess) is the northern climate. It must be the harsh climate and the dramatic changes in the weather that make people more considerate, she says, without expanding on the causal connection. Including her husband in the exchange, she goes on to stress the intelligence and skills of northerners. Children have a lot of common sense (again hinting at the climate as an explanation; the children probably read a lot since it is too cold to be outside most of the time), the education system 'is really something round here'; above all, the education level is higher than in the south. In short, she highlights the orderliness, self-composure and considerateness of northerners.

After praising northerners, the south – encompassing the southern stretches of the former USSR – is brutally invoked as a constituting other. Marina is shocked whenever she visits her parents in Ukraine; she probably should not feel like that, she admits, but simply cannot help it, 'the things that go on there, awful things'. As opposed to the good manners of the northerners, southerners 'steal and swindle'. Ivan, for his part, seems to position himself as the Westernizer, claiming he has no knowledge of the post-Soviet backwoods Marina is referring to. He has been 'more or less everywhere in Norway, but never made it to the south of Russia'.[4] Marina picks up on this, comparing her own perception of the Russian south with how she believes foreigners see Russia: 'They're really shocked with the chaos everywhere.' She is quite vehement in her characterization of southerners: 'There's so much rudeness there. People are evil.' She admits that the northern climate is probably not good for one's health – her husband mentions its effect on people's eyesight[5] – but everyone wants to return to the north after a stay in the south, she maintains. Something pulls them back. Lots of people have a flat they've been allocated in the south, but remain in the north, unable or unwilling to cut the ties.

When the interviewer asks Marina whether she feels Ukrainian, she swiftly answers 'No,' arguing that the life she has created for herself – with two sets of qualifications, two children and two flats combined into one (giving her the luxury of three bedrooms and two bathrooms) – would have been impossible had she stayed in Ukraine. She describes the 'misty-eyed' reaction of former classmates to her description of life in the north at a twenty-year school reunion in Ukraine. 'When I compare myself to the others … well, no, comparison's out of the question.' Why the north is better is explained by Marina at length. The buildings are dreadful in the south. There is no street lighting. It's filthy (although they are used to it down there). In the north, everything is so lovely and clean! And when she tells her southern friends about how kids in the north can travel abroad on exchange programmes, they simply cannot believe it. Again, Ivan takes the opportunity to mention his Scandinavian experience when Marina touches on the Barents collaboration. Instead of giving a traditional, elaborate Russian toast at a function where this was probably expected of him, he just uttered the Norwegian drinking toast 'skål!'.

After a brief intermezzo about Scandinavians,[6] the three dinner guests ponder the possible influence of St Petersburg on society on the Kola Peninsula. Ivan takes the initiative. After a word about Moscow as the Russian capital, he likes Piter, he adds, because it is 'more civilized'. He likes how people there read books all the time, or at least pretend to. The scientists who built up Apatity and the officers and crews of the Northern Fleet came from St Petersburg (or Leningrad, as the city was called at the time), he maintains. And that was all an advantage for the new communities on Kola. 'We're well organized, and that's thanks to Piter.' Even the Kola dialect is Piterish, 'good, normal, human Russian'.

Ivan ridicules the long 'a' of the Moscow dialect, possibly hinting at a perception of Moscow as an inward-looking, 'eastern' or 'southern' peasant community, as opposed to the civilized, intellectual, 'western' and 'northern' old Russian capital of St Petersburg. We shall return to this later in the chapter.

In the concluding part of the interview, the interviewer asks how they feel about the environment. Marina admits – after a long silence – that her feelings are rather negative, but again she reverts to the advantages of life in the north. The children have to spend more time indoors because of the climate, but then again people can afford to pay for transport and after-school activities for the children because wage levels are higher in the north. Actually, she argues, there is so much for kids to do, they hardly have any time to spend outdoors anyway. Perhaps anticipating a response citing the health benefits of fresh air, as far as she is concerned, she goes on, she was always ill when she lived in the south, but felt much better the minute she moved up north. When the interviewer finally asks what sort of future they see for themselves in the north, Ivan again invokes his connections with Norway. Probably referring to his personal experience of various exchange programmes (and possibly the Norwegian interviewer's numerous visits to the Kola Peninsula), he jokes about having 'annexed' Norway and made it part of Murmansk Oblast, or even the ninetieth federal subject of the Russian Federation.[7] Marina, for her part, continues listing evidence of northern prosperity, now in the form of a skyrocketing Severomorsk birth rate the previous year, the only town in Russia, she contends, where births exceeded deaths. Yes, it is really very nice with all these healthy children, she muses. You don't have to drag suitcases full of fruit and vegetables with you any more when you return home from holidays in the south. The picture is complete: we have everything we could possibly need here in the north.

Extract 2: 'If you'd asked me last year, I would have said Murmansk was the best place in the world'

Nastya and Sergey are a married couple in their late twenties, both with university degrees and juggling academic careers with work in private business. They meet the two Norwegian interviewers in their apartment for an evening meal. Both speak of themselves as Ukrainian. Nastya was three when the family moved to Murmansk. Both parents are Ukrainian. Sergey was born in Murmansk. His father is Ukrainian, his mother from Murmansk. Nastya's father used to live in the Moscow metropolitan area and accepted the offer of a flat in Murmansk, hoping it would speed up his return to Ukraine. 'He has been here for thirty years,' she says.

Nastya: Northerners are intelligent, well educated, friendly, not easily peeved or mean.
Sergey: Not particularly talkative, nor emotional.
Nastya: For example, when you go on holiday, I usually take the train to Moscow, and [change trains for] Ukraine: two completely different experiences. The Murmansk–Moscow train is quiet, civilized [kul'turno]; the train from Moscow to Ukraine is full of southerners, people are more talkative, it's noisy, never a dull moment ... on the Murmansk train to Moscow you don't really talk to anyone; but from Moscow on to Ukraine people are chatting from the word go. Everyone invites everyone else into their compartment. Both are OK, but like night and day. If you pressed me, I'd say I prefer the Murmansk – Moscow journey.
Sergey: I think people in the south are a bit like the Italians – not that I've ever spoken to an Italian, but from what I've heard ... for instance, a couple of Italians are talking to each other, people think they're arguing, but they're not, just talking ... the difference, it's on the outside.
Nastya: People tend to lose their manners when they're unhappy. That's why people make a spectacle of themselves down south. Part of it's cultural, part poverty. It's getting like that up here in the north too, what with the harder times. We used to get perks for living in the north, they're gone now, and other benefits with them. People are hard up and not as well behaved as before.
Sergey: My parents lost all their accumulated benefits.
Nastya: People are on edge, you can see that on the street.
Interviewer I: Why are people quieter in the north?
Sergey: There's always been a lot of outsiders here, it's been good to live here. People came to make money [za dlinnym rublyom = 'for the long rouble'], and only stayed temporarily. There are lots of specialists here, many highly qualified people. Many say northerners are a bit cold, buttoned up.
Nastya: No, that's not right. I'll tell you a little story. I was in a shop and there was this lady buying apples. Before she got round to paying for them, a new load of apples arrived, much better quality, so she went back and asked if she could exchange hers with some new ones, and the assistant said she could, she even said 'be my guest'! When I told this to people in Ukraine, they just wouldn't believe it was true. It would never happen down south. It just goes to show, people are more civilized in the north.
Sergey: Ok, Ok, colder and less outgoing ... people in the north travel more, they're more mobile. You don't ask 'when' people are going on holiday, you ask 'where' are you going, it's understood that you'll be going somewhere. In Ukraine, a holiday means doing up the house or tending the garden.
Interviewer I: What about Belarusians?
Nastya: Not many, but Belarusians do some business here. They come here to sell clothing, among other things. Ukrainian women are known for growing rather ample with age, and finding the right sized outfit in Murmansk can pose problems. So these small businesses, manufacturers, from Belarus, they come and cater to that market.

Interviewer I: Do people want to leave Murmansk?
Nastya: Absolutely. Among our friends, for example, almost all have connections with Ukraine in some shape of form, either from having come from Ukraine themselves, or their parents, partner, what have you. Lots of people are called Nikolayevich. Nikolay was a popular boy's name in our parents' generation, and many in our generation are called Nikolayevich. It was different before; the older people want to leave, now many of the young want to get away. Many are trapped in the north. There's a programme to help folks move from the northern areas, but it doesn't work: it's supposed to encourage people to move to 'the middle belt' [srednyaya polosa], build homes there; but there's so much corruption. Businesses simply swindle the government. They get money to build homes, but do nothing – while people sit and wait.
Interviewer II: I remember reading a letter in Polyarnaya Pravda from an elderly lady who'd experienced that herself…
Sergey: Happens all the time.
Interviewer II: What draws people back [to the south]?
Nastya: The life's hard here, it's difficult if you're old; my mother, for instance, she's used to living in a milder… to fruit, relatives close by.
Interviewer II: [talking to Interviewer I in Norwegian: It's so obvious what draws them to the south, they hardly comprehend the question.]
Sergey: Used to having her relations on hand.
Interviewer II: Do you know people who've lived here for several generations?
Nastya: Yes, I do.
Interviewer II: Why did they stay so long?
Nastya: They've got a dacha.
Interviewer I: In the south?
Nastya: Yes.

[talk continues about their impression of Scandinavians]

Interviewer I: What about the natural conditions?
Nastya: If you'd asked me last year I would have said Murmansk was the best place in the world, but after last winter, I think it's awful. The polar night, it made me ill, really ill. It wasn't a very hard winter either, but the gloom, it sort of invaded me, I couldn't understand what was happening, big changes in the temperature – perhaps that was it? Something connected with [atmospheric] pressure? Was I getting old? I asked my dad, what's happening? People say it's normal, you'll get over it. But I wanted to get away from Murmansk, to Ukraine, even Moscow; the sea, mountains… I never get to see them anyway, all I see is my flat and my office, that's it. I only get to see the countryside in the holidays.

[conversation proceeds to issues concerning nuclear safety in the region, leading to a discussion about why Russians don't trust the state]

Sergey: I'd like to pick up on that question about the environment. What's so brilliant about the north is its uniquely beautiful natural environment, that's the first thing I want to say.
Nastya: It was a great autumn, and a great summer, berries, mushrooms…
Interviewer I: And the climate, what's your opinion?

> *Sergey: I know the younger folks don't think much of the northern climate, but that's because they haven't seen the effects yet. 'Night's' the culprit, not the cold, but it's obviously not good for the organism, even if I can say for myself that the polar night doesn't bother me very much. But it's harder getting up, and when I was a kid, I couldn't see very well when I was here in the north, but on holiday in Ukraine, my sight was ok. Don't know why, but that's how it was.*
>
> ---
>
> *[We look at photos of Murmansk and Ukraine – Ukraine: 'Oh, the sea!' (Akh, more!), Murmansk: 'Oh, the greenery!' (Akh, zelen'!)]*

Nastya and Sergey begin by listing some of the positive attributes of the north noted by Marina in the previous interview: northerners are intelligent, well educated and friendly. They are 'not talkative, nor emotional'. Nastya gives a vivid account of the difference in practice between northerners and southerners by comparing train rides between Murmansk and Moscow, and Moscow and Ukraine. On the first stretch, from Murmansk to Moscow, it is quiet and civilized (*kul'turno*). From Moscow to Ukraine, on the other hand, there's a lot of noise as people enjoy each other's company. Interestingly, she says nothing dismissive of the south, unlike Marina. For Nastya, southern chaos equals 'never a dull moment'. While north and south are both ok, at the same time they're 'like night and day'. Only when she is urged to expand does she express her preference for the Murmansk–Moscow part of the journey. Like Marina, however, she speaks about the poverty of the south, which partly explains why people are prone to 'make a spectacle of themselves down south': 'People tend to lose their manners when they're unhappy.' The same is happening in the north, as the economic climate worsens: 'People are hard up and not as well behaved as before.'

When Sergey hints that northerners are a bit cold, his wife objects and tells the story about a lady who was treated with unexpected courtesy and friendliness in a Murmansk shop.[8] They let her exchange a bag of apples she was about to pay for[9] with fresher ones that had just arrived – and they even said 'be my guest'. People in Ukraine refused to believe it, said Nastya, which goes to show that people are more civilized in the north, despite the fact that southerners might appear friendlier at first sight. Nevertheless, both agree that many people would move south if they had the opportunity. They describe how mobility programmes are fraught with corruption, so that people are trapped in the north despite governmental financing of new flats for them in the south.

At some point in the interview, Nastya loses her ability to speak only positively of life in the north. If we had asked her a year before, she would have called Murmansk the best place on earth. But last winter was difficult. 'The polar night, it made me ill, really ill.' A sense of gloom seemed to invade her, without her understanding why. Perhaps it was the swings in temperature or atmospheric pressure? She complains about life in general. What's the point of beautiful scenery if all you get to see is your flat and office? After some gloomy remarks about the risk of nuclear radiation in the region, Sergey tries to clear the atmosphere: 'I'd like to pick up on that question about the environment. What's so brilliant about the north is its uniquely beautiful natural environment, that's the first thing I want to say.' Does he feel his wife's picture of the region is too depressive? This does not prevent him, however, from commenting himself on the negative effects of the northern climate on the human body. If younger people tend not to think too much about it, it is only because they lack the experience. It is obviously not good for the organism, he contends. Although it gets worse with age, even children succumb. When he was a kid himself, for instance, his eyesight was worse in the north, but picked up again on long holidays in the south.

Notably, Nastya and Sergey look to the natural environment for explanations of problems with their health. Nastya wonders whether wide and sudden differences in temperature or atmospheric pressure can explain last winter's depression. Sergey admits to not knowing exactly why his sight was so poor in the north when he was a child, but he seems convinced that the northern climate in general is not good for the human organism, including eyesight.

All in all, however, Nastya and Sergey's account is more balanced than Marina, Ivan and Anton's in our first interview (and of participants in our next interview, too). It becomes apparent when they look at photos of Murmansk and Ukraine after the interview. 'Oh, the sea!', they say with longing in their voices looking at pictures from the south. 'Oh, the greenery!', they sigh to pictures of the north, obviously with a certain pride.

Extract 3: 'The north is like a bottomless pit dragging you down'

In this interview, we meet a married couple in their mid-fifties. Elana and Nikolay came to Murmansk with their two-year-old daughter some thirty years ago. They have both worked at the same small business for many years and put in a lot of hours. Elena and Nikolay meet our Russian interviewer at their apartment. The conversation proceeds in a warm, homely atmosphere although the subject matter is far from cheerful. Both interviewees were briefed beforehand about the likely questions, and are clearly apprehensive. For Elena and Nikolay, they touched a sensitive nerve.

Interviewer: I'd like to begin by asking you whether you enjoy living in the north.

Elena: [imitating] Enjoy, enjoy. We're hostages of the north. We came when we were young, with a child of two. We thought we would be here a couple of years and then go back home to the south. But we've been here nearly thirty years.

Nikolay: She spoke the truth, the children's nurse, when she told us: 'You'll never move anywhere else, mark my words when you give your daughter away in marriage in Murmansk. The north is like a bottomless pit dragging you down'.

Elena: You're so right, I'd forgotten. We were young back then, and thought we had our whole lives ahead of us. But life sort of evaporated without us noticing. We've spent our whole life in darkness and permafrost. I handed in my notice every year so I could take my little angel [detënok] to the sun. Now, I'm 53 and miss my home more than ever.

Interviewer: Home, where is home?

Elena: Where I was born, went to school, got married; the place where all my relations live. Tell you the truth, the north is the affliction of my life, because for all of these thirty years, I've had this idea in my head of one day being free. We never wanted to fix up this flat, we didn't even swap it with a bigger one when the opportunity arose. In short, I've been living in the north temporarily for thirty years.

Nikolay: Now, now, let's not dwell so much on the sad things. We've had our share of good things, too. Our wages, you can't compare them with what they earned in the south, and back then we could afford to spoil ourselves as well. And where else can you see snow in the amounts we get here, and the sunshine...?

Interviewer: Has the northern environment affected you in any way?

Elena: I've never managed to walk for long spells in the forests in the autumn. The ground isn't firm enough. You're walking along, and everything seesaws under your feet. But a little way from the road, I really like it outdoors.

Nikolay: We've even got our own favourite place off the Leningradka [St Petersburg–Murmansk road]. Before we got the car, we had no idea there were so many lovely places. It was slog, slog and then more slog.

Elena: And just see how it's changed: on Fridays, if the weather's nice, it's virtually impossible to find a place to park the car outside of town. And if you look down from a height, there are columns of smoke in every direction [where picnickers are grilling food]. We had a shashlyk picnic with some friends once, but we'd forgotten to bring the matches. We heard laughter, and went towards it, and right there, almost next to us so to speak, there was this group having a rare old time, and they lent us matches.

Nikolay: Shops probably lose a lot of custom on those days. Murmansk turns into a ghost town.

Elena: Oh, I don't know. The supermarkets do a very good trade. You can't have a picnic without food and drink [laughs]. We are Russian after all! We need something to grill, something to drink, something to eat. Even if we can't be bothered to make shashlyk, we take along different sorts of sausages and meat cakes and what have you and grill them on a skewer.

Nikolay: The funny thing is, it tastes good even when it's burnt, underdone or overdone.

Elena: I don't want to talk about all the unhappy things again, but the nice things can't make up for what we've suffered in the north.

Nikolay: Now, now, don't upset yourself [tries to calm his wife].

Elena: No, we've been asked, and I want to answer. Living here is really hard. Your whole system gets worn out, like you drive a car till it falls apart. And no one can mend or prevent it, and no reason to either. You go out and buy a new car. The government don't care about us. People at the top have other concerns. And to think we gave our youth and health to the state. It doesn't count. You've only got yourself to rely on. Nowadays, there's no point expecting any help from the government.

Nikolay: Well, obviously I agree with you by and large. As far as the state's concerned we're expendable, use and throw.

Interviewer: In what sense?

Nikolay: In the ordinary sense. We're vassals to the state, full stop. Abroad, relations between the state and citizens are governed by a social contract or partnership. You work while you're young and take it easy when you're old. You know you can look forward to a dignified old age. What I call a dignified life, and I want to make this perfectly plain, is not a life of luxury or great wealth. But look what they've done to our old people. They're poverty stricken. And we're not getting any younger ourselves.

[talk about their impression of Scandinavians]

Interviewer: So what do you think, is there any difference between northerners and southerners?

Nikolay: In our country?

Interviewer: Yes, if we were talking about our former union.

Nikolay: We tend to simplify the differences, categorize people as northerners and southerners. But if you want a complete picture, you need to ask both groups. Northerners will see southerners as sociable, eccentric, impulsive and pretty miserly. But to themselves, northerners are kind, sympathetic, reliable ... and, you see, they'd give all the positive attributes to the northerners. Southerners' impression of northerners, on the other hand, is buttoned up and cold, dull, wealthy, lucky etc. etc.

Elena: Northerners are more like Muscovites today, in that department.

Interviewer: In what way?

Elena: I'll explain it to you. Muscovites think they're the bees' knees. Everything was created for their benefit. The rest of us are rubbish. And we're the same, we northerners, we think we're the most honest, kindest, best etc. But in reality all that's relative. If they took away all the perks we northerners enjoy, and cut off

> our *mazut [oil fuel used for heating homes], you'd soon see how kind and honest we are. But if you want it in a nutshell, there are differences between southerners and northerners as regards the peoples' characters, habits, cuisine and language. And any one of those characteristics can be used as a pretext to ignite national conflicts.*
>
> *[talk about the environment]*
>
> Elena: *Anyway, young people who want healthy children shouldn't live here. I want to go home myself, to the sea, where it's warm in the spring...[dreaming].*

The interview starts in a far from comfortable tone. Elena imitates the interviewer when asked if they enjoy living in the north: 'Enjoy, enjoy. We're hostages of the north.' The couple had imagined staying a few years at first, but are still here thirty years on. The atmosphere takes an ominous turn when Nikolay recalls what the children's nurse predicted: 'You'll never move anywhere else, mark my words when you give our daughter away in marriage in Murmansk. The north is like a bottomless pit dragging you down.' Elena is clearly very distraught. The north, she says, is 'the affliction of [her] life'; she has been dreaming for thirty years of 'one day being free'. She feels she has spent her whole life in darkness and permafrost. They thought they had their whole lives ahead of them when they arrived, but life evaporated without them noticing it. Elena is well into her fifties and misses the south more than ever. Opportunities to live a more comfortable life in the north were passed over. They could have exchanged their flat for a larger one, for instance, or redecorated the one they had. But no, they would be leaving soon enough, they reminded themselves.

Nikolay tries to comfort his wife by reminding her of the good things about living in the north ('we've had our share of good things, too'), as Sergey did in our last interview, but at a far more serious level. For a moment, amusing stories about picnics in the countryside and the episode with the forgotten matches seem to distract Elena. There is a sense of cosiness, but also of solidarity among northerners, all trying to make the best of things under harsh climatic conditions. Elena speaks of the need for good food and drink – even in the most uncomfortable settings – as a distinct marker of Russianness ('We are Russians after all!'). Nikolay joins in. Food cooked on an open fire in the countryside tastes good whether it is burned, underdone or overdone – even in the north. But these nice things cannot make up for what they have suffered in the north, Elena interjects. When Nikolay again tries to calm her down, she protests. They were asked their opinion, and she wants to answer.

'Living here is really hard. Your whole system gets worn out, like you drive a car till it falls apart.' She starts criticizing the Russian authorities who, she thinks, have let northerners down (and probably the Russian people at large): 'The government don't care about us. People at the top have other concerns. And to think we gave our youth and health to the state. It doesn't count. You've only got yourself to rely on.' Nikolay draws a comparison with other countries ('abroad'). They have a social contract between the state and its citizens. You work while you are young and relax when you get old. In Russia, the authorities have no such contract with the people. Or rather, they did in Soviet times, but no longer.[10]

The most interesting part of the interview is Elena and Nikolay's attack on the usual stereotypes of northerners and southerners. First, they remind us, it is all too easy to categorize people. Second, if you still want to define northerners and southerners, the least you can do is look at things from the other side's point of view as well. While northerners tend to view themselves as kind, sympathetic and reliable, southerners would perceive them as cold, dull and buttoned-up. This does not prevent Elena from giving a rather categorical description of people in the Russian capital: 'Muscovites think they're the bees' knees. Everything was created for their benefit. The rest of us are rubbish.' Her point, however, is that northern complacency – 'we're better than those southerners' – is no better than Muscovite complacency. Echoing Nastya's views above, Elena links northern considerateness to the region's healthy economy: 'If they withdrew all the perks we northerners enjoy and cut off our *mazut*, you'd see how kind and honest we are.' There are differences between different regions, of course, but one should avoid stereotyping. At the end of the day, stereotypes can be used to ignite national conflicts. As for herself, she doesn't seem to like what she takes as the prevailing upbeat image of the north.

Much like Marina, Elena seems eager to round off the interview by restating her main point (which is the opposite of Marina's), though the conversation has now turned to another theme: 'Anyway, young people who want healthy children shouldn't live here.' Period.

Negotiating stereotypes about north and south

These interviews illustrate the stereotypes in use by and of Russian northerners: well educated, hard working, calm, considerate and friendly. To Marina, that is how Russian northerners actually are, unlike the southerners (i.e. inhabitants of the southern belt of the former Soviet Union[11]), whom she denigrates: uneducated, uncivilized and mean. Nastya repeated Marina's list of positive attributes about northerners, but also saw some good sides to southern 'noisiness'. Nevertheless, she too called southerners mean, uncivilized even, though they cannot be blamed for it: 'People tend to lose their manners when they're unhappy. That's why people make a spectacle of themselves down south.' Elena and Nikolay go even further and criticize northerners' complacency. By cultivating a self-image as better than people in the south, northerners are no better than haughty Muscovites. And however good northerners might be, it's thanks to comfortable standards of living. Without the perks and *mazut*, 'you'd soon see how kind and honest we are'. The interesting thing is that while the interviewees in this chapter disagree about how northerners actually are (or at least about how they would have been without the perks), the discussion revolves around the same basic traits. It seems generally accepted that this is how northerners 'are believed to be'.

The same thing is evident in the rest of my interviews. Some interviewees confirm conventional wisdom, others challenge it, or at least try to nuance it. But all seem to take the same stereotypes as given. First, the interview transcriptions are full of adjectives like competent, calm and kind of northerners and the exact opposite of southerners. Some even rival Marina in their characterizations: 'Southerners are simply very envious. They always count other people's money' (female, mid-forties). 'Even Rottweilers are kinder here [in the north]' (female, mid-fifties). '[Southerners] are by nature disposed towards gossip' (male, late fifties). Several interviewees (like Nastya in our second interview) disagree with the conventional perception of southerners as open-hearted, indicating that this is just on the surface of it, that northern kindness is deeper and more genuine. In the following interview extract, Maria (mid-twenties) ridicules the myth of southern openness, while her husband Sergey (around thirty) tells a story about genuine northern kindness.

Interviewer: What do you think, is there any difference between northerners and southerners?

Sergey and Maria: [as if in one voice] Of course, there is. Obviously.

Interviewer: Could we try and see what the differences are?

Sergey: Northerners are more considerate, polite. Southerners are hot-tempered, but open-minded.

Maria: Well, in my opinion, northerners are really, really nice. Really nice! [She says this emphatically, as if to ward off expressions of disbelief.] Southerners are alright in their way, but they're so uptight.

[brief spell of silence]

[to Sergey] Are you saying southerners are open? I don't think they are! What I think is ... southerners are 'nice' and open on the surface.

[Maria jumps out of her chair and mimics a southerner.] 'Hi!' [She exclaims in a loud voice, opens her arms and gives an imaginary friend a triple hug and kiss in Russian style.] 'How's things? How's life treating you? When did you get here? And tra la la, tra la la ...' But in reality they've forgotten you as soon as they asked how you are and probably never registered your response, anyway. The northerner is more reserved – he's not given to tittle-tattle. And he's more genuine by a factor of about a hundred.

Sergey: Southerners – they're just putting on an act. Northerners are different. Last summer, we were travelling home after the holidays, and my wife was carrying little Dashka [their daughter] in a bag. And there was me, loaded like a pack-ass, dragging bags, rucksacks, suitcases – everything my wife and daughter needed for a three month holiday. I can tell you, by then I was pretty fed up. And on the underground, this woman comes up to us – this was a woman [pauses, in turn looking the others in the eye] – and says: 'Excuse me, won't you let me give you a hand?' We thanked her but said we'd manage. But the bags were really heavy, so we changed our mind and accepted her offer, and she helped us all the way to the station. And d'you know something? [dramatic pause] It turned out she was FROM MURMANSK!

Here we find a story, as a sub-category of narrative (see Chapter 1). According to Czarniawska (2004, p. 19), stories are distinguished by the existence of a plot that brings the recounted events into a meaningful whole. Sergey's last narrative would have had little meaning for us without the last sentence (except as an illustration of the widespread practice among Russian northern men to send their wives and children to the south for at least three months a year). It would have related a series of events about how a family struggles to get their holiday luggage from the underground to the railway station, the husband 'loaded like a pack-ass', and a kind woman who insists on helping them. Then comes the endpoint that brings meaning to the events: it turns out – why had they not understood this before? – that the woman is *from*

Murmansk! As Gergen (2001, p. 250) points out, endpoints in stories are typically saturated with value. In this case, it serves to underscore the kindness of northerners. The woman is even from their own home town of Murmansk, and the couple's joy at the kindness of a stranger is reinforced by pride in the good human qualities of their fellow citizen.[12] The following brief narrative holds a similar moral. This time the narrator is at the giving end:

> In Maykop [...], I was at the market buying fruit. And the old lady (behind the stall) says, 'You're not from here, are you? You must be from up north.' I say, 'How on earth did you know?' And she says, 'you're very polite' (female, around forty).

Many of my interviewees grew up in southern parts of the USSR and moved north because of their qualifications. Some of them equate northern life with 'life as led by specialists and highly educated people', while the south remains a place for people without more ambition than growing fruit trees or running a small business.[13] It is reflected in the following brief extract from our interview with Viktor (about fifty) and Anna (about thirty). They are both technical experts and from the south.

> *Interviewer*: You know a lot about people from the south and the north in our country from first-hand experience. Are there any differences between them?
> *Viktor*: Well, so that we get our terminology right from the outset, I want to say I consider myself a northerner, despite being born in Crimea.
> *Anna*: Me too, I'm one too [seemingly happy to play along]. Here – that is here in the north – there's a higher level of education because there's nothing else to do apart from getting qualifications. But the southerners, their mindset is more ... [obviously thinking hard to find an appropriate expression] more of a dacha-and-orchard level thing (*ogorodno-dachnyy*).

Others are more eager to challenge conventional wisdom, or at least underscore that they do not simply reproduce myths; their opinions of northernness are based on their own observations. One young man started the interview in the following way, 'You probably think we're going talk about how kind and honest northerners are and how nervous and uptight southerners are. [Pause] And that's how it's going to be! [Pause] No, I'm just kidding, just kidding. Let's get started!' (male, early thirties). He went on to describe northern orderliness (referring to a well known saying, 'my police force protects me') and the anarchy of the south ('It's completely lawless there. Everything can be bought and sold. It doesn't even count as corruption. It's just the way things are.') – all in line with conventional wisdom, and without any attempt at substantiation beyond statements like 'this is how we are, and that is how they are'. This interviewee plays with conventions while reproducing them. As a young woman remarked, people don't always live up to the stereotypes. 'People are different, everywhere. You can find altruists and skinflints in the south and the north. My mother, for example, is a native of Murmansk and my grandparents have always lived in Murmansk. One shouldn't discuss one's parents, but mamma, she's so emotional and impulsive, she's more southern than the southerners. And she's good at counting the money' (female, early twenties). Implicitly, this interviewee confirms the myth of southerners as emotional, impulsive and stingy, but her point is that also northerners can be like that. To some interviewees, the once clear differences between north and south are receding into the background: 'Earlier, the dividing lines were clear. Northerners were friendly, southerners were not. Northerners were quiet and calm, southerners were noisy and hot-tempered. Northerners were rich and unselfish, southerners were envious and greedy.[14] And so on. But now the dividing lines are becoming blurred' (female, mid-forties). The other interviewee at this session blamed this development on the increasingly difficult economic climate in the north: 'Of course [the differences] are blurred. Social conditions in the north have deteriorated, which explains a lot. Wage differences are smaller, and they've removed perks, but the perception of the rich northerner persists still' (female, mid-forties). According to these two women, economic developments in the post-Soviet era have shown northerners 'life as it is', that is, without the 'artificial' conditions created by Soviet authorities: '[Southerners] think northerners are naïve. That's not good, the way I see it. People need to be wary. In that department, southerners are better adjusted to life. They're smarter, in a positive way.' 'I agree. We're like chickens used to the warmth of an incubator. But then they suddenly turned the lights out and everybody fell ill, and now we're all in danger of perishing. We're obviously defenceless against outside forces and changes.'[15] Another interviewee poignantly describes the balancing act required of a northerner in post-Soviet Russia.

What do northerners do? They've all got a regular job. Nobody makes money from a smallholding. And relations are usually miles away.

You can't expect anyone to come and help you. If you can't make it in the normal way – you're lost. You'll freeze slowly but surely to death [*Tikho zamërz i vsë*]. A southerner, on the other hand, can exist on the margins. If you get laid off, you've still got your little farm, and if the harvest is a failure, you can rely on a big extended family, and if you're evicted – at least it's warm on the streets. And so on and so forth. (Female, around forty)

The vocabulary available – identity as narrative

The labels used by my interviewees to characterize Russian northerners resonate more with the ideals of the Soviet conquest of the north than with romantic images of the north as the 'real', indigenous Russia (see Chapter 1). The north, as presented in the interviews, is not Solzhenitsyn's land of moral salvation or an echo of the mythical 'bell, sounded long ago', a trope of so-called countryside literature. My interviewees centre their narratives rather on the Arctic myth of the early Communist period, with aviation and expeditions – and, above all, the taming of the northern wilderness with people and industries. As we saw in Chapter 2, forced labour kept the wheels turning before World War II in the Kola Peninsula; after the war, economic incentives attracted workers. Those incentives were probably real enough, as the following extract shows: 'D'you remember what Lena told us about her husband being relocated from Ukraine to Murmansk, with a promise of 150 roubles a month? And she had replied, "What on earth are we going to do with all that money?"' (female, late thirties). But people obviously also took pride in being part of the 'conquest of the north'. According to one of the few published studies about identities on the Kola Peninsula (albeit in Russian), this is the case even today, see Razumova (2007, p. 146). The field of 'local cultural studies' (*kraevedenie*) in the Kola Peninsula, Razumova says, is particularly advanced. In her interviews, she found several stereotypes featured in historical and popular literature about the region. 'On the Kola Peninsula, you can find the whole of Mendeleev's periodic table': 'the conquest of the north'; 'the storming of the Khibiny [mountains]'; 'the towns grew before our eyes'; and 'it was necessary to survive the harsh climatic conditions of the north'. 'The concept of the history of the region can be defined as "the myth of the north", subjugated by Man, the creator of civilization', she writes (ibid., p. 147) [my translation].

The main public narrative (see Chapter 1) in my interviews is 'the good life in the north'. Standards of living have 'always' been higher than further south, although the gap has allegedly narrowed in recent years. In Soviet times, the authorities paid the northern population so well, people 'did not know what to do with all the money'. Although incentives do not exist to the same extent today, wages are still generally high and job opportunities relatively good for people with academic (especially technical) qualifications, and people continue to improve their qualifications because 'there is little else to do' (as Anna remarked above). 'The good life in the north' is summed up by Marina's '2+2+2': she has two sets of qualifications, two children and two combined apartments – all inconceivable in the south, she claims. And with financial and material security come good manners. When you know you and your family will be taken care of, you don't have to 'make a spectacle of yourself' the way people often do down south. The level of education, the high living standards and the harsh northern climate (see discussion below)[16] are represented by the four Cs of Russian northernness: Competent, Cultured, Calm and Considerate.

The category of northerner is not static; 'becoming a northerner' definitely makes sense. And it is not restricted by happenstance such as place of birth, or open to happenstance such as present location (although one must have lived for a time in the north obviously). Northernness can only be acquired by merit, depending on one's ability to fulfil the four Cs. One has to live in a specific place, but it demands something in addition. You are not a northerner the moment you move to the north. Both time and adjustment seem to be needed. It is absolutely an attractive category of which to be a member, cf. how Viktor above found it appropriate to stress his perception of himself as a northerner despite being born in Crimea, and how Anna – obviously with a far shorter period of residence in the north – is eager to be included: 'Me too, I'm one too.'[17] Just because she lives in Murmansk, she seems to be saying, her northern credentials might not be obvious. On reflection, though, she feels she deserves to be called a northerner, too.

Another prominent public narrative mentioned only in passing so far, is to explain how you react, mentally and physically, by phenomena in the natural environment. We remember how Nastya sought for an explanation of last winter's gloom in the different temperatures and changing atmospheric pressure,[18] and how her husband Sergey – despite painting a generally happy picture of life in the north – believed it is not good for 'the organism' (a word very frequently used in the interviews in discussions about how the northern climate affects one).[19] On a similar note, one interviewee explains how the northern environment influences her: 'If your organism is one of those that's immune to changes in the weather, living here is obviously good. When I was young, I didn't notice anything either. Today, though, I can feel it when the pressure falls and [getting through] the dark days of winter is hard, it's, er, everything...[waves her arms around]' (female, mid-forties). Another interviewee blames other natural phenomena for northerners' health problems: oxygen discharges and magnet storms, 'Ah, let's see. Well, to start with, the north itself affects people most of all. Often because of changes in the air pressure, oxygen discharges, and all sorts of magnetic storms. The effect grows as you get older – and we're not getting any younger [smiles knowingly to her friend]' (female, around forty). Another interviewee also points the finger at magnetism and, moreover, to the lack of oxygen in the north. 'Whatever's in store for us here it's unpleasant. Murmansk is a magnet, twice as strong as Sochi [on the Black Sea]. There's 20 per cent less oxygen, and the temperature fluctuates wildly from one day to the next' (male, about fifty). A dentist (male, around forty) and his assistant (female, late twenties) explain how the northern climate even affects their work:

Interviewer: So what kind of effect does the climate have on you?

Dentist: Well, since I'm a doctor, I have to say it's clearly unhealthy living in the north. The winters wear the organism down, and it becomes increasingly difficult to get one's strength back for every passing year.

Assistant: And it's not only us – we can see it in our patients. For instance, when people have teeth removed, the organism gets back to normal more quickly in the autumn because of the vitamins one has absorbed during the summer. One shouldn't pull teeth at all in the spring. Immunity is at a low, and one's strength is declining. [She smiles and begins to sing 'Strength fails when wounds bleed' – a verse from a popular song.]

The most interesting part of this extract is arguably the dentist's opening line, where he uses his academic credibility ('since I'm a doctor, I have to say...') to state beyond any doubt ('clearly', literally: *konechno* or 'of course') that it is unhealthy to live in the north. Similar formulations are found in many of my interviews – we already heard Sergey's concern in our second interview extract – but here it is given added weight as an objective fact put forward by a doctor (albeit a tooth doctor).[20] It is presented as the baseline, the point of departure for any further discussion. We can go on and on about good and bad things about life in the north until we're blue in the face, but one thing is beyond discussion: *healthy* it is not! This puts a serious dent in the happy picture of life in the north presented above. Yes, we are competent, cultured, calm and considerate, we northerners, but it is our destiny to live in a place where people were never meant to live. The Soviet experiment involved building a human incubator in the Arctic wilderness, but the lights have gone out, and those who have not left yet for lack of courage or money, run about like demented hens in the dark and cold. Elena and her like are fear-stricken and blame the Russian authorities for not taking care of the people of the north any more. Others criticize the idea of populating the Russian north in the first place. Viktor, whom we saw was eager to stress his northern credentials, called building a city for a population of half a million north of the Polar Circle a crime. On the whole, letting people live in the north is 'inhumane' [stresses *in-hu-mane*].[21] Even among those who are less categorical, a distance to the northern environment is visible. People watch the colours of the changing seasons with admiration (as many interviewees reportedly do), but sort of from the side. They are not unconditionally 'inside' their natural environment, like people who have lived for generations in the same place (especially indigenous people) are generally believed to be. We remember Elena noting how she was never able to walk for long in the forests in the autumn, 'The ground isn't firm enough. You're walking along, and everything seesaws under your feet.' On a similar note, another woman told us,

> When I moved to Murmansk from Bashkiria, it was ten years before I visited the countryside. The forests didn't seem like forests to me, and the wet ground sank under my feet. But now I can't get enough of it all. I hug the trees, devour them so to speak, and I feel the better for it. (Female, mid-forties).

Changing borders?

Does northernness strengthen people's sense of Russianness, or is it rather a way of distancing oneself from what is typically Russian and opening up for relations with the West? Has the opening of the border with Scandinavia had any influence in this respect?[22] In the next chapter, we will see what impression people have of their Scandinavian neighbours in general; here just some notes about how some of my interviewees weave observations about the Scandinavian countries into their narratives about Russian northernness.

In our first interview extract, Marina comes across as a fierce and consistent defender of northern virtues, as we saw. Her opinions of

Figure 3.1 Sunny winter day in Murmansk

Scandinavia, however, lead in different directions. She speaks about the BEAR collaboration in positive terms, saying how much her Ukrainian friends envied the opportunities children in the north have to visit Norway and Finland on exchange programmes. Asked about her impression of Scandinavians, she hesitates before giving a rather faltering answer. This isn't what she personally thinks, she says, but what people in general think about Scandinavia. That is, it's quiet and clean, but rather boring.[23] The Norwegians one comes across in Murmansk are not very cultured,[24] but perhaps people from southern Norway are, she wonders. She sees in Scandinavia the same positive attributes as the Russian north (both are quiet and clean), but in Norway these virtues are more likely to be found in the region around the capital; northern Norwegians are the uncivilized crowd there. A bit later, when everyone is pondering 'the Piter factor' (see below), she interrupts, as if she feels a point has been missed, with a harsh description of the Norwegian education and health systems. There is a Russian girl she knows who married a Norwegian (a typical consequence of the opening of the border; see Chapter 2). Contrary to popular belief in the West that Russian girls are eager to marry Western men in order to live in the West, this particular girl, Marina assures us, was not keen on moving to Norway at all. Why? Because

Figure 3.2   A quick snack during working hours

she wanted her children 'to go to a normal kindergarten, where they could learn something'. Marina then comments the Norwegian school system, which allegedly produces 'subnormal' (*degenerirovannye*, literally: 'degenerate') children; obviously the children don't learn very much at school. She recites a litany (Ries, 1997, pp. 84ff) of problems supposedly connected with living in Scandinavia, 'And the health service there! I wouldn't trust the medical system in Norway if you paid me!' After another round of allegations against Norwegian schools, she concludes (she 'lands' her litany) with the words, 'That's just how it is.'[25] Marina, while consistently categorical in her depiction of Russian northerners and southerners, is sometimes inconsistent when she speaks about life on the other side of the border. She might have hesitated because the interviewer is Norwegian and she does not want to appear impolite. Or she might simply be ambivalent about her Nordic neighbours and interaction with them. Clearly, she is proud when she can tell her Ukrainian friends about the exchange programmes in the Barents region. But this does not mean, she seems to want to say, she is uncritical of whatever the opening of the border implies. She obviously has some information, or has heard rumours, about Norwegian schools and hospitals and their standards[26] and is adamant that Russians have nothing to learn from their Nordic

Figure 3.3   A Russian northerner fixing his car outside his private garage

neighbours in that department. For Marina, then, the opening of the border seems, if anything, to have made her more conscious or proud of her Russianness, not the other way around.[27] Even more interesting for the topic of this chapter, Marina does not ascribe the same good qualities to northerners on the other side of the border as she does to Russian northerners. Actually, she likens the Russian north to Scandinavia as such, but with the northern parts of Scandinavia (i.e. those that are engaged in cross-border collaboration with north-western Russia) as a possible exception!

Marina's fellow interviewee, Ivan, thinks along similar lines. Unlike Marina, he says not one deprecatory word about Scandinavians at this interview, but despite his apparent wish to appear knowledgeable about cross-border schemes under the Barents programme, he has not one positive word to say about them either. Explicitly, he promotes a specific form of northernness – which is neither that of Polar romanticism or harsh Stalinism, nor of outspoken Westernism, for that matter. No, his idea of northernness is the mild, 'civilized' version springing out of St Petersburg, Russia's 'northern capital' and 'window on Europe'.[28] He openly declares his admiration for St Petersburg; and what goes for Piter by and large also goes for Murmansk, he insists ('we've always relied on Piter'; 'even our dialect is Piterish').[29] Implicitly,

Figure 3.4 Shopping for food

he draws a connection between this desirable form of northernness and that which is developed at the border in the Barents region ('we've annexed Norway as part of Murmansk Oblast', i.e. into the Piterish Russian north).[30] More than anything, Ivan's rather acute comments in this interview point to a specific form of northernness that is open to Europeanness, but not the West per se. His opinions are similar to those of Müller's (2008) respondents, Moscow IR students who engage selectively with European signifiers. Identifying oneself in some situations as European does not mean relinquishing one's Russianness (as identification with Westernness would probably require), although it acts as a foil to 'ordinary' Russianness. This is exactly what Ivan and his friends do when they speak pejoratively about Russian southerners, but also aim some blows at the West. They probably would have spoken negatively about southerners even in the absence of cross-border partnerships in the north, but the latter presumably serve to give their sense of northernness yet another pillar to rest on. Engaging selectively with some Scandinavian attributes while discarding others strengthens their feeling of Piterish northernness. Although someone has to state – as Marina did clearly and loudly – it does not mean slavishly adopting Western ideals. We will return to this in the next chapter.

Conclusions

Prevailing stereotypes of what it means to be a northerner – competent, cultured, calm and considerate – fill out the dominant public narrative I term 'the good life in the north'. A high level of education and material wealth ensure good manners, orderliness and civilized relations among people. There is a strong element of othering in this narrative: southerners are uncivilized, stingy and mean, at best 'fun to be around, but oh so superficial'. Then there is a competing narrative of life in the north as fundamentally 'unnatural'. Even doctors and psychologists say that life in the north is, beyond any shadow of scientific doubt, not good for the organism, and most people seem to agree. We hear them worry about the affliction called Arctic eyesight, about winter depressions and a general lack of physical well-being; and we hear them blame the problems on magnetic storms, atmospheric pressure and lack of oxygen. We see them admire the northern landscape, but from a distance, as something almost unreal ('the forests were not forests'). And we hear them say that building a city like Murmansk north of the Polar Circle was a crime and liken it to an unlit incubator, where you risk slowly perishing from cold if you forsake the conventions. This alternative narrative hardly figured at all in the interview with Marina. It was breaking through the surface in Nastya's story, and had taken over the entire picture of 'the good life in the north' for Elena.

As mentioned several times already, there is a conspicuous tendency for interviewees to alternate between sets of opinions or attitudes. Obviously, one can call Murmansk the best city in Russia and at the same time call its construction a criminal act without contradicting oneself. The same applies to the wish to be a northerner, and believing people should not be living in the north. Is 'being a northerner' essentially a way of distinguishing oneself from the uncultured, dacha-and-orchard mentality of southerners – thanks to Anna for this wonderful expression! – or simply from 'ordinary' Russianness? Nor is there any obvious opposition between enthusiasm over cross-border cooperation and dismay over what the other side has to offer. The first interview in this chapter took place in an amicable atmosphere, though the interviewees held highly divergent opinions. Ivan subtly boasted about his visits to Norway, while Marina performed something close to a character assassination of the same nation. The interesting thing was *the absence of an argument*; everyone smiled and nodded at each others' comments, signalling agreement. Marina and Ivan leaned in different directions, but there seemed to be no fundamental disagreement between them. Could each of them perhaps have used the other's more extreme arguments (i.e. Marina praising and Ivan scolding Norwegians)? In this case, I can confirm that not only could they, they did. (I have interviewed them both on other occasions.) I heard Ivan deride Norwegians for lack of culture and Marina praise Norwegians for orderliness and competence. What do they really think, then? Ok, they might be picking selectively from the 'syllabary of possible selves' (Gergen, 2001, p. 253) available to them, but do they have no core identity that ensures consistency on a subject? Or is it meaningless to search for an inner conviction, a central 'truth'? Is 'truth' being true to narrative conventions (or a logic of appropriateness, see Chapter 1)? Is it simply so that these conventions – in this particular case – give individuals flexibility to switch between positions as long as these positions are of a certain type? In this chapter, we identified a specific set of narrative resources available to north-west Russians related to northernness and southernness. These resources can be used selectively, we found, depending on the situation; they do not require internal logical consistency. Actors behave rationally as long as they draw from the set of stereotypes about Russian northernness, *but these stereotypes can be played with, tested out, twisted and torn apart.* Perhaps the closest we can get to defining Kola northernness is *engagement, in some form or other, with these stereotypes.* That said, we should not lose sight of the fact that the majority of my interviewees still embrace, or rather do not question, the conventional wisdom of northerners as competent, cultured, calm and considerate.

Hence, the two competing narratives on life in the north might present reality in very different ways, but the distance between them is not insurmountable, to say the least. Who would have thought it, that the first one to travel south of this chapter's interviewees would be Marina? Shortly after my interview with her, she left her double flat in Severomorsk for good and took her three children (she was pregnant when the interview took place) and Anton with her to settle on the shores of the Black Sea. She continues to complain about southerners, though.

4
How to Be a Russian: Distinguishing East from West

In Russia driving through the red light when the police is not watching is an acceptable practice; there, public opinion would be more critical of eating ice cream on the subway, a practice classified as foreign or 'uncultured' behaviour. (Boym, 1994, p. 289)

Introduction

Now we turn to a discussion about how the inhabitants of the Kola Peninsula distinguish themselves from people on the other side of the East–West border in the region. What's their opinion about the Nordic countries, what do they know about people there and how they live? How are they different from Russians? Which stereotypes exist, and what narrative resources are at hand for north-west Russians to define themselves as Russian as opposed to Scandinavian northerners. And what has the opening of the border implied in this respect? Again we start with three relatively long interview extracts. To retain the character of each interview, I have kept most of the discussion about northerners vs. southerners in two of the interviews.[1] I have, however, removed sections specifically dealing with the topic of our next chapter, notably nuclear safety. In the ensuing discussion, I quote my interviewees more frequently than I did in the last chapter because, as we shall see, opinions are more widely divided on the issue of East vs. West, than on that of northerners vs. southerners.[2]

Extract 1: 'Their eyes are always wide open'

Again we meet a married couple, this time one in their mid-forties. The interview takes place in the office of the female spouse Larisa after working hours. She is a technical specialist and teaches at the university. Born in Russia's middle belt, she married a military man, Andrey. They lived in one of the closed military towns on the Kola Peninsula for about a decade, but they have lived in Murmansk for nearly as long.

Interviewer: What are the differences between people who live in the north and people who live in the south in your opinion?

Larisa: Well, first of all, what you mean by 'south' needs defining. For me, for example, south means Crimea. I lived in Crimea for a number of years, given that 'certain people' [referring to her husband] were studying there. But Samara, where I was born, isn't south to the same degree for me.

Interviewer: But that apart, for people like us who live in Murmansk, middle Russia is south.

Larisa: Well, it might be in principle. And it is true that the natural environment and people are different. Southerners are different from us temperamentally; they are more active, emotional. We are compelled by the climate to be more conservative, even-tempered. Because of the weather we've learned to take things as they come, so we're more patient than southerners. They can't take criticism; you can't say anything negative about them, but here, people say whatever they like about you. Me, for example, I never quarrel with people I don't know, fellow travellers for instance, and I don't often see others involved in quarrels of that sort, because I live here in the north.

Interviewer: And all these differences can be ascribed to natural conditions?

Andrey: It's difficult to be categorical. It's not very hot up here, so people try to spread a bit of warmth in their personal relations. What else? People observe the traffic rules. Just yesterday I saw a girl stop at a zebra crossing when the lights turned red, and she stood and waited till they turned green, even though there were obviously no cars there and none could be seen approaching – and the street was quite narrow. It was on Marata [Marata Street. There's a tiny crossing at a point where the road narrows considerably].

Larisa: That could never have happened back home in Samara. People don't care two hoots about traffic lights – everybody walks and drives just as they like. People believe traffic lights restrict their freedom and don't feel obliged to follow them. What's more, it's very quiet on our public transport here. If people talk, it's never very loudly, and people don't snarl at each other so much. I don't get tired of the noise on the way home after work. Once, in Samara we were going to the theatre, and it took one and a half hours to get there. Before we'd even arrived, all interest in the theatre had evaporated.

Andrey: Not to mention that we're all dependent on the sun in those cases, and we notice it when the sun's shining. Life suddenly seems more interesting and you feel better too.

Larisa: I experienced something interesting once. I'd travelled in connection with work to Piter, and one morning in February I got on the tram near the hotel. Since this was the first stop on its route I was the only passenger until the next stop. It was early morning, but the sun was already shining; it's so unusual for us, I just sat there smiling to myself. It immediately made me feel good. At the next stop a man of a certain age got on, looked at me and thanked me – for smiling! He said my smile had cheered him up and been a real tonic.

Andrey: Yes, the bright sunshine didn't affect him either way, because it's like that every day there. But we don't get sunshine every day, and are all the more grateful when it does shine.

Interviewer: What in your mind is the difference between Russians and foreigners, such as Scandinavians?

Larisa: I don't know that I've met so many foreigners, so I can't really say for certain what I think. But judging from what I do know, I'd say they were more emancipated. It's always surprised me why they're not afraid of foreign countries, not afraid of us, and they're not put off by not knowing the language. They feel at home everywhere. They think it's interesting to learn something about us, to get to know us, mix with us. You can always tell a foreigner.

Interviewer: How's that?

Larisa: Their eyes are always wide open, and you can see the interest in them. They can express an interest even by a short glimpse; they're interested in everything.

Andrey: But they're interested in slightly different things than, let's say, Russians on a visit from the south. They're not interested in the blessings of nature, they live in the north themselves, at the end of the world so to say, they know everything there is to know in that area, so they're more interested in the people, or us in other words.

Interviewer: Would you like to travel abroad yourselves?

Larisa: Move there for good – no, but to have a look – yes. I'd soon start feeling pretty inadequate abroad, even deficient in some respects, because I don't know the language, which would be a real drag. I wouldn't be able to converse normally with people or explain myself should the need arise.

Andrey: It sounds like a case of inverted chauvinism, directed against yourself. Get rid of your complexes, wife! Having a look – obviously it would be thrilling. It's one thing seeing it on television, but being there and seeing it for yourself is completely different. But to move there, no, that's for the young. It's too late for us. I have to say though that when they show something from Norway on TV, it looks remarkably similar – same buildings, bridges, landscape.

[talk focuses on the northern nature and nuclear safety]

Larisa and Andrey, like many of my interviewees, have little experience of foreigners and do not really know what they think of them. Based on what she has seen, Larisa is impressed with how self-assured and outgoing Scandinavians are. They are obviously not afraid of foreign countries, even if they do not know the language. They seem to feel at home everywhere. But perhaps they look a bit naïve, 'their eyes are always wide open'. Asked whether she would like to travel abroad herself, Larisa would like to have a look, she says, but not move to another country – she would feel awkward not knowing the language. Andrey tells his wife to get rid of her complexes, but agrees that moving abroad is not for them, 'that's for the young; it's too late for us'. Larisa and Andrey seem slightly apprehensive, preoccupied with language-related problems. They would have felt uncomfortable abroad without being able to converse normally with people. They are impressed with Scandinavians who come to Murmansk not knowing Russian, and obviously not ashamed of it or restrained by it. But are Scandinavians considered 'simple' because they don't seem embarrassed?

Extract 2: 'As nations, they're on the decline'

Both of my next interviewees are psychologists. They used to work together and are still friends. Ashot, fiftyish, was born and raised in Armenia, but has lived in Murmansk for many years. Natalya, a woman in her early forties, grew up in one of the closed military towns on the Kola Peninsula and is married to a serviceman from the south. They live in Murmansk now as well. The interview takes place at Natalya's flat and proceeds in a friendly, easy atmosphere. The interviewees come across as very emotional – they caress each other, rave and rant – but that seems to be how their relationship works.

Interviewer: So what would you say, is there a difference do you think between people of the north and people of the south?

Ashot: Well, I was born and bred in Yerevan and have an Armenian accent, but I'm very fond of the north, however barmy that probably sounds. I count myself as a northerner. [Addresses a grinning Natalya] And it's nothing to laugh about!

Natalya: No, no, I'm not laughing. It was just such an unexpected revelation. A northerner-Armenian. I'm a blue-blooded native myself, born in a closed military town. And I married a serviceman. I'm proud of being a northerner, and, now, a citizen of Murmansk. When I visit my mother-in-law in Sevastopol', I can never stay for very long – I'm just itching to get back home again.

Ashot: So neither sun, wine nor fruit [exaggerates his accent on purpose] makes you happy, or what?

Natalya: Well, obviously, I like them, it's just that everything here is my own. People down south get on my nerves. They're so eccentric and tense – puts me off the fruit altogether.

Ashot: So don't talk to them, just enjoy the holiday!

Natalya: But you can't live in a vacuum. I'm a gregarious type, as well, you know.

Ashot: You're a bit manic yourself, that's why they get on your nerves. You are a psychologist, after all. You know the saying about only seeing in others what you've got in yourself. Me, for example, I think most people in the north are internationalists. In the north, all nations merge into one.

Natalya: Which makes one big nation – of northerners!

Ashot: I agree with most of what you say, Natash. Yerevan may be my birthplace, but after twenty days on holiday, subconsciously, I'm longing to get back home again.

Natalya: [sarcastically] And 'home', I take it, is Murmansk.

Ashot: [vexed, even irritated] Yepp, it's Murmansk. My grandchildren were born here, among other things, so 'home's' not the worst word you could use.

Interviewer: But what are the differences between northerners and southerners, in a nutshell?

Ashot: We have more common sense, we have more patience, and we're generally more open to other people.

Natalya: But southerners are open – too open.

Ashot: [reacting to Natalya with anger and irritation] No, that's where you're utterly wrong! Didn't you work for years as a psychologist!? Let me explain in simple terms. Southerners talk nineteen to the dozen because it's in their nature. But they don't lay bare their souls to any Tom, Dick or Harry. Being open, it means getting to the heart of the matter, not beating about the bush. Southerners' superficiality isn't openness, it's a pose. They'll launch into any and every conversation – but the chances of catching them going on about personal matters are microscopic. If you rely on what they talk about, you'd think none of them had any money, but any number of dachas, villas and cars – who's going to talk to you about them? [interjects without waiting for an answer] No one!

Natalya: And, I might add, southern men don't give women flowers. Which I know from personal experience, my husband being born and raised in Sevastopol'. Flowers don't count as a present down there. Better to buy a box of chocolates. It's enough to get you down.

Ashot: Well, there's an obvious explanation. Down south, you can't take a step without tripping over a flower. There's no point in giving a lady from the south flowers – she wouldn't appreciate them. Not much of a gift, she'd think. You probably pinched it from your neighbour's garden anyway, and never spent a kopek. Women who live very, very far south, they generally prefer gold as a gift. And I should know [raises himself up in a show of pride].

Interviewer: How do you like the countryside and wildlife here in the north? Does it affect you in any way?

Ashot: Well, it's pretty stunning, of course – untouched. But the trees up here, they're sort of 'short' [not a word usually used of trees]. Although a winter which lasts for all of nine months, I can't stand it. Then the snow melts – I like it. [His non-Russian background shines through in these abrupt sentences.]

Natalya: The constant whiteness day after day makes northerners depressed. It's a scientific fact. Though you wouldn't hear it said officially. It's been a virtual state secret since Soviet times. In any case, depression is a relatively new idea in Russia – Soviet people wouldn't dare to even think of anything so absurd. We all worked for the sake of the country, but people's health was not valued. Which, by the way, hasn't really changed.

Ashot: You're so right. We did a study fifteen years ago of the impact of living in the north on health, and they didn't even give us permission to publish the results. Even then, 45 per cent of the kids had rickets, and 30 per cent of babies had biliary dyskinesia. That's the truth. So why I'm still living here is beyond my comprehension.

[talk about nuclear safety]

Interviewer: D'you have any experience of foreigners, and what do you know about our neighbours?

Natalya: My God, my God! I just have to learn English. How many opportunities haven't passed me by? I haven't even been abroad – ever! But I'd really like to. But I can't even talk to people: I took German at school you see.
Ashot: [ironically at Natalya's expense] So take a trip to Germany then. But this is really something you should ask the younger generation.
Interviewer: But in your words...
Natalya: Helpless, but under the strong protection of the state. Seems to me, people over there are extraordinarily naïve. Live in an incubator. They've got food and water and heating and...
Ashot: [lets her finish] As nations, they're on the decline. Especially Scandinavia, but Europe as well.
Natalya: True, true. There's something seriously wrong with the blood over there. They're all brothers and sisters. If they'd only let some fresh blood in... They marry our young girls, you know.
Ashot: And insult us in the process, if you get my meaning. We're better than these foreigners! But the girls leave for the sake of the money and a better standard of living.
Natalya: And with good reason. I would have gone myself – just don't tell my husband!
Ashot: [in jest] I don't think wizened old women are exactly what they're looking for. You stay here with us. But your daughter, may be worth giving it a thought on her account.
Natalya: No, it'll be up to her. But if that's what she wants, I won't interfere.

I think it is a delight to read this interview extract: Natalya and Ashot are extremely witty, articulate and amusing. (See, for instance, how Natalya weaves together various myths about the Russian south, 'They're so eccentric and tense – puts me off the fruit altogether.') Most of the interview concerns differences between northerners and southerners; northerners, says Ashot, tend to be internationalists. ('In the north, all nations merge into one.') With a question about their experience with foreigners, the interview atmosphere becomes suddenly tense and forced. After brushing away the question with a coquettish 'Oh my God, my God! I just *have* to learn English!', Natalya admits she has never been abroad, and regrets, like Larisa in our first interview, not being able to speak with people in other countries in their own language. Ashot believes travelling abroad should be left to the younger generation, echoing what Andrey said in our first interview. When the interviewer asks them to say something at least, Natalya doesn't mince her words. Scandinavians, she says, are helpless and extraordinarily naïve. It's as if they live in an incubator. And as nations, they are on the decline, Ashot follows up. 'True, true', Natalya responds, 'There's something seriously wrong with the blood over there. They're all brothers and sisters. If they'd only let some fresh blood in ...' Then they start talking about Scandinavians who marry Russian girls, 'and insult us in the process', Ashot says. 'We're better than these foreigners!' The atmosphere clears when Natalya says she understands girls who marry foreigners – they're looking to improve their living standards. 'I would have gone myself – just don't tell my husband!' Which gives Ashot an opportunity to mock Natalya; 'wizened old women,' he says, are probably not exactly what they've got in mind. Becoming serious again, he agrees that she might think of a foreign husband for her daughter. Natalya sounds sincere when in the last lines of the interview she says that if that is what her daughter wants, she will not interfere.

Extract 3: 'Everything over there predisposes them to equanimity'

This interview is with a group of three women in their mid-forties. Tamara and Olga are colleagues at a firm in the private sector, and Vera is their friend. The interview takes place inside during the lunch break. Since the weather is bad, no one is interested in going outside anyway. They are not pressed for time, and are well disposed towards being interviewed. As it turns out, one of them is particularly well qualified to have an opinion of the opening of the East–West border.

[long discussion about north and south]

Interviewer: What do you know about our northern neighbours? What would you say in your opinion distinguishes people who live in Russia from people who live in Scandinavia?

Tamara: I think people are people, in Africa too [Russian saying]. If you're nice to them, they'll be nice to you.

Olga: My daughter happens to be married to a Norwegian, so you've come to the right place.

Interviewer: Now that's interesting! Is there anything you've noticed in particular?

Olga: To take one particularly conspicuous example: my daughter's wedding. After the ceremony the groom's parents wanted to lie down, even though the celebrations were far from over. They said they just needed to rest. You could have knocked me down with a feather! Here we all are running around, busy as you like, and the only thing on their minds is the state of their health! After five years [of marriage] my daughter's more like [all those] Ibsens and Amundsens; she lies down and doesn't lift a finger if she doesn't have to. On the one hand, though, I'm happy for her, but on the other, it takes some getting used to. I mean, they're not exactly slow; I like their equanimity and reticence in fact. That's something we should learn from them.

Vera: Everything over there predisposes them to equanimity. Even the animals are cool and collected, and have no fear of people. [Turning towards Olga] D'you remember that photo you showed me, the one with your daughter and her husband feeding sardines to a fox in the forest? Where would you see something like that in Russia, I ask you?

Tamara: My husband told me about a fox that used to live in the vicinity of the Finnish–Russian border. The Finiki [Finnish border guards] were fond of it and gave it food. But 'our' lot went and shot it when it strayed into our territory. That episode soured relations between the Finnish and Russian border guards for quite a time afterwards.

Vera: I'm ashamed of 'ours'.

Tamara: There you have another difference between us and southerners. Here we are having a nice conversation about Scandinavia. We've all got ties in that direction, or we know people who have.

Olga: That's because we've started making international families, and there's a lot in common between us.

Tamara: Very true. For southerners, even Moscow is abroad, but to us it's a transit town. Because we all go south for our holidays every year.

What do they think of Scandinavians, the interviewer asks. Tamara sets the scene by declaring that people are people everywhere, 'if you're nice to them, they'll be nice to you'. Then it turns out Olga has a daughter who is married to a Norwegian, and she gladly shares her experience. She mentions her daughter's wedding as a 'particularly conspicuous example' of how Russians and Scandinavians differ: after the wedding ceremony, the groom's parents needed to rest, even though the wedding was not over yet. The bride's family were shocked. ('You could have knocked me down with a feather!') These Norwegians only cared about their health – in the middle of their son's wedding! And now, after five years of marriage, Olga's daughter is like all those 'Ibsens and Amundsens',[3] 'she lies down and doesn't lift a finger if she doesn't have to!' Olga is not judgmental; she is happy for her daughter, and she sort of likes Norwegian calmness, although it requires some getting used to. But 'everything over there predisposes them to equanimity', Vera says, without further explanation. (Based on the other interviews and conversations, though, I assume she is referring to what Russians suppose is the comfortable life in the West, where people do not have to toil like Russians do to make ends meet.) On the other side of the border, even the animals are cool and collected, and unafraid of people. Wild animals are treated so well. Vera reminds Olga of a picture of her daughter and son-in-law feeding sardines to a fox in the forest. 'Where would you see something like that in Russia, I ask you?' Tamara adds a story of a fox that used to live in the Russian–Finnish borderlands. The Finnish border guards used to feed it, but the Russians shot it. Vera is ashamed of the Russians' behaviour. The interview rounds off as the company comments on how typically northern it is to sit and have a nice conversation about Scandinavia, 'We've all got ties in that direction, or we know people who have.' In short, these women seem to admire the gentleness and humanity they have observed in Scandinavians, and they take pride in the geographic and cultural proximity to them.

Exploring stereotypes about Scandinavians

In two of these three interviews, we meet people who say they have little or no experience of Scandinavians, or of foreigners in general. They try to avoid saying what they feel about their Nordic neighbours. Leave that to the younger generation, they say (despite most of them being in their forties). One of the couples, Andrey and Larisa, describe Scandinavians with some admiration as a fearless lot, but perhaps a bit naïve. To the two psychologists Natalya and Ashot, Scandinavians are 'extraordinarily naïve'. But their explanations and conclusions are less nuanced than Larisa's and Andrey's. 'As nations,' we are told, 'they're on the decline, especially Scandinavia, but Europe as well'. 'There's something seriously wrong,' moreover, 'with the blood over there – they're all brothers and sisters'. They feel 'insulted' by Scandinavians who 'marry our girls', and consider themselves 'better than these foreigners'. Nevertheless, Natalya would have married a foreigner herself, and if her daughter wants to she won't stand in her way. Ashot seems to agree. For our last interview, we had 'come to the right place' if we wanted first-hand experiences of Scandinavians; Olga's daughter is married to a Norwegian. Olga is struck by the tranquillity of Norwegians, which she and her friends link to the comfortable life over there. Further, people are more considerate; even animals are treated with respect.

If we compare these observations about Scandinavians with what we heard about southerners in the previous chapter, what strikes is the wider range of adjectives used to describe the former. Not only do most interviewees have far less to say about Scandinavians than about southerners,[4] they don't seem to have a common pool of characteristics to give structure to the discussion. Many seem unsure of what to say or how to respond. Some are categorical, but don't really say very much. (Nor do they have much first-hand experience from which to draw conclusions.) A few – those with personal experience – describe Scandinavians using a richer, more balanced vocabulary.

While many interviewees have no personal experience of Scandinavians, they have watched them in the streets of Murmansk or heard stories about them. They tend to characterize them as 'different', even 'strange', based on physical appearance or reported behaviour. In many instances, interviewees talk first about the difference in appearance before rehearsing their assumptions about 'how they are over there'.[5] Aleksandr and Tatyana (both in their early thirties), who are colleagues and personal friends, touch upon clothes, roads, Scandinavian dullness[6] and respect for the law[7] in this brief extract:

> *Interviewer*: What do you know about our northern neighbours? How would you describe the difference between people in Russia and people in Scandinavia?
>
> *Aleksandr*: I wouldn't live there for love or money. It's excruciatingly dull [*skukotishcha u nikh tam zhutkaya*] in my opinion. And the roads are so narrow! As an experienced driver, I'm amazed to see how enormous transport vehicles negotiate the roads [moves some glasses around on the table to illustrate his point].
>
> *Tatyana*: On the other hand, vehicles stop if you're at a zebra crossing to let you over. [Addressing Aleksandr] As a driver, you form your own opinions, but I look at it from the pedestrian's point of view. It'll never be like that here.
>
> *Interviewer*: What about the people over there, what d'you think of them?
>
> *Aleksandr*: Frost-resistant [laughs]! We wear fur, they wander round in casuals, jackets undone. This is an example from everyday life. They're also extremely honest. They don't like getting involved in anything fishy [*afera*].
>
> *Tatyana*: Best not to even try, because they are also extremely law-abiding. It wouldn't occur to them to try and con anyone. Anything goes wrong, they give themselves up, intestines and all.

Viktoria and Julia, two women in their late twenties, blame Scandinavians' poor posture and inability to dress on the welfare state:

> *Viktoria*: There's no two ways about it – they're pofigists [*pofigisty*, people characterized by indifference to and disregard for the feelings and opinions of others]. And their clothes are dreadful. You can spot them a mile away from the clothes they're wearing. Even though everything is available in the shops, they still can't dress properly.

Julia: It's because they don't have a clothes cult. You said yourself they're all 'pofigists' [impersonates Viktoria]. And it's really true, they sort of lumber around all floppy like. The government's given them everything, so they don't have to keep fit. Not like here.

Elena and Nikolay, the elderly couple we met in Chapter 3 who felt as if they were hostages to the north, have similar thoughts on the subject and tell a story purporting to illustrate the different ways Russians and Scandinavians tackle everyday challenges.

Interviewer: Since we're on the subject of abroad, what do you know about your northern neighbours? Are the people who live in Scandinavia like us?

Elena: Well, I think their life's a lot easier than ours.

Nikolay: They don't need to use up all their energy on all sorts of everyday problems. Living there's more enjoyable. But to get back to the question, hear what Zadornov says. [M. Zadornov is a humorist specializing in making fun of foreigners, especially Americans. His most trenchant statement so far regarding the latter is: 'Well, they're stupid' – in contrast to Russians who are intelligent and inventive]. They're wilting under all that wealth. Here, it's like this: if you can't find a screwdriver, you use whatever you've got at hand. *They* call the local service station.

Elena: Ay, d'you remember what our friends told us? Some foreigners came here with flies to fish with, probably Finns or Norgs.[8] They board this helicopter, and off they fly to the tundra. They'd brought along a piece of Swiss cheese, but forgotten the knife. [Parodying the fishermen, she throws out her arms in an expression of helplessness] A disaster! One of our boys, the helicopter mechanic, seeing their horrified expressions thought something really serious had happened. So what does he do? He cuts a length of wiring, fixes a piece of wood at either end, and uses this contraption to carve up the cheese. He'd probably never felt more proud of his own people than at that moment.

One of the most conspicuous features of the interview material – totally unfamiliar to Norwegian discourse (if not insulting to me as a semi-northern Norwegian) – is the reference to 'the blood factor' (see interview with Natalya and Ashot), that is, there has been too little mixing of blood in the northern parts of Norway. My first experience of this metaphor was during my own interview with Nastya and Sergey (see Chapter 3). I failed at first to understand what Nastya was referring to, 'There's a widely held view here in Murmansk that there's been too little mixing of the blood in the Scandinavian countries, they've been very shut off and haven't had the infusion of fresh blood. The towns are small, the communities over there.' A rather extreme variant is found in our interview with Tolik, Kolya and Genya, three colleagues and workers at a private enterprise, all in their early thirties:[9]

Interviewer: What do you think about foreigners then?

Tolik: Once more – let's clarify what we're talking about. What foreigners are you interested in?

Kolya: Indians or Ukrainians? They're all foreigners to us nowadays anyway.

Interviewer: Let's stick with Scandinavia.

Tolik: They're the most ludicrous countries. Even their flags are idiotic.

Interviewer: Could you expand a little on that?

Tolik: Yes. In Norway, for example, you're better off saying you come from Russia than from Northern Norway.

Kolya: How's that?

Tolik: Some friends showed me a picture once of eight people. Only one of the faces had the merest glimpse of intelligence. The others, some had disproportionately large heads, others disproportionately small. It wouldn't be insulting to call them completely deformed.

Kolya: And the intelligent-looking guy, he wasn't Russian by any chance?

Tolik: Precisely! Didn't I say? But you're right. It was the first time I saw the photo. Since then it's been explained to me scientifically. To put it briefly, population density in Northern Norway is extremely low, so there's a particular blend of blood and what have you.

Genya: Well, they'll probably do something about it now, what with technological progress.

Tolik: And which technology did you have in mind [smiling]?

Genya: Well, cars, 'planes – was that what you were thinking [general laughter]? They use 'planes over there like we use taxis.

Kolya: But conversely, it costs a lot more to take a taxi there!

Tolik: Mmm, but something has to be wrong with them too.

Then there are the more nuanced accounts from those who have personal experience with Scandinavians. Valeria (female, around forty) and Katya (female, early twenties) work at the international department of an institution of higher education and have visited the Nordic countries on a number of occasions.

Interviewer: Both of you know a lot about foreigners from personal experience. Could you tell me what you think about the differences between people living in Russia and Scandinavia respectively?

Valeria: Well, I mix with foreigners mainly out of interest. It's always interesting to learn new things about people living nearby. They're sort of next door [pointing in the general direction], but their worldview couldn't be more different. In the very beginning, after I'd started going around with foreigners, a lot of things shocked me. For instance, what I found weird was normal to them.

Katya: You're right, but after you've met a few of them and got to know them, you realize they're human just like us. And you start accepting these foreign bodies as they are instead of trying to get them to be like us.

Valeria: But that's something you learn from experience ... [exhales audibly, as if she is thinking of something with regret]. So many thoughts whirling around ... To start with you think everything here is just how it's supposed to be – and not there. But then everything seems good there, but not here [gestures right and left as she speaks]. I'll tell you about the washing machine – all my friends know this story. [Recounts the story with great passion.] I'd been dreaming about buying a washing machine, because I DIDN'T HAVE ONE. Finally I managed to buy one – I'm pleased as Punch and tell a Finn. I mean, I tell him how much time I'm saving, and how my hands will benefit etc ... Then he asks me twice in a row, 'so you've bought a dishwasher.' And I say 'not a dishwasher, no, not me nor any of my friends or acquaintances – that's a luxury for us.' So he says, 'I can't imagine how anybody can live without a dishwasher. Whenever ours stops working I call the repair man immediately or have to go and get a new one. Otherwise there'll be mountains of dirty dishes in the house.' I can tell you, I felt really, really put out! On the one hand – in what way am I worse [= *this is unfair!*], and on the other – how can you not wash dirty dishes for days on end?

Katya: Precisely. That's how they raise their kids too. And it's not right!

Valeria: Well, let's get back to the question, what's right and what's wrong. What is it about this 'right' [*Gde ono eto 'pravil'no'?*]?

Katya: Aaaah. That's just the way it is over there. They've progressed faster than us over the past forty years. Perhaps you'll find yourself saying to some underdeveloped African in forty years: What??? You don't say you haven't got a dishwasher! How awful! How d'you manage without one [smiles]?

Valeria: I'd like to talk more about the children. Abroad, the way they raise children is less dramatic than here, they don't go round shouting and screaming. They leave their children to get on with their own affairs. Here it's the opposite. We keep on looking after them till we're old and grey. Other people's children too – on the street, in the shops.

Katya: You're so right. Children in other countries go shopping on their own and choose their own clothes. I've seen it with my own eyes! There was this small kid of about ten, and he picked a pair of trousers and bought them himself. I thought they were absolutely awful, but he wouldn't have anything else. Children over there are allowed to make choices from a young age. Here, on the other hand, some mothers are still buying clothes for us – and yes, I'm referring to myself here.

Valeria: But there's more to it than that. Take my kids, for example. They were supposed to be going to the sea. Their dad gave them 13,000 roubles [she explains she doesn't live with the children's father]. They went and blew the lot. What d'you think they bought? They came home with a suitcase full of clothes. All sorts of Chinese T-shirts and pants in a livid scarlet hue. And all in a style which they'll grow out of in six months. They're just not ready to manage a budget, and us parents can't afford to give them things, because there's no money left over. Just you wait till you get children yourself. You'll soon find out.

Valeria and Katya switch back and forth, describing Scandinavians first in a positive light, then a negative one. You start off thinking everything is better at home, Valeria says, before changing your mind, and everything is suddenly better abroad. The truth, she seems to be implying, lies somewhere in between. Foreigners 'are human beings just like us', Katya adds. Once you've realized this, you can start accepting them as they are and not try to fit them into a Russian mould. Valeria recounts her story about the washing machine, and how a Finn thought she was talking about a dishwasher and couldn't understand how anyone could survive without one. But dishwashers are luxury items, says Valeria, and neither she nor any of her friends could afford one. But the episode was not all fun – she actually felt quite put out by the Finn's remarks. What made him think he could speak to her like that? How is he better than her? Katya supports her friend, 'it just isn't right!' Then they wonder what 'right' means, and they discuss the pros and cons of the way children are brought up in Russia and abroad. Russian-style parental care is preferable to Western 'freedom', they agree.

Interviewees with little first-hand experience of the Nordic countries, almost always speak of them as prosperous. Viktor, who said it was a crime to build a city like Murmansk (see Chapter 3), continues to lament the state of Russia, which he compares to Scandinavia:

> The whole country is so pathetic. I can't stand those old houses. In Saratov, for instance, there are some barns. You're travelling along the road, and there they are, weather-beaten barns [extends his arms to indicate both sides of the road]. It's not like Scandinavia – looked after, respectable small houses, a light in every window and a proper drive to the front door.

The words to say it – identity as narrative

As we have seen, my interviewees entertain a wide range of views of Scandinavians. Scandinavians are different and strange; they are alright when you get to know them; they're gentle and naïve. At the other end of the scale, they're considered mentally and physically impaired. Among these different descriptions, one discerns an underlying theme, a common thread in almost all of the narratives in my sample. It is the idea of 'the good life in the West'. Many interviewees are explicit about what they believe is the prosperity of the Nordic countries. People over there are positively 'wilting under all that wealth'; they 'live in an incubator', are 'given everything by the state' and 'don't lift a finger if they don't have to'. Even the least impressed interviewees seem to imagine Scandinavians as a rich and comfortable lot. The three young men who found hardly a trace of intelligence in the Nordic faces portrayed in the photograph, for instance, believe their Western neighbours 'take 'planes like we take taxis'. They state that 'something has to be wrong with them too', indicating that by and large Scandinavians are pretty well off. And the psychologists Natalya and Ashot, according to whom the Scandinavian countries are on the decline from lack of fresh blood, agree that it would be a good idea to settle there if one had the chance.

But while 'the good life in the north' portrayed in Chapter 3 was an ideal to strive for (or an idealized reality they had been promised by

Soviet authorities), the 'good life in the West' is a good life *in quotation marks* for my Kola inhabitants. It is a hollow 'good life', like a horror film, the heaven you don't want to end up in, a disinfected Barbie world where all the pretty people are gone, leaving ghastly, deformed hobbits behind, so heavy they're hardly able to carry the weight of their own bodies. And with so much in-breeding, they're all sisters and brothers. It is indeed a 'life in plastic, it's fantastic'[10] – with high levels of personal wealth and highly organized, *but with no soul*.[11] It is a place of 'extraordinary dullness' and monotony, where parents can't even endure the wedding of their own children, where people eat for the sake of nutrition and not for pleasure,[12] where schools produce 'degenerated children', where you can hardly tell the difference between a man and a woman, where people are incapable of handling unexpected situations – like how to divide the cheese when you've forgotten your cheese knife, or what to do with the dirty dishes when the dishwasher breaks down. Just watching people move shows you how weak they have become. But they don't have to keep in shape because the state literally supports them. What they need is a strong dose of Russian zest, initiative and spirituality.

While 'the good life in the north' is well within the bounds of accepted Russianness (although it also offers a means to distinguish oneself from outright *ordinary* Russianness, characterized by a lack of *kul'turnost'*, the alleged bane of the south), 'the good life in the West' is the exact opposite of what is considered to be the essence of the good Russian, that is, the *shirokaya dusha*, or 'wide soul' comprising passion, generosity, open-mindedness, hospitality, unlimited kindness and a certain amount of recklessness (see Chapter 1).[13] 'The good life in the West' is, in this sense, a representation of 'Anti-Russia' – for better (a certain amount of law and order is acceptable at times), but most of all *for worse* (it's not worth it if a soulless society is the alternative; 'puts you off law and order completely', to paraphrase Natalya). Sergey from our second interview in Chapter 3 explains: 'Scandinavians, Norwegians … they're widely believed to be pretty unemotional, very calculating, no unnecessary movements, a bit niggardly'. And his wife adds, 'Scandinavians are generally believed to be physically robust, they can wear casual clothes, like I've got to wear a fur [in the winter], but you can manage in a jacket'. See also Aleksandr's characterization above of Scandinavians as 'frost-resistant': 'We wear fur, they wander round in casuals, jackets undone.' Is it a case of 'Scandinavia is nature, Russia is culture'?

But there is another narrative, a modified version of the 'life in plastic + hobbits' image of Scandinavia. Of my interviewees with experience of

Figure 4.1 Typical Russian kiosk, perhaps prepared to welcome guests from the other side of the border ('nord' meaning 'north' in the Scandinavian languages)?

personal contact with Scandinavians, almost all were surprised by what they saw as the unruffled temperament and tranquillity expressed in these people's behaviour. Olga, who has the Norwegian son-in-law, was taken aback by the slow pace of life in Norway. Nevertheless, 'that's something we should learn from them', she said. Her friends admire Finns' and Norgs' treatment of wild animals. And Valeria relates how parents in Scandinavia bring up their children 'without shouting and screaming'. In the following interview with two young women, Tanya and Sveta (both in their early twenties), they compare different approaches to the disabled:

> *Interviewer*: What do you know about our northern neighbours?
> *Tanya*: They're clever, in the sense of having a more advanced culture than ours. They don't throw rubbish all over the place and they keep to the traffic rules, you know...
> *Sveta*: I'd also mention their attitudes towards people with disabilities. Wherever I've been, Norway, Finland, England, they don't treat the disabled as though they're not fully human. Unlike in our country. This is important for me. [Sveta has a child with a congenital disability.] I may start thinking some day about trying

to give my child a future abroad, because disabled people are human just like everyone else.

Interviewer: How do your initial impressions of Scandinavians compare with your current opinions, now that you've had some experience of them and been abroad?

Sveta: The differences were much greater I thought at first, but I've friends in Norway and Finland now. They're just ordinary people. Like to enjoy themselves, love their children, they're not mean or nasty. And they have fewer problems in their lives than we do.

Tanya: My opinion hasn't changed so much. I think they're bored in their own countries and visit us for the adrenalin kick. Which we've got enough of here.

On the whole, my interviewees are less inclined to define themselves by othering westwards than southwards. Everybody seems to have a very distinct idea of what it means to be a Russian *northerner*, and how that identity differs from that of southerners. My interviewees have a harder time nailing down the Scandinavians – some have nothing to say at all, some opinions are quite categorical but lack the supporting evidence; only a few know enough from first-hand experience to be in a position to put flesh on the bone. Hence, narratives about life in Scandinavia might serve to shape north-west Russian identity by confirming already established images of Russianness, though presumably with less force than narratives about southerners. Even in my scattered sample, a thread runs through the interviews, an image of relatively wealthy Scandinavians, but a spiritually impoverished bunch in comparison with the Russians. The othering westwards might be less outspoken than southwards, but the conclusion is no less clear: even those who say they would have settled in the Nordic countries if they had the chance (which quite a few of them do, actually), express the same sentiment: 'this is not what we want *for Russia*'.[14]

New borderlands?

How has the open border with Scandinavia influenced north-west Russians' perceptions of themselves as Russians?[15] I said above that othering westwards is less pronounced than southwards, but if the border had not been opened at all,[16] people would probably have had far fewer reference points in the western direction. Until the early 1990s, foreigners were a rare sight in the streets of Murmansk – and Russians in Tromsø, Luleå and Rovaniemi.[17] There was no Internet, and media

Figure 4.2   A Russian security officer

coverage of events on the other side of the border was presumably not very common. So fifteen or so years before I conducted my interviews, the chances of people on the Kola Peninsula having any personal experience of Scandinavians would have been slim. Most people would only know what they were taught in school. By the mid-2000s, the majority of the inhabitants of Murmansk (and probably the other towns on the Kola Peninsula, except the closed military towns) would have at least *seen* foreigners (in most cases Scandinavians) with increasing regularity in public places. A substantial number would have met Scandinavians through their work, had friends and acquaintances in one of the Nordic countries or known people who did. Finally, a large proportion of the north-west Russian population is in touch with Scandinavians on a more or less permanent basis either because they have lived abroad themselves, have worked or had personal relationships with Scandinavians. In my interview sample, these three categories are represented fairly evenly.

One notices a difference between interviewees who deal with Scandinavians, either sporadically or regularly, and those that do not. Almost without exception, the former group has at least something positive to say about their Nordic neighbours. Hardly any of them accept uncritically everything that goes on on the other side of the

Figure 4.3   Norwegian oil giant Statoil, a piece of Norway in Murmansk

border (although some say they did so in the beginning), but they agree that 'there are things there I hadn't thought of before, they're not all that stupid after all'. They may have noticed Scandinavians' interest in other people, their temperament, respect for wild animals, the well-kept gardens, respectful treatment of people with disabilities or the amount of freedom children enjoy in Scandinavia compared to what is usual in Russia.[18]

Some have only seen Scandinavians from a distance – in public places, in the media or through hearsay. Although these interviewees also spoke of Scandinavians as materially affluent, they were much quicker to criticize them than people who actually know Norwegians, Swedes or Finns themselves. They direct their criticism at the bad manners, poor posture, lack of style, practical helplessness and unintelligence, and invoke 'the blood factor' as an explanation. In practical terms, their reference group tends to be Norwegian tourists in Murmansk, mainly comprising middle-aged and elderly men in search of women and booze. We remember from Chapter 3 Marina's initial response to the question about Scandinavians, 'Most people have heard about the Norwegian tourists...', and how she went on to talk about Scandinavian peace and quiet (plus boredom, of course), but she obviously did not find it necessary to define what she meant by 'the tourists'.[19] Later, though, she

Figure 4.4   Russian-orthodox church

told a story in which Norwegians figure as 'our four-footed friends', that is, drunks. As Sergey from the second interview of Chapter 3 said, 'A lot of the people who've hardly ever met a Norwegian think they come here for the vodka rather than to do business. This is because the vodka is cheap and they can be anonymous in Murmansk.' Then he goes on to tell a story about a Norwegian delegation of feminists visiting Murmansk, who, 'on their last night here, got well and truly sloshed and had to be literally manhandled onto the bus and sent home the day after; they didn't even pay their bill – we had to do it for them.' So in Norway even feminists get sloshed – at least they do when they visit Murmansk.[20]

Finally, there are a few people in my sample with practically nothing to say about Scandinavians (apart from remarks about Scandinavian affluence). One was a housewife in her mid-fifties. 'I know absolutely nothing about them, so there's nothing really I can say – nothing of interest at least. I only know what they say on the telly: "They live for themselves and have no worries" [Russian saying].' Larisa in the first interview of this chapter belongs to this category, although she has met a few foreigners. She has nothing particularly negative to say about Scandinavians, but is palpably curious about them. A bit para-doxically, then, it does not seem as if the opening of the border has had unequivocally positive effects in terms of bringing people on either side of the border closer together. Yes, those of my interviewees who have had dealings with Scandinavians on a more or less regular basis understand them better and seem to have a relatively balanced view. But those with more limited contact – who have watched their neighbours from the side, so to speak – are more inclined to have a negative opinion than those without any such experience at all. To generalize a bit, then, *cross-border contact seems to actually worsen mutual perceptions, until a certain point where it starts to improve them beyond the point of departure.*

As we saw in Chapter 2, most East–West collaboration in the European north – notably the BEAR partnership, but also the different institutional arrangements set up to protect the northern environment – is mainly intended to improve Russian know-how in various areas. See also how Browning (2003, p. 58) more generally speaks of how Europe has taken upon itself the 'self-endowed role of civilising the barbarian learner, or European apprentice, not quite fully European but on the way to getting there – as long as it attends the lessons and does its homework.' Interestingly, the possibility of learning from one another is virtually absent from my interviews. As the discussion above suggests, what Russians think about being taught by the Nordic countries comes through loud and clear: 'thanks, but no thanks'.[21] Perhaps training is not what first comes to mind when you are used to counting 'competence' as one of your attributes as a Russian northerner (cf. the discussion in Chapter 3), especially not, one might add, when what you see on the other side of the border is a not particularly inviting mixture of drunkards and spineless hobbits. Without concluding whether the East–West collaboration has been successful or not – as noted in Chapter 2, it has had its ups and downs over the last fifteen years[22] – it might be worth noting that learning from the West does not seem to be an element of the narrative repertoire of ordinary north-west Russians (while on the Nordic side it looms large). This might have to do with people's opinions of Scandinavians, or there might be a more general explanation. Ries (1997, pp. 35ff) argues that 'practical problem-solving' is not a speech genre to the same extent in Russia as it is in the West:

> Just as improper or odd grammatical constructions would call forth the criticism, 'that is not Russian,' so might unusual discursive genres seem to be 'not Russian.' I had the experience many times of having my remarks during conversations completely ignored, or met with strange looks, as if I had mangled pronunciation or syntax. [...]

The more I learned and practiced not just proper language but proper *genres*, the more I was able to participate fully in conversations with Russians and the more I was able to belong. This does not mean, however, that I was able to communicate everything I wanted to say. My adoption of Russian speech genres meant putting aside certain key attitudes, ideas, and approaches to life which American speech genres supported and contained, but which Russian genres did not. One particularly American genre of speaking to which I was inclined could be termed 'practical problem-solving.' For example, in conversations about food shortages (a very popular topic, since shortages kept getting worse and worse at this time), I tended to ask questions about how Soviet food-distribution systems are operationally structured, assuming that it would be interesting to try to imagine (although, of course, in very crude ways) how these might be improved. I eventually realized that my Russian interlocutors did not find my question appropriate for discussion. They seemed more interested in impressing and astonishing each other with increasingly dire accounts of shortages and tales of how difficult it was becoming to buy anything. My genre not only did not fit in with theirs – in fact it contradicted their genre and threatened to deflate it if they engaged it seriously; this they managed to avoid by ignoring it altogether in ritualized speech settings. (Ibid., pp. 35–6)[23]

Conclusions

The narrative resources available to north-west Russians for describing their Nordic neighbours are not as rich as those available for descriptions of southerners, but are probably growing as contact between the nationalities increases. Othering southwards was seemingly a central component of the Kola identity as it was constructed in Soviet times, but the leading narrative of 'the good life in the north' arguably lost some of its hold on the northern population with the financial and social crises of the 1990s. At the same time, the opportunity for increased othering westwards – but also of identification with the Nordic countries – arose with the opening of the border and more extensive East–West contact. As the discussion in this chapter suggests, my interviewees do identify (or wish to identify) with the Nordic countries to some extent, but the general picture is one of othering. But unlike othering southwards, this othering is multisided, less categorical. Othering southwards is fluid in that established truths of the good life in the north can be played with, turned inside-out and fragmented (just like interviewees alternate between admiration for and contempt of Scandinavia), but the pool of such accepted truths is very limited (i.e. rich in detail, but limited in scope). The corresponding pool of 'truths' about Scandinavians is more diverse, although some common ground exists here too. In short, my interviewees' general impression of Scandinavia is that it is everything Russia is not. On the one hand, Scandinavia represents orderliness, gentleness ('humanity'), law and order, which Russia does not (although the Russian *north* to some extent does). On the other hand, the Nordic countries lack the 'wide soul' of the Russians, implying generosity, excitement, inventiveness and fun. One is tempted to ask how this impression has come about. Is it based on a careful examination, or does it involve logical inference from more scattered observations? (If something over there is the exact opposite of how it is at home, then it must be so on a general basis?) Is it an example of how a narrative base can fuel the production of recordable opinions? When Natalya and Ashot exclaim that the Scandinavian countries are on the decline because there's a shortage of fresh blood, is it a considered opinion, or something they say 'off the cuff' in lack of such an opinion? Must they then resort to one of the 'social voices' available to them, but which do not necessarily reflect any particular personal point of view? Is there something in the speech situation – two competent and eloquent people and dear friends cultivating the art of conversation – that calls for yet another cutting or penetrating remark? In a similar vein, when Tolik, Kolya and Genya say 'shocking' things about Scandinavians' physical attributes, is it a symptom of 'male bonding', something they wouldn't have said in a different interview situation, for instance with their sisters or wives? I can't say therefore whether Natalya means this or Tolik means that, but nor is that the point. The interesting thing is that images of deformed heads and decadent nations (both ascribed to 'the blood factor') are aspects of the narrative repertoire of northwest Russians when the Nordic countries are the topic of discussion. Activating the repertoire presumably helps boost people's feeling of Russianness. Interesting also is the observation (though I am aware of the problems of generalization; see Chapter 1) that othering in the western direction is most intense among people with some, but not much experience of Scandinavians (having seen them only from afar in public places). Those with no experience seem less prejudiced, while those with close, lasting ties with Scandinavians avoid the most extreme criticism of the Nordic physique and intellectual capacity. (But again, are they only adapting to a Scandinavian speech mode when they are interviewed for a Norwegian research project?) The most sustainable conclusion we can draw on the basis of this chapter, however, is that the 'wide soul' occupies a central place as signifier of Russianness in the north-west Russian narrative repertoire. My interviewees need the wide soul attributes to survive, they say, and this is something they do not see on the other side of the border. Nobody seems interested in trading Russian excitement and soulfulness for Nordic welfare, law and order.

5
Living in the Northern Environment

We wanted the best, but it turned out as always.[1]

Introduction

As we saw in Chapter 2, Western governments, including those of the Nordic countries not least, are concerned with the pitiable state of the environment in the Kola Peninsula. The nickel smelters at Nikel and Monchegorsk are responsible for much of the pollution, but it is the inadequate storage conditions in which radioactive waste and spent nuclear fuel are held that give rise to the gravest concerns. An accidental meltdown of the reactor at the Kola nuclear power plant is the most serious threat to health and environment in the region. As I have earlier argued, Russians tend to dismiss Western environmental worries as slightly hysterical (Hønneland, 2003, pp. 124–5). While Nordic governments, media and NGOs call the peninsula a catastrophe area, 'lunar landscape', 'nuclear war zone' and 'black desert', Russians, while admitting that the nickel smelters cause pollution, give the environment much lower priority than do their Scandinavian neighbours. The Kola Peninsula, they insist, is located in a largely pristine corner of the world, blessed with many natural attributes and boasting the purest water and air. They are not inclined to 'go all hysterical' about the pollution which they don't deny. It is a bad thing. But there are many other bad things in life and, what's more, you can't have industrialization without pollution.[2] And as a third point, they put more confidence in their experts than public opinion. As a friend of mine in Murmansk once said: 'I don't understand all this Norwegian fuss about our nuclear complex. There's nothing to worry about. Our experts know what they are doing.' In this chapter, we will see if these views are reflected in the opinions of my current interviewees. More interesting, however, is to ask whether opinions about the environment also say something about what it means to them to be a northerner or Russian.

Extract 1: 'Nothing wrong with the environment here, despite the slight lack of oxygen'

We met Valeria and Katya briefly in Chapter 4, where Valeria told the story of the washing machine, how she was insulted by a Finn who mistook her new appliance for a dishwasher and was incredulous at how she had managed to live so long without one. As mentioned there, they both work at the international department of an institution of higher education. The conversation takes place at the end of the working day. We sit round a table in a room for ourselves and have a friendly chat – over a cup of tea.

[Extended discussion on the interviewees' impressions of Scandinavians]

Interviewer: What are your thoughts about the environment in the region?
Valeria: Nothing wrong with the environment here, despite the slight lack of oxygen.
Interviewer: And what about nuclear safety?
Katya: Well, our region is one of the cleanest by any measure. There's a POTENTIAL danger, but it's one we can live with. We've got too many problems already without having to worry about that too every day. It's something we have to live with, accept and get on with our lives.
Valeria: I don't think there's any pollution here, because it's being monitored all the while. And with Scandinavia, like I said, next door, they've got their ear to the ground alright. At least, that's what people secretly hope.

[Conversation continues on topics concerning nature in the north, and comparisons between north and south]

Inviting Valeria and Katya to talk about the environment is not particularly successful. According to Valeria, there is nothing wrong with the environment in the region, except 'the slight lack of oxygen', which concurs with what I have been led to believe is public opinion on pollution in the Kola Peninsula. But her response also reflects one of the narratives we identified in Chapter 3: it is not 'natural' for humans to live as far north as the Kola Peninsula. When the interviewer asks about nuclear safety in the region, Katya answers first. There is absolutely nothing wrong in that department either, she protests. And echoing Russian respect for expert opinion (see introduction), the risk of nuclear contamination in the region is just that, a risk, not a fact. Nordic NGOs are wrong, she seems to be implying, to give the impression of higher levels of radiation on the Kola Peninsula than are good for your health. It could, in principle, be a problem, but an insignificant one in the hierarchy of everyday problems. Russians have too many problems already without having to worry about what might go wrong, but probably will not. The risk in this case is 'one we can live with'. Valeria joins in. There isn't any pollution in the region, she believes, because it is continuously monitored. And being neighbours with Scandinavia is a reassurance in that respect; 'they've got their ear to the ground alright', she avers. Perhaps she expresses a doubt in Russian experts and their monitoring capabilities, pinning her hopes on Scandinavians as an environmental backup. This is confirmed by the additional cadence: 'At least, that's what people secretly hope.' Between the lines, she says she has little faith in the Russian system of environmental monitoring and management.

Extract 2: 'Russians in general are a lucky bunch of people. Foosht! Foosht!'

We met Tanya and Sveta too in Chapter 4. They are both in their twenties, Tanya a teacher and Sveta a teaching assistant at an institution of higher education. Sveta is the young woman with a disabled child. Like the first interview, this one takes place at their workplace.

[We converse for some time about north and south.]

Interviewer: Does our northern nature affect you in any way?

Sveta: It affects both us and our kids. Come May, everyone will be busy sending their kids somewhere, away from here, until September if possible. Kids with a grandmother in the south, they're fortunate, and the ones that don't – it's enough to make you weep! In our family, both grandmothers live in the north, and they're still working what's more.

Tanya: Personally, I enjoy all varieties of nature. Doesn't matter if it's 'southern' or 'northern'. I can't understand how someone could like a birch tree, but not a baobab tree. Either you like every living thing, or you prefer metal, glass and concrete. I teach my children to enjoy nature. But the weather and natural conditions obviously affect me. First of all, our climate affects our health. You probably couldn't find a single person in the Kola Peninsula who's completely fit and healthy.

Sveta: The way we dress reflects the climatic conditions, and how much it costs us. Southerners don't have to have as many warm clothes as we do, for example. And another thing, I don't spend money on clothes [that appeal to me] because I can't wear them in Murmansk. It's a real shame. Three years ago, for example, I bought a lovely summer outfit. Expensive it was, too. But because of the weather I could never wear it in Murmansk. So I visited relations down south. That gave me a chance to try it on, but it was only a fortnight out of the whole holiday. The year after I managed to wear it for another fortnight. Then the third time I visited, the following year, I looked forward to wearing it again, but my grandmother said, 'Please, dearie, don't wear that dress again. People'll think you haven't got anything else to put on. Every year you go around in the same old clothes.' There you have the drawback of living in the north. But then again, southerners are very touchy about what others say.

Interviewer: Do you have any thoughts about nuclear safety on the Kola Peninsula?

Tanya: Well, we live in a peaceful nuclear environment. In inverted commas, I mean, obviously. In my view, we've had a run of good luck so far. Russians in general are a lucky bunch of people. Foosht! Foosht! [spitting twice over her left shoulder].³

Sveta: Not to mention superstitious. Touch wood! There's a lot they don't tell us in general. There's probably a ton of problems on those submarines and elsewhere too. There are nuclear-powered vessels in the middle of town, and we've got the Kola power station in our back yard.

[We continue talking for a while about north and south.]

Tanya: Live and die in blissful ignorance, tra, la, la. We depend on a good dose of Russian avos' [faith that nothing unpleasant will occur], and, I might add, on our European neighbours.

Interviewer: In what sense?

Tanya: We still believe 'foreigners will come to our aid' [old expression]. They aren't particularly keen on dying just because we're idiots. So they're keeping an eye on the environment. And our leaders aren't interested in international scandals. So we're better off than the other regions.

Sveta: [Cries out cheerfully] I understand, I understand! Our Russia is big. If anything happens, we can always escape to another region. But their countries are small – they've got nowhere to run. So they care about the environment [smiles].

Tanya: Well, if there's enough time you might be able to find a safer place, but we all know that story about the sheet.⁴

[Conversation continues on their impressions of Scandinavians.]

In this interview, views on the environment are woven into the overarching discussion about north and south. If only indirectly, the two young women give an impression of liking the natural environment in the north. ('Personally, I enjoy all varieties of nature'.) But what surprises most is their attack on the myth of 'the good life in the north'. When Tanya says that she does not understand how someone can like a birch (found in the north), but not a baobab tree (found in the south), she is presumably confronting the idea shared by many Russian northerners of the superiority of their local natural environment to that of the south.⁵ Further, when they describe how hard everyone works to send their kids south for five months if possible as soon as May arrives, it chimes with the 'alternative' narrative that we proposed in Chapter 3. Tanya probably gives best expression to this view: it would be difficult to find a single person in the Kola Peninsula who is completely fit and healthy. Interestingly, she does not refer to pollution or radiation, which a Scandinavian would probably expect, but to the northern climate. When asked upfront about nuclear safety, however, her tone changes. When Tanya says 'we live in a peaceful nuclear environment', she is being ironic. Unlike Valeria and Katya in our first interview, the risk of a nuclear accident cannot be ignored in her opinion. Quite the contrary, she concludes. They have had their share of good luck – so far. Sveta expresses distrust in Russian authorities. 'There's a lot they don't tell us in general. There's probably a ton of problems on those submarines and elsewhere too.' Interestingly, she does not depart from the Russian expert discourse mentioned above. She does not attack Russian experts (scientists), but Russian officials in general, possibly Russia as a *state*. Direct reference to Russianness is given in the key statement in this interview, 'We depend on a good dose of Russian *avos*', and, I might add, on our European neighbours.' Like the two girls in our first interview, Tanya cites trust in foreign countries' monitoring of radiation levels on the Kola Peninsula, but unlike them she challenges the assumption that nothing will go wrong. She even labels not taking precautions as typically Russian, preferring instead to avoid thinking about what could happen, encapsulated in the untranslatable Russian word *avos*'.[6] Another key citation is Sveta's remark: 'Our Russia is big. If anything happens, we can always escape to another region. But their countries are small – they've got nowhere to run. So they care about the environment.' It is unclear whether she shares this view or is being ironic at the expense of those Russians for whom environmental problems are not something to worry about. My impression is that she deplores the lack of environmental consciousness, but at the same time finds it hard to disagree with people whose argument relies on Russia's size – there'll always be somewhere safe to escape to. Tanya's concluding remark, however, seems to hint that it is time to take the nuclear threat seriously. 'We all know that story about the sheet.' If there is an accident at one of the atomic installations on the Kola Peninsula, other than wrapping yourself in a sheet and creeping towards the church yard, there is not much you can do.

Extract 3: 'I loathe Russia as a state!'

Like the interviewees of our first two extracts, Olga and Valentina are colleagues, and both around forty. Olga is head of an accounting department at a large private enterprise, Valentina is deputy head of the same department. The conversation is held after working hours on the firm's premises. Accountants often need to work longer hours to get through the workload, and the meeting gave them an opportunity to relax for a while. The conversation flows freely, and the interviewees appear to feel quite at ease.

Interviewer: What do you know about the radioactive waste deposited underground in the Kola Peninsula, and how do you feel about it?

Olga: I'm CATEGORICALLY [ka-a-a-ategoricheski] against it. It would've been much better in my opinion if we weren't making the stuff in the first place – we can't use the waste and don't need it. The environment round here is already saturated with poisonous substances. In our country, you know, everything is for sale. That's just how it is. Someone makes a decision, and the waste is dumped underground. They don't ask us.

Valentina: That is so true! Russians as a nation are all for sale [prodazhnyy narod], and especially the bureaucrats. They...er, I mean Russians...obviously have their good points, but putting them into practice is difficult. I personally, my roots are Jewish, and I feel closer to the Jews, despite being Russian as well, strictly speaking.

Olga: Russian or not – you don't want to live in Russia do you?

Interviewer: Is it like that? And if it is, why don't you?

Valentina: [Exclaiming loudly] I loathe Russia as a state! They're pumping up oil both in Norway and here, but they have different attitudes to sharing the pickings. [Bangs her fist on the table top.] Just compare the Nords[7] with us, just as an example. If you think back to Albania – everybody was lifted, from the ordinary man in the street up to government ministers! But here, no one gets up and protests about anything. So I'm looking for a nice place in Old Europe [v Starushke-Evrope] for my daughter [aged twelve]. And I'm investing stacks of money in her education. I can't see any future for my kid in our country.

Interviewer: What sort of impact does our northern nature have on you?

Olga: Ah, let's see. Well, to start with, the North itself affects people most of all. Often because of changes in air pressure, oxygen discharges, and all sorts of mag-netic storms. [The effect] grows as you get older – and we're not getting any younger [smiles knowingly to her friend].

Valentina: But the landscape is very special – goes without saying. Everything – and I mean everything – is unique here. It always amazes me, the intensity of the autumn colours, for example. And when everything suddenly turns green in the spring. It's like they say, 'I don't know where it's come from – it wasn't there yesterday'.[8] You go home in the evening, and everything's the same, and you look out of your window the next morning to read the temperature and you notice the trees have got tiny leaves already. It's lovely. And the long days [polyarnyy den'], it's all completely unique.

Olga: [The 'white nights'] are so unusual that when I moved here, I couldn't sleep in the summer. I hung curtains in front of the windows. I'm used to it now, of course. And the children, they grew up here. Doesn't bother them at all.

> *[A long intermezzo while we talk about Russians and Scandinavians, northerners and southerners.]*
> *Valentina: I'm telling you. Get the kids off to Europe. That's the place to live life!*
> *[Vot tam zhizn'!]*

Instead of raising the environment or nuclear safety in general as topics of discussion, the interviewer here asks how the two women feel about the depositing of radioactive waste underground on the Kola Peninsula.[9] That might explain why their initial response differs so sharply from the first two interviews (less from the second than the first, though). Olga is *categorically* against it, she exclaims. The environment is already saturated with poisonous substances. Unlike the interviewees we have met so far, she believes something is wrong with the Kola environment, and she specifically refers to 'poisonous substances'. Interestingly, however, she does not say what these substances are, where they come from or how they are deposited. Instead, she segues directly into a lament about Russia's misfortune, 'In our country, you know, everything is for sale. That's just how it is. Someone makes a decision, and the waste is dumped underground. They don't ask us.' Valentina agrees, 'That is so true! Russians as a nation are all for sale, and especially the bureaucrats.' She explains that she herself is of Jewish descent and feels closer to the Jews 'despite being Russian as well, strictly speaking'. When the interviewer asks why she does not want to live in Russia – her friend has already mentioned her wish to live abroad – Valentina enunciates the key citation of this interview: 'I loathe Russia as a state!' She is angry about the unequal distribution of resources in Russia, which she compares with Norway – the country's oil wealth is shared on a far more equal basis by the population – and Albania, an allusion possibly to the levelling out of living standards under Communism. Not only does she incriminate the Russian authorities and their unjust politics; she also criticizes the lack of initiative shown by the Russian people, 'no one gets up and protests about anything'. She is unable to see any future for her daughter in Russia and is already looking for 'a nice place in Old Europe' for her.

In the remainder of the interview, the two women speak about pros and cons of the northern climate and landscape (we recognize some of the citations in Chapter 3). It might be easier for the generation that was born in the north to withstand the northern climate, Olga says. It does not seem to bother her children, at least.[10] Valentina poignantly concludes, 'I'm telling you. Get the kids off to Europe. That's the place to live life.'

General views on the state of the environment

Three different views on the state of the Kola environment are expressed in the three interview extracts. First, we hear that nothing is wrong with the local environment. The risk of a nuclear accident is there, but people can live with it. Second, some people are unaware of how serious the situation is; sometimes they get concerned, but by and large prefer not to think about it. Third, the situation is disastrous, and something needs to be done. All three views are represented in my interviews, with the majority of respondents falling into the second category. Conspicuously, only a small number adhere to the disaster perspective, and only few refuse to acknowledge the existence of environmental problems altogether. In a number of interviews, all three views are represented, sometimes even by the same person.

The disaster perspective is represented by Valentina and Olga above, although they do not go into much detail about what the problem consists of. Our two psychologists Natalya and Ashot (see Chapter 4) express similar views on nuclear safety, but weave them into views of the negative effects of the northern climate, so it is difficult to see where they think the problem really lies. In any event, they use the type of disaster metaphor that is usually only found in statements from Western NGOs (which in itself is ironic given Natalya and Ashot's limited experience of and negative attitude towards foreigners; cf. Chapter 4).

Interviewer: What are your feelings about nuclear safety on the Kola Peninsula?

Ashot: What, indeed, should one's feelings be? There was a Japanese delegation here for a five-day conference – they lasted a single day and then made for home. It was the risk of radiation that unsettled them. Each had his own radiation detector. But for us, levels were within normal limits.

Natalya: I think nuclear safety should count as one of the disadvantages of living in the north. And people should be compensated, the sooner the better. Get special terms, compensated in their wage packets. We were just comparing with southerners – they live down there in a mild climate and normal levels of background radiation.

Ashot: [Pensively] Mmmmm... Yes. Nuclear safety is a complicated issue. On the one hand there's the constant [risk of] harm, which we don't see but feel all the same.

Natalya: [Starts talking before Ashot has finished] Yes, it's harmful, especially in our climate, which does absolutely nothing for the human organism. And the children, what sort of childhood are we condemning them to? I have a daughter – a teenager. And I buy a couple of kilos of apples for her every day, so she gets at least some vitamins.

Ashot: [Addressing Natalya] Don't interrupt! On the other hand there's the constant likelihood of random, unavoidable death. If the truth be told, we're sitting on a time bomb. So the idea of safety is wrong, we ought to be talking about 'nuclear danger' [*yadernaya opasnost'*].[11]

The second view – 'there's probably something wrong, but we're afraid to think about it' – is represented in our interview with Irina and Andrey, two friends in their early thirties. At the end of this excerpt, though, they seem to be edging towards the first category – 'there's nothing to worry about, really':

Interviewer: What do you think about nuclear safety in the north?

Andrey: [Addressing Irina] What should people think when they've got children, Ira? They're like tender blades of young grass, you're afraid of breathing on them. One minute they've got the 'flu, the next a sore has appeared somewhere or other. We pack them off to the south whenever possible.

Irina: It's common knowledge that we have higher radiation levels round here. They often say on the weather forecast, 'radiation level is at 9 micro-röntgen per hour [µR/h], and within the range of natural background radiation' [a stock phrase]. Everybody knows it isn't true. But there's nothing we can do about it. Some of us go round secretly hoping nothing's going to blow up, no accidental discharge of radioactive substances. But if you go round worrying about it all the while, you'd go mad.

Andrey: Radiation used to worry people more in the past. They bought iodine pills. But people seem to have got used to it. Radiation is invisible, after all.

Irina: Remember that story? It wasn't about us. Some journalists uncovered information about a radioactive release from a nuclear power station. [Addressing Andrey, who's looking anxious] No, no, it wasn't here, take it easy. And everyone went out and bought iodine pills. Now as it turned out there hadn't been an accident. But a bunch of people ended up in hospital with iodine poisoning.

Andrey: Situations like that always [*voobshche-to*] call for a good cognac.

None of my interviewees dismisses the risk of a nuclear accident altogether, but there are problems everywhere, many remark, not to mention *possible* problems. As one young woman says, 'I'm too young to think about it. And honestly I don't care. I'm not afraid of radiation because wherever you look you can find something that's not quite right. Gas emissions, polluted water. You can die of anything.' Another interviewee (female, late twenties) claims, 'Well, we don't think much about [nuclear safety]. I for one consider Murmansk to be one of the safest places right now.' Her fellow interviewee (male, around forty) responds, 'I agree. In Moscow there are terrorist attacks, and in the south – if it's not a fire, it's a flood!' Another man (around forty) concludes, 'In any event, it's better to live here than anywhere else – it's calmer. There are neither earthquakes nor all manner of tornados and tsunamis in the north. The nuclear fleet and the nuclear power plant – we can put up with them'. Another typical answer is this that occurred in an exchange between Larisa and Andrey, see first interview extract, Chapter 4:

> *Larisa*: [Deliberately elongates the syllabic stress. The expression is well known in Russia from its use by a satirical comedian] 'Aaaaaaaah, now that's a veeeeeeery intereeeeeeeesting question.' Nobody notices any radiation round here. Strictly speaking, it's the same everywhere, because wherever it explodes it'll affect everyone. The nuclear waste found here needs guarding. There have been instances where people who don't know what it is have stolen different radioactive substances. But I would say, generally, that it's not much more dangerous to live here than other places. And we have no choice, we've got to live here.
>
> *Interviewer*: But can you be absolutely certain everything is safe?
>
> *Andrey*: When you live in this country, there's nothing that's completely safe. The technology can be super-safe, but people can make mistakes. I'm relaxed about it, don't think about it at all. I comprehend its importance intellectually, and the risks, but this is where I'm going to live anyway. Things like that are not a good reason not to live here.
>
> *Larisa*: I can say that working with nuclear devices is dangerous, but it has its benefits. Take Andrey [asks Andrey if it's OK to proceed]. He's a submarine seaman and has worked on these diesel-fired submarines, but several of his classmates have worked on nuclear-powered submarines. There are quite a few perks and extras. They've all been pensioners for ages now, and as far as

money goes, they aren't exactly beggars. At the end of the day – it's OK to live here, and this is where I want to live.

In sum, my interviews with ordinary people on the Kola Peninsula reflect a wider selection of views on the environment than my interviews with scientists, civil servants and environmentalists in the same region. In a series of interviews with Russian environmental experts and stakeholders on a possible offshore oil industry in the Barents Sea (Hønneland et al., 2007), few saw any use in thinking about what *might* go wrong. Going on the historical evidence, there will probably be some minor oil leakages, but no serious accidents.[12] The lack of precautionary thinking was striking.[13] Even environmentalists, reassuring the public, say there is nothing to fear – as long as drilling hasn't started yet. You can't expect people to protest *before* an accident actually happens.[14] In a separate round of interviews with environmental government officials in the Russian north, including Siberia, very few saw any immediate danger to Russia's natural environment (Hønneland and Jørgensen, 2005). Pollution's no big problem, they often said, because the Russian Federation is so enormous: 'we are saved by our expanses of land' (cf. Sveta's remark above: 'Our Russia is big. If anything happens, we can always escape to another region'). Others, however, take this statement as a symptom of rationalization: since everybody thinks Russia extends forever, it is difficult to galvanize the public behind environmental causes.[15] My interviews with ordinary people confirm this lack of precautionary thinking – or fear – but nevertheless show an awareness of problems that could affect the environment. They just don't see any point in letting the thought upset them.

'The Russia tale' – laments evoked by the environment

In Chapter 4, we noted the tendency of people on the Kola Peninsula to characterize Scandinavia as everything Russia is not – mainly to Scandinavia's disadvantage. When talk centred on life in Scandinavia, most interviewees extolled Russianness directly or indirectly by using derogatory terms about the neighbouring countries such as dull and decadent. Some saw signs of positive, 'humanistic' values across the border, but no one used it as a launch pad to lambast Russia on that account (apart from mild remarks to the effect that some things are in fact better on the other side). Interestingly, interviewees didn't deplore how things are done in Russia when Scandinavia was the topic of discussion, but they did so when talk centred on the environment. We saw Valentina in our third interview expressing her loathing of Russia as a state, after she and her friend Olga had talked about the depressing environmental situation, the lack of public and governmental initiative and widespread corruption among Russian government officials. Valentina and Olga were not the only ones to complain. The following remark is very typical: 'Now the danger posed by radiation in my estimation is extremely serious. And as history shows, if something goes wrong on a submarine or at a nuclear power station, we're the last to be told' (female, late twenties). A taxi driver called Dima (mid-forties) and Lyuda (around forty), a friend of his, also express disillusionment:

> *Interviewer*: What are your thoughts about nuclear safety in the Kola Peninsula?
>
> *Lyuda*: Well, I don't think there's much point in asking the question around here. Everybody has their own opinion, some stronger than others.
>
> *Dima*: You're right, you know. Why (*Chë*)[16] bother to ask at all? Not as long as we have absoluuuuuuuuutely no power to change anything. Nine hundred and ninety-nine in every thousand would tell you, if you asked them, that living here is harmful, dangerous and scary – but nothing changes. Our votes count when somebody wants to be elected to something or other, but afterwards, they count for nothing.
>
> *Lyuda*: In my opinion, young people should get out of here (*otsyudova*).[17]
>
> *Dima*: No, they should not get out [imitating]. Everything needs reforming. But it's a slow, painstaking process. Much more exciting to rake in the money and invest it all in themselves. The rich decided that they wanted to build a village.[18] I often take them out there in my cab. They want to live where the air's nice and clean and avoid being blown to smithereens. And, what's more, avoid the unpleasant sight of the jealous poor unsettling their peace of mind.
>
> *Lyuda*: They don't like our entrances [to apartment buildings] [uttered out loud with a sense of resentment]. Everything's so filthy and disgusting. So do something about it then, so it doesn't look like that! [She enunciates each word clearly, as if she is investing each and every one with profound meaning].
>
> *Dima*: Let's face it, cleaning up the entrances isn't going to get us very far. These things are more serious and comprehensive than that. The problems stem from a lack of order, and that stems

from people not having enough money – which in turn stems from government policies, etc. The government doesn't care two hoots about ordinary people. The government – it's the same bunch of rich people who want to fence themselves off and live in a clean environment, without [ordinary] people[19] giving them a hard time.

Lyuda: And when people start talking about the needs of the government, the government gets irritated and jumpy. But we're not asking for miracles, after all. Just give us what we've worked for!

Read in the context of the other interviews, it reminds us of what Ries (1997, pp. 42ff) calls 'the Russia tale'. This is the story of Russia as a mythical land where everything is geared towards going wrong: a gigantic theme park of inconvenience, disintegration and chaos.[20] 'You know what this country is, Nancy?', one of her interviewees asks her, 'this country is *Anti-Disneyland!*' (ibid., p. 42). It was the punch line of a conversation in which people traded examples of social chaos and absurdity in late Soviet Russia. 'Our fairy-tale life' is another metaphor used by her respondents, referring to the monstrous political projects of the Soviet state (ibid., p. 43). Laments about Russian fairly-tale life typically ended with the following statement, 'Such a thing is only possible

Figure 5.1   *Shashlyk* in the countryside

in one country – here, in Russia' (ibid., p. 49). However, Ries argues, 'Anti-Disneyland' also carries positive cultural value for Russians. Even when 'Russia tales' had tragic elements, they were appreciated for their fascinating, amusing and astonishing epic. They made people feel personally part of the intense Russian drama (pp. 49–50). While Russians may feel ashamed of their country when they are abroad, as one of her respondents puts it, 'within themselves they are all very proud that they are Russians, that they come from such a country, which has such a strange history' (ibid., p. 50).[21]

> The 'Russia tale', an epic absurdist genre, with boundaries flexible enough to admit all kinds of novel material, was a form of narrative familiar and widespread enough to provide a mode of cultural connection among vastly different people; it is one key thread in a web of communicative exchange and transmission. [...] Belonging to the web means regularly fashioning personal narratives that embed the self in the larger, ongoing tale. It means keeping certain basic types of stories, anecdotes, absurdisms, and laments 'in the air', more or less, not stopping the performance or altering its inherent morphology. (Ibid., p. 51)

Figure 5.2 Entering Murmansk by car

Scandinavia and the environment

I remarked earlier how many Russians find Western preoccupation with Russia's environmental issues rather hysterical, scientifically unfounded and even offensive (Hønneland, 2003, p. 103).[22] They have everything under control, maintain the Russians (see comment in the introduction to this chapter, 'our experts know what they are doing'); foreigners have too much faith in people without expertise, such as environmental NGOs. Many also interpret Western environmental initiatives in Russia in a 'Cold Peace' context (see Chapter 2). The West, some believe, is utilizing environmental collaboration with Russia, often channelled through NGOs, to camouflage intelligence gathering. When the aims of other states are not immediately comprehensible to Russians – Norway, for instance, had the declared goal of 'helping Russia' throughout the 1990s – there is space for speculation over whether the entire Norwegian nuclear safety mission might not really be part of a cunning, calculated plan to destroy eventually Russia's nuclear power capabilities. One could, for instance, see Norway's insistence on the closure of the Kola nuclear power plant as a condition of development aid as an attempt to prevent progress in the area since alternative energy

Figure 5.3 Enjoying the northern countryside

sources are not present. And it would mean the total destruction of the town of Polyarnye Zori, whose existence is dependent on the power plant. And why did Norway want to take care of the old storage vessel *Lepse* (see Chapter 2) when it represented no threat to Norwegian territory? Or provide generous financing terms to enable the building of a new treatment facility in Murmansk when liquid low-level radioactive waste doesn't put Norway at risk?

There is virtually no such speculation about dubious Western motives in my interviews with ordinary people on the Kola Peninsula. There is a general belief in Murmansk, according to some interviewees, that Scandinavians are trying to take advantage of them. For instance, Nastya in Chapter 3 says, 'Many people believe [northern Norwegians] live off Russia, take our resources. Like "it's not our fault, blame somebody else".' She does not share this view herself, she points out, but many people in Murmansk do, she says. We also remember her husband's characteristic of Scandinavians: 'they're widely believed to be pretty unemotional, very calculating, no unnecessary moves, a bit niggardly.' Nastya and Sergey here refer to suspicions that Scandinavians are out to feather their own nest, often under the guise of altruism. When the discussion turns to the environment, however, the Scandinavian countries come in for praise. Some ridicule foreigners for worrying: 'only foreigners are afraid of all that' (female, around thirty). Nevertheless, their monitoring of radiation in the area is appreciated by many. As expressed in the interviews above: 'They've got their ear to the ground all right. At least, that's what people secretly hope'. 'We still believe foreigners will come to our aid. They aren't particularly keen on dying just because we're idiots. So they're keeping an eye on the environment.' For one young woman, Russians are incapable of overseeing nuclear safety, 'I'd say the mentality is different in other countries. In Russia, safety regulations will always be broken.' Another young woman explains how they have become dependent on the Scandinavian countries for information about accidents in their own region:

> [Responds to the claim made by her friend that they are the last to know if an accident takes place at a nuclear submarine or a nuclear power plant] Or we learn about it from our Scandinavian neighbours, which was how it happened to a friend of mine. She lives in Murmansk and has relatives in Arkhangelsk. And a friend of hers lives in Norway. And you know what sort of friend we're talking about [winking to her friend]. When a building collapsed in Arkhangelsk, he rang and asked her, 'is everybody alive?' But she had

no idea of what had actually happened. The officials didn't release proper information until the following day.

Conclusions

There is a perception in my interviews about life in the northern environment of a very real risk of a nuclear accident, but the risk is something people can live with. All the different regions have their problems, and this happens to be the affliction of the north (in addition to the climate). On the good side, they avoid tornados, tsunamis and terrorist attacks. And for most people, the threat of nuclear radiation is rather academic, something they can lament at the intellectual level, as they would probably respond with if asked about climate change or overpopulation – it's bad for humanity, but we'll probably not be affected personally. Some are genuinely worried, though. Hardly anyone mentions pollution or other environmental problems, however.

The subject of the environment offers an opportunity rather to complain about things that go wrong in Russia, but which the Scandinavian countries are good at. Asked about nuclear safety, quite a few respondents evoke 'the Russia tale': stories of calamities, absurdities and counterproductive governmental action – in a country where everything that can go wrong, will go wrong. Even the prime minister who so wanted the best for his country, had to conclude that it ended 'as always' (see epigraph at the beginning of the chapter). Interestingly, my interviewees complain less about actual environmental problems; they are more agitated over Russia's eternal hopelessness, as they see it: no one takes responsibility, and everything is for sale. Luckily, they can put their trust in their Scandinavian neighbours – foosh! foosh!

Perhaps the most interesting observation is to see which narratives are invoked about Russia and Scandinavia when the subject is either 'our Scandinavian neighbours' or 'our northern environment'. As we saw in Chapter 4, most people are protective of Russia and what they conceive of as Russianness when asked to share their impressions of Scandinavians. Admittedly, there were some positive things across the border, but their main message was 'don't you think we see Scandinavians as any better than ourselves!', followed by examples of Russian inventiveness, soulfulness and intellectual achievements. Asked about nuclear safety, on the other hand, the term *avos'* was used to describe Russian unpredictability and excitement. Sometimes the stakes are too high, though. When no one takes responsibility and everything is for sale, it might in fact lead to disaster. While Scandinavian discipline and diligence, in turn, might signify utter boredom, they might, in certain situations, save your life. Again, I am careful not to draw hard and fast conclusions concerning the opinions of my interviewees. Listening to 'Russia tales' might make foreigners feel sorry for the Russians, but as noted by Ries, such laments may actually make Russians feel alive. Likewise, the positive accounts we now hear about Nordic diligence may be a play of mirrors, an illusion. Is it something people say to reproduce myths about Russianness, not to characterize their neighbours? I do, however, find support for the proposal set forth in the two preceding chapters: the important thing is not so much which conclusions are drawn on particular issues – whether northerners are cultured or not, whether Scandinavia is boring or not, or whether there is something wrong with the Kola environment or not – but that your opinion is drawn from a specific set of recognizable narratives. Or as Ries said: keeping certain types of stories, anecdotes, absurdisms and laments 'in the air'. And we have learned something about which situations are more likely to evoke specific narratives. If you want a Kola inhabitant to say something nice about people on the other side of the border, don't ask him what he thinks about foreigners, ask about nuclear safety.

6
Narrative, Identity and International Relations

> The stories we tell define not only what we want, but also who or what *we are like*. Yet there is an important difference between these two kinds of stories: the narratives through which our selves are constituted are always the more fundamental; stories of selves are preconditions for stories told about interests. (Ringmar, 1996, p. 76)

Introduction

As we saw in Chapter 2, the north-western parts of Russia have been drawn into extensive political partnerships with the Scandinavian countries since the end of the Cold War. While this international cooperation is particularly widespread in the areas of nuclear safety and environmental protection, it extends to the joint management of the Barents Sea fish stocks and people-to-people projects under the auspices of the Barents Euro-Arctic Region (BEAR). Judging from the evidence of my own fieldwork in the area over many years, Western assistance was largely welcome during the 1990s, although hand-outs to relieve poverty were viewed with disdain by some. Russian perceptions of the international cooperation began to shift around the turn of the millennium, however, and projects aimed at transforming Russia into a Western-style liberal democracy were greeted with increasing scepticism. Above all, there was a pervasive suspicion of what the Russians presumed to be the West's hidden motives behind seemingly altruistic ventures in Russia. Why would Norway insist on precautionary fisheries management (including reduced fish quotas) if not to damage the Russian fishing industry? Why would the Nordic countries be so interested in nuclear safety on the Kola Peninsula if not to gain access to the naval shipyards and other military installations in the region? And why would these countries want to 'invade every nook and corner' of north-west Russia's bureaucracy in any case?[1] When Murmansk governor Yuriy Yevdokimov was ousted in spring 2009, he was vilified precisely for his willingness to work with the Nordic countries. Before he resigned, the president allegedly gave him one final warning: stop fooling around abroad, and concentrate on domestic problems. He was accused of 'betraying Russian interests in the Arctic' and of trying to 'detach the region from Russia and give it to Scandinavians and Americans who are fighting for their interests in the Arctic' (see Chapter 2). As we shall see, however, during more than twelve years in office Yevdokimov had continuously juggled a cooperative stance towards the Scandinavian countries with public statements about their suspicious motives in their dealings with Russia.

I declared my intention, at the beginning of this book, to use the stories of my interviewees to reflect on the political processes underway in northern Europe. I cannot prove any causal connections – that is, that the president and governor speak as they do because Vanya and Masha in Murmansk do so, or Russia acts as it does because the governor speaks as he does – but the narrative resources available to north-west Russians (or the Russian population) might say something about the governor's (or the president's) room for rhetorical manoeuvre.[2] Hence, my aim in this chapter is to discuss whether the Russian perceptions described above of East–West relations in the European North can be fleshed out and given weight by our more extensive presentation of the narrative base of the north-west Russian population.[3] I start by reviewing some of the key words I found in my interviews before summarizing the main narratives I singled out in Chapters 3–5, reflecting also on the constitution of north-west Russian identities. I stop for a moment to contemplate the phenomenon I have chosen to call 'narrative juggling', the tendency of one and the same person – be they a politician or a regular Ivan – to jump back and forth with apparent ease between different positions drawn from a given narrative pool. The rest of the chapter discusses the theoretical and practical implications of my investigation. How can narrative analysis contribute to the study of international relations? Do my findings provide any lessons for practical collaboration between East and West in the European North?

The key words

We saw in Chapter 5 that *narod* ('people') was Ries's (1997, p. 27) 'key "key word"'.[4] This is one of the most common words in Russian talk, but it was one she felt sheepish trying to use herself: 'it was like borrowing someone else's slang, or, more accurately, like saying someone else's prayer'. In my investigation, the word *kul'turnorst'* ('culture', or literally 'culturedness' or enculturation) arguably occupies the same position, both as the central concept around which much of the discussion revolves, and as a word I feel extremely awkward (or extremely Russian) trying to use myself. It obviously refers to a person's level of education, both formal training and qualities as a human being. It probably also includes the other three Cs (in addition to C for cultured) I identified in Chapter 3 as the primary characteristics of northernness in the words of my interviewees: competent, calm and considerate. In my interviews, they come across as the most important criteria for judging people individually or collectively. *Kul'turnost'* is in our context first and foremost a marker of northernness, but it also distinguishes Russia from the West. While there is obviously little culture to be found among southerners, in the discussions comparing East and West it could be ascribed to both sides. My interviewees do not say right out that Russians are a very cultured people, but they do so implicitly when they speak of Scandinavians' lack of culture or breeding. Scandinavians have no food culture, no clothes culture, no inventiveness and little soulfulness. On the other hand, they have something Russia lacks: order. The word cultured is used by my interviewees when they describe how Scandinavians follow traffic rules and safety regulations or try to keep public areas tidy.

Then there are a couple of words linked to the human physique that appear with a higher frequency in my interviews than I had expected: *organizm* ('organism') and *krov'* ('blood'). *Organizm* is the magic word that shows that the fairy-tale version of life in the north is an illusion. 'The good life in the north' is one of many Soviet myths about the good life just beyond the horizon, what Communism was supposed to promise. It is a beautiful state, but unfortunately not realistic. The human *organizm* is simply not built to live in the northern environment, with its swings in temperature and atmospheric pressure, with its magnetic storms and lack of oxygen. *Krov'* – the blood factor – is introduced to explain Scandinavians' lack of culture, their disproportionate heads and their poor posture. People have lived for generations in small settlements separated by mountains, fjords and the sea, so there's probably been too little mixing of blood in Scandinavia. I was surprised by these body-related explanations simply because they are not used in my own cultural sphere. Norwegian inbreeding is obviously not a theme; even hinting at in-breeding in other societies is a cultural taboo. Claiming that the human body is not fit for life in the north is similarly absent in the Norwegian discourse. While the phenomenon called Arctic eyesight is obviously well known in Murmansk, I have never once heard it mentioned in Norway. On a more general note, the Russians seem more inclined than Scandinavians to invoke nature, biology, physiology, including the human body, to explain social phenomena.

The word *inkubator* ('incubator') is used by several of my interviewees as a metaphor for what they term the artificial life of the Soviet north, or Scandinavia. Again the myth of 'the good life in the north' is presented as a human construct, not a natural thing. The Soviet plan economy made acceptable living conditions possible even north of the Arctic Circle, but with the introduction of a market economy, the lights went out, and people fell ill from cold and darkness. *Inkubator* is also used to describe the Scandinavian welfare state. The wealth of these countries has allowed them to provide a public welfare system, whose negative side-effect is to deprive people of responsibility for their own lives. Hence, *inkubator* works together with both *organizm* and *krov'*. It creates an artificial condition enabling the *organizm* to survive in the Russian north, and it works in synergy with the blood factor to produce feeble Scandinavians, devoid of physical strength, intellectual virtue and practical creativeness. My interviewees do not see the *inkubator* as unequivocally bad. It is obviously comfortable to live in one, but doing so has regrettable implications. As one of my interviewees put it: '[Southerners] think northerners are naïve. That's not good, the way I see it. People need to be wary. In that department, southerners are better adjusted to life.' Finally, the word *avos'* is a clue to understanding the Russian concept of fate: we're not good at preparing for the future, but luckily we're good at believing nothing bad will happen. Without that ability, life would be unbearable. From the side, one can speculate whether it is easier to celebrate the absence of pessimism than to take precautionary measures in a society where such action is generally not encouraged.

Key narratives, northern identities

In Chapters 3 and 4 we singled out two main narratives: 'the good life in the north' and 'the good life in the West'.[5] In the north, high educational levels and material wealth ensure good manners, orderliness and civilized relations among people, according to my interviewees. Southerners, though, are uncivilized and mean – at best amusing, but superficial and somewhat simple. This narrative is supplemented by another depicting life in the northern environment and climate as unnatural. There is no necessary opposition between these two narratives. Rather, many people say they struggle to find belief in the possibility of a good life in the north, knowing deep inside how the climate works against them – like a battle between man and nature. We remember Nastya in Chapter 3 counting all the good qualities of life in the north, but admitting towards the end of the interview that her faith was slipping (only at the very end again to praise the northern landscape and climate, as if she felt ashamed of complaining about it in front of her husband and the interviewers). As noted in Chapter 3, the labels my interviewees use to characterize Russian northerners resonate more with the 'Arctic myth' and the ideals of the Soviet conquest of the North (McCannon, 1998) than romantic images of the north as the 'real', indigenous Russia. Razumova (2007) arrived at the same conclusion in her study of Kola identities (see Chapter 3): 'The concept of the history of the region can be defined as "the myth of the north", subjugated by Man, the creator of civilization' (p. 147, my translation).

'The good life in the West' is something my interviewees have watched more from the side. They say good and bad things about life in Scandinavia, but almost all agree life is easier on the other side of the border. And although some – especially those with first-hand experience of the Nordic countries – mention a few good qualities (like equanimity, gentleness and order), most of my interviewees place Russia unequivocally above Scandinavia when asked to compare. As I said in Chapter 5, 'the good life in the West' is a good life in quotation marks, as my interviewees present it. It is a hollow, plastic version of the good life – there is wealth and structure, but there is no soul. 'Boring' is my interviewees' favourite adjective for Scandinavia. It resonates with the image of Russian soulfulness (Hellberg-Hirn, 1998, 1999) and old representations of the West as alien and heretical (Boele, 1996). We also see represented the intriguing Russian disdain for plain everyday life, the *byt* (Kelly, 2004) or *poshlost'*, 'the incommensurable everyday routine, obscene by virtue of being ordinary and evil by virtue of being banal' (Boym, 1994, p. 41). The 'plastic factor' – the well-kept gardens, the shipshape roads and general orderliness of the Nordic countries – in turn evokes old Russian conceptions of Western Europe as excessively clean and tidy: 'The lack of dirt seems to reveal a lack of sincerity, humaneness, and truthfulness' (ibid., p. 97). Finally, Scandinavian taciturnity parallels old Russian perceptions of European manners as affected and theatrical: 'Whatever its style, the Russian national mythology continues to counterpoise its dramatic sincerity, pure-hearted (and pure-blooded), against the self-conscious social theatricality characteristic of the civilized and mercantile West' (ibid., p. 102).[6]

Other narratives about the Nordic countries – and also of Russia itself – appear when nuclear safety is the topic of discussion. Now the flipside of the coin becomes visible: Scandinavian orderliness implies not only dullness, but also human security. 'They've got their ear to the ground all right', as far as radiation is concerned. Being a neighbour of these countries is an asset as far as nuclear safety is concerned. Talk about this topic similarly gives rise to complaints about everything that can go wrong in Russia, and, indeed, often *does* go wrong. It is a country where everybody fights for their own corner, and no-one takes responsibility or thinks of the common good, according to many of my interviewees – and indeed to established truth in Russia. While the positive aspects of Scandinavians are easy to see, the picture of Russia is more variegated. My interviewees are seemingly contemptuous of Russia – one of them cries out that she loathes Russia as a state – but stories of Russian absurdities and calamities can also be interpreted as a means of 'feel[ing] personally part of the intense Russian drama' (Ries, 1997, p. 49). These descriptions of Scandinavia, in turn, allude to the mild, 'civilized' (or intellectual) Russian version of northernness, springing out of St Petersburg. It makes it possible to open up for certain European qualities, if not the West per se (Müller, 2008).

Kola identities are negotiated along a north–south and east (Russia) – west (Scandinavia) axis. People's self-perception seems firmly rooted in the mythology of the Soviet conquest of the north. My interviewees are almost unanimous in their praise of northern virtues. The category of northerner requires more than just geographical location; becoming a northerner implies or presupposes certain skills or attributes. First, you are most likely well-educated if you go there in the first place. The Kola Peninsula is the land of *specialists*: scientists, engineers and military personnel. Second, not everyone dares to face the northern wilderness. It requires boldness, dedication, physical and mental fortitude. Third, and most important, living there strengthens you as a person. The northern climate hardens you and forces you to treat others with respect; we're all in this together. Most of my interviewees see these factors as their main identity (in addition to their national identity as Russians, which was not an issue as such in my interviews): they're northerners – they're proud of it and happy that life gave them the opportunity to become one. Many say they would like to move south, but none of them say they would like to become southerners. Marina (Chapter 3) grew up in the south and after two decades in the Kola Peninsula moved back; she still speaks of herself as a northerner.[7]

The opening of the border between Russia and the Nordic countries might have changed the character of the Kola Peninsula as a borderland – and north-west Russian identities – but only to a limited extent, judging from my interviews. Those without personal experience of collaboration with Scandinavia – presumably the large majority of the Kola population – seem little affected by the changes in East–West relations.[8] Many admit to knowing nothing about their Nordic neighbours. As expressed by one of my interviewees: 'I only know what they say on the telly: "They live for themselves and have no worries"'. Those who do have some experience with Scandinavians tend to report certain peculiarities that they like, and some of them use cross-border cooperation to cultivate a sense of 'civilized northernness slash Europeanness'. All the same, most of my interviewees say they do not want this for Russia. Essentially (and ironically – we will return to this), Scandinavians lack the *northern virtues*. They are spoilt, feeble and uncultured. And their good qualities, among them orderliness, are also equated with dullness unfortunately. People who obey traffic rules and safety regulations are obviously good for society, but at what price?[9] More than anything, the opening of the border seems to have strengthened people's sense of Russianness. Observing and interacting with their Nordic neighbours has made them more aware of who they are and who they want to be – Russians, after all.

Narrative juggling

One main finding of my investigation is the freedom with which my interviewees seem to jump back and forth between seemingly incongruous conclusions. A person who says Murmansk is the best place on earth may later call it a crime to have built a city of half a million people north of the Arctic Circle. One can praise the human qualities of northerners, but say that people should not be living in the north. Most notably, one can express admiration and loathing of the Scandinavian countries, even when one and the same Scandinavian quality is the topic of discussion. Scandinavian orderliness, for instance, can be a symbol of lifesaving diligence (like at the nuclear power plant) and, almost simultaneously, utter, soulless boredom (in everyday life). Western wealth can be desirable, but despicable. Ashot says in Chapter 4: 'we're better than these foreigners', but urges his friend Natalya to send her young daughter abroad. It is certainly no novelty that people can express diverging opinions,[10] so the interesting thing is whether there is a regularity in a person's alternating between seemingly incompatible points of view.

There seems to me to be a continuum in my interview material where Soviet, or possibly old Russian, stereotypes are contrasted with or balanced against 'post-Cold War' stereotypes. I am referring to the tendency in early post-Soviet Russia to turn old truths about the world on their head. Communism was good. Now it's capitalism. Democracy is good, even if it means the press can print lies with impunity. Isn't that democracy, many Russians would ask laconically, letting the papers write whatever they want. If some old truths were supposed to be turned upside down, did that imply that none of the old truths were valid anymore? In the old days, people took pride in being northerners. Most say they still do, but some have started to doubt this attitude as they see that the state is no longer prepared to take care of the northern population. Back then, people were not supposed to admire the West (and probably only a few did; if there was envy it was of Western material wealth). Suddenly they are all expected to imitate Western behaviour and adopt Western ideals – market economy, democracy, trash culture. What are people supposed to believe?

I contend that the narrative base of north-west Russians grew substantially with the fall of the Iron Curtain. Old truths still form the basis – whether about the good life in the north or the so-called good life in the West – but 'new truths' have also appeared. Open admiration of the West is legitimate, as is continued contempt of Western values. This narrative base is fuelled by the old Russian dichotomy between Slavophilism and Westernism. In the late Soviet era, Westernism was largely limited to a small circle of intellectuals in Leningrad and Moscow. In all probability, it would not have been widely supported in the militarized and technocratic Kola society. With the end of the Cold War, not only were Russian official values turned on their head; the Kola Peninsula itself became a spearhead of regional cooperation between Russia and Western Europe. The region is still heavily militarized – even more so in the late 2000s than it was in the 1990s – and has remained open towards collaboration with the Nordic countries (despite, as we have seen, a cooling off since the early 2000s). Could it be that the narrative base of Kola inhabitants in the mid-2000s contained both elements to such an extent that many people found it natural to juggle pro- and anti-Western positions, as well as traditional and modern positions about life in the north? Could the opening of the border in fact have given the positions a sharper definition, making them more accessible to people, but without coalescing into a single repertory? Take for instance Marina, whom we saw in Chapter 3 recommend the student exchange programmes in the north to her Ukrainian friends, but criticize the Scandinavian health and education systems in front of the Norwegian interviewer. Before the border was opened, she would probably not have had anything to either praise or criticize in this respect. Working with Scandinavians showed her something of Scandinavian life, and she seems more confident in her opinions whether she speaks about how bad Norwegian schools are or how good it is that Russians students have a chance to attend them.[11] Both narrative options are open to her. Speaking to Russian southerners, the new climate in cross-border cooperation gives her a platform to cultivate her sense of northernness; speaking to people from the Nordic side, she can now emphasize her Russianness with more authority. Or might the juggling have less to do with the political changes in Russia, and in fact be a specific Russian speech genre?

There is a similarly conspicuous tendency at narrative juggling among Russian politicians. We saw former Murmansk governor Yuriy Yevdokimov warning against Norwegian intentions in Russia (although he said it was 'normal' for states to be at loggerheads) at the same time as he pioneered Russian BEAR participation.[12] During the economic crisis in 1998, he appealed for humanitarian aid to the governments of Norway, Sweden and Finland. In the Russian press, however, he ridiculed the aid that came from Russia's north-western neighbours: 'There is no tragedy, there is no catastrophe in our region. There is no reason to expect 50,000 refugees on Norwegian territory. We can cope without their humanitarian aid.'[13] We saw a number of examples in Chapter 2 of Russians involved in cross-border projects in the north alternately praising and criticizing them. One is struck again by the facility with which one and the same person could switch from one extreme to the other in the same setting. The nuclear power boss could speak warmly about international cooperation, but then accuse Norway and the US of taking part only to destroy Russia. The chairman of the Russian State Committee for Fisheries told the Norwegian minister of fisheries what a good job he was doing ruining the Russian fishing industry. This remark came in a conversation between the two politicians about joint interests, efforts and good relations. At the country's highest political level, the Kremlin officially commends collaboration with the Scandinavian countries in the European north for proceeding smoothly and to the advantage of both parties. This does not prevent representatives of the president's political party from accusing Yevdokimov of giving away the Russian north to Scandinavians and Americans fighting for their own interests in the Arctic. Political actors can speak with different tongues to different audiences: praising international cooperation on the international stage while criticizing it for home consumption. They can also avail themselves of different narrative resources for different purposes. The president's aides, for instance, accused Yevdokimov of lacking patriotism because they wanted to get rid of him and knew the charge would be readily accepted by the Russian public. But something remains of my hypothesis about narrative juggling as a specific Russian speech genre. When the Russian top fisheries bureaucrat casts doubt offhand on Norwegian intentions in the middle of an upbeat comment on joint interests, it breaches the Norwegian speech mode. It is something a Norwegian minister arguably would not expect to hear in that particular setting; he might dismiss it as an anomaly (or put it down to faulty interpretation). It is something I have observed on a number of occasions, both as a researcher and participant in Norwegian–Russian joint ventures myself. 'He didn't really say that', the Norwegians, looking decidedly suspicious, would ask the interpreter. Well, often he did say just that, that is, something the Norwegian delegation was not expecting to hear in the given context, based on what had been said up to that point in the conversation. This tells me the Russians have a narrative repertoire that allows for more variation, more juggling, than Scandinavians do. As I concluded in Chapter 3, actors behave rationally as long as they draw from a definite set of stereotypes about Russian northernness, *but these stereotypes can be played with, tested out, twisted and torn apart.* The important thing is not whether northerners are cultured or not, whether Scandinavia is boring or not, or whether there is something wrong with the Kola environment or not – but that your opinion is drawn from a specific set of recognizable narratives. These can be used selectively, depending on the situation; they do not require internal logical consistency. To the extent that this is the case, we might be talking about narrative juggling as a Russian speech mode on a par with Ries's (1997, p. 37) litanies, mischief tales, shopping tales and 'the Russia story' (to mention just those of her speech modes I have referred to earlier in the book).

Narrative analysis, international relations

Now let us take a step back and see what it is exactly I claim to say something about, and what lies beyond my theoretical and methodological ambitions. In Chapter 1, I reviewed literature from different academic fields according to which identity is constituted through narratives. (See, in particular, Somers, 1994; Gergen, 2001; Meinhof, 2002.) The main assertions are: i) people become who they are by telling stories; and ii) there is a limited number of stories available to people in a certain society at a certain time. This is not something I have sought to test empirically. It wouldn't be easy anyway. The furthest one could go would be to map speech regularities in a society or note discrepancies between observed and reported facts.[14] I am not looking to identify lack of correspondence between what people say about the world and how the world really is, but I am looking for regularities in how people talk.

I accept the claim that narrative is constitutive of identities (because it 'sounds reasonable', although I cannot say that it is necessarily 'true'), and my main ambition is empirical: to circle in Russian identities in a north European borderland, the Kola Peninsula, based on the public narratives that are at work in my interviews. But I also have a more ambitious aim: to begin reflecting about the relationship between these identities and cross-border political practices.

We also saw in Chapter 1 the burgeoning literature on the role of identity in IR studies (see, for instance, Lapid and Kratochwil, 1996; Neumann, 1996; Goff and Dunn, 2004b). This body of literature is dominated by theoretical reflection and discussion of empirical research at the macro level, including the identity of newly independent states in the Third World or post-Soviet area. Then there is scattered use of the term narrative also in IR studies. Williams and Neumann (2000, p. 363) echo the linguistic and sociological literature in describing the narrative resources available to political actors as neither infinite nor unstructured, but 'historically and socially constructed and confined'. For Joenniemi (2008, p. 121), narratives represent symbolic power and can be used to facilitate or impede the granting or denying of identities to people. Ringmar (1996) elaborates a narrative theory of action that, he claims, under certain circumstances explains states' behaviour towards other states as a defence not of their interests, but of their identity. Again, the sociological argument comes through. 'It is through the stories that we tell that we make sense of ourselves and our world, and it is on the basis of these stories that we act' (ibid., p. 66). Identity-driven explanations, argues Ringmar (pp. 90–1), can be used instead of interest-driven explanations when i) traditional interest-based explanations produce ambiguous, highly contested and perverse results (e.g. there were no obvious interests to be defended in the specific case); ii) the action in questions takes place at a 'formative moment', that is, when new metaphors are launched and individuals tell new stories about themselves, and new sets of rules emerge through which identities are classified; iii) the actor is engaged in the process of identity formation; and iv) the actor has experienced a loss of recognition under humiliating circumstances, a 'loss of face'. Krebs and Jackson (2007), for their part, present a model of 'rhetorical coercion':

> While claimants may deploy arguments in the hope that they will eventually persuade, their more immediate task is, through skilful framing, to leave their opponents without access to the rhetorical materials needed to craft a socially sustainable rebuttal. Rhetorical coercion occurs when this strategy proves successful: when the claimant's opponents have been talked into a corner, compelled to endorse a stance they would otherwise reject. (Ibid., p. 36)

Researchers should therefore avoid focusing on unanswerable questions about actors' motives and examine instead what actors say, in what contexts and to what audiences.

> We cannot observe directly what people think, but we can observe what they say and how they respond to claims and counter-claims. In our view, it does not matter whether actors believe what they say, whether they are motivated by crass material interests or sincere commitment. What is important is that they can be rhetorically maneuvered into a corner, trapped into publicity endorsing positions they may, or may not, find anathema. (Ibid., p. 42)

It is not my ambition in this book to explain events or actions in Russian foreign policy. My aim is to trace north-west Russian identities, based on the assumption that the construction of identities takes place as much in the everyday lives of ordinary people as it is orchestrated by the political elites (Müller, 2008). But then there are theories saying that political action is dictated, or can be explained, by actors' identities. Is there evidence in my material of this? Based on ethnographic interviews, I have identified central components in north-west Russians' talk about who they are as northerners and Russians, assuming that this also says something about their identities. In brief, my interviewees say they are proud of being northerners and of being Russians, contrasting themselves to southerners and Scandinavians. *Southerner* seems to be a relatively fixed category (although some like what they see, others not); there is more see-sawing between showing respect for and contempt of what they see as typically Scandinavian values. I have discovered patterns in more anecdotal evidence showing how Russian political actors talk about cross-border collaboration with the Nordic countries. Again, there is alternation between enthusiasm and disdain. Russian politicians at federal and regional levels generally speak about international cooperation in the Barents region in favourable terms, but occasionally hit out at their Nordic partners: 'We do not think mutual gain is possible to the extent that you say; we do not think your intentions are as unselfish as you say; and we certainly do not need your humanitarian aid!' I see similarities in ordinary people's talk and the political rhetoric. Are politicians then just like ordinary people who draw on the same pool of narrative resources? Does the political elite know its audience and adjust rhetorical style to what the population is likely to accept? Or is ordinary people's talk just a reflection of how the elite has 'instructed' them to talk, for example, through propaganda?

My answer to these questions is, of course, more reflection than science. I do think there are traces of (earlier) political indoctrination in the way my interviewees talk. Pride in the conquest of the north was essential to Soviet propaganda aimed at attracting people to the north, and is still evident today in how my interviewees present their northern credentials. I also think politicians are ordinary people, too, who sometimes speak (and even act) off the cuff. What they say (or do) may reflect *who they are* (or rather: *establish* who they are) more than their well-calculated interests. Ringmar's (1996) narrative theory of action seems suitable to explain why north-west Russian political actors starting in the late 1990s were increasingly dismissive of Nordic initiatives. Such dismissals were usually verbal, but could occasionally be accompanied by action. In one such case, the Norwegian coordinator of the AMEC partnership (to decommission nuclear submarines at the naval shipyards in the Kola Peninsula; see Chapter 2) was denied entry to the Russian Federation in 2007 (Rowe, 2007). Russian authorities later accused her of having used her position in the AMEC collaboration to get hold of sensitive information. During the same year, Norway withdrew from AMEC (continuing only as observer). As we saw, Ringmar (1996, pp. 90–1) sets forth several requirements for substituting an interest-driven explanation for identity-driven explanations. Applied to our situation, it is, first of all, not immediately comprehensible why the given act was in Russia's interest. If Russian authorities had not denied the Norwegian coordinator entry to their country (or started a rhetoric that led up to the denial), Norway might have remained party to AMEC, and continued to transfer money to the cause. Second, the act took place at a time when new identities were taking shape, and the actor (whether we consider 'Russia', 'Russian armed forces' or 'Russian security services' to be the actor here) had 'lost face' under humiliating circumstances. The Soviet Union had collapsed, Communism had been conquered by capitalism and the reputation and financial foundation of Russian armed forces and security services had waned. Both the 1990s and the 2000s were decades of confusion for many Russians as far as Russia's place in the world was concerned. During the 1990s, Westernizers were largely successful in their efforts to help Russia rebuild itself according to Western ideals. After the turn of the millennium, Putin re-launched a form of 'official nationality' ideology (see Chapter 1), and suspicion of the West was mounting. While disagreeing with Nordic proposals was not necessarily to Russia's economic advantage, it might have helped consolidate Russians' sense of self-respect. In Ringmar's (1996, p. 14) words, 'It is only as someone that we can want something and it is precisely this "someone" that the action in question is designed to establish.'

Finally, I think that sometimes politicians avail themselves of devices from the population's narrative toolbox for strategic purposes. The president's administration took advantage of popular scepticism to the West when it tried to get rid of the governor of Murmansk Oblast in 2009. It is generally believed that the 'real' reasons were political disagreements about the mayor elections in Murmansk City (where Yevdokimov supported a challenger to the president's candidate) and/or financial interests in the Shtokman development. There were also allegations that the governor had misused state funds (see Chapter 2). All these explanations were aired in Russian media, but the presidential administration chose to hit at Yevdokimov's international engagement. He travelled to Scandinavia all the time and was even named Commander of the Royal Norwegian Order of Merit. Suspicious or not? This is an example of how narratives about international relations can influence internal politics. Accusing governor Yevdokimov of being too friendly to cunning Western states is a way of 'talking someone [in this case: the governor and his supporters] into a corner' (Krebs and Jackson, 2007). Naivety – or even worse, disloyalty – in relations with the West is simply something you can't argue away in Russia. Traditional suspicion and disdain of the West in the public mind made it narratively possible for the Kremlin to give a veneer of legitimacy to the sacking of the governor.

Borderland Russians, Nordic neighbours

'The North is a white field, a blank space [...], a quintessential periphery questioning the dominant narratives of modernity', said Medvedev (2001, p. 94) in the epigraph at the beginning of this book. While the east, west and south have relatively fixed meanings in international politics, the north lies open to the construction of new transnational identities. My investigation confirms Medvedev's opinion, to a point: the Kola Peninsula does not emerge as north in the form of a 'blank space'. On the one hand, the slogan of the political partnerships initiated by the Nordic countries in the European North in the early 1990s – 'brotherhood in the north' – obviously struck a Russian chord. 'North' was something the Russians could relate to. Paradoxically, however, my investigation raises questions about whether the 'north' presented by the Scandinavian countries to their Russian neighbours is indeed the 'north' in which the Kola inhabitants take pride. The BEAR programme, for instance, uses phrases like 'harsh living conditions', 'closeness to nature' and 'distance to national centres' to characterize life in the new transnational north. Russians may well subscribe to the notion of tough climatic conditions, but the Scandinavian endeavour arguably involves an attempt to make people take pride in 'being inside the harsh northern environment'. As we have seen, my interviewees talk about the northern climate as something external to them, something almost unreal ('the forests were not forests'). They talk about unnatural whiteness, lack of oxygen and magnetic storms, all of which make it difficult for the human *organizm* to live at such high latitudes. And while the Scandinavian northerner is generally portrayed as self-made, reckless, noisy and extrovert (i.e. in the Scandinavian public),[15] my interviewees portray the (Russian) northerner as well-educated, cultured, restrained and introvert. As we have seen, not all Russians are impressed with what they saw on the other side when the border was opened.

My interviewees' descriptions of Scandinavians should similarly be of interest to those on the Western side involved in cross-border cooperation with Russia in the north. At least in Norway, north-western Russia has been portrayed as impoverished almost continuously since the early 1990s.[16] When I lecture on north-west Russian politics and society to Norwegian students, I often start by asking them about their impression of the region. 'One of Russia's poorest regions', is the most frequent answer. This is actually quite far from the truth; Murmansk Oblast has been one of the few net contributing regions to the Russian federal budget for many years. As we saw, Kola inhabitants speak of themselves not only as cultured and competent, but also as well off in material terms. In my interviews, there is virtually no mention of Russians having anything to learn from the Scandinavian countries.[17] Much more is said to the opposite effect: Scandinavians should come to Russia 'to learn how to enjoy life'. Although many say they think life is 'easier' on the other side of the border, Scandinavians are pitied more than envied.

The views of Scandinavia that emerge in my interviews are actually quite condescending. Key terms include in-breeding, rude behaviour, deformed bodies, nations on the decline. As I have repeatedly under-lined, descriptions like these do not necessarily imply that people really *mean* what they say about dumb and decadent Scandinavians. As I have also repeated a few times, my aim is not to find out what people mean. The interesting thing is that statements about decadence and decline are readily available from north-west Russians' narrative repertoire when their Nordic neighbours are the topic of discussion. Repeatedly, we saw people hesitate and stutter when we asked for their opinion of Scandinavians. Then, instead of cautiously reasoning their way to a considered response, they jump straight to the argument's conclusion with a categorical 'this is how they are and it's not good'. My point is not only that this is one of the ways north-west Russians represent the Nordic countries to themselves, but exactly that such statements are *readily available*. They might even be *the most readily available* statements about Scandinavians in the Kola Peninsula. This is what you say unless you happen to have a better argument based on observation, I assume.

According to a narrative theory of action, this particular vocabulary not only makes people who they are, but it also affects how they act. Based on my interviews and general experience in the north European border-land, I do not think vocabulary dictates action in all situations, though it may have an effect in situations where the outcome is uncertain, where there is no specific material interest to defend, and where a decision is nevertheless required of an actor. Whenever activated, I assume often-repeated narratives have an effect (at least a larger effect than any more 'arbitrary' comment) because they are familiar, because they confirm old truths people know are widely accepted in society. As long as a state-ment is in line with such accepted truths, the amount of argumentative work needed is limited. I venture to say that it's 'easy' for political actors in Russia to throw out allegations about Scandinavian bad will towards Russia – or about Russian participants in cross-border cooperation being suspiciously friendly towards the West – simply because the home audi-ence is very receptive to such claims. As noted in Chapter 4, I did not discover a large amount of suspicion towards the Nordic countries among my interviewees, but there was substantial derision and contempt. Such sentiments resonate with age-old Russian perceptions of the West, but in my interviews I got the impression that they were found not too far under the surface – ready to be activated when someone demands an opinion of Scandinavians from you, but possibly also ready to be modified in encounters with alternative narrative practices.

Notes

1 Introduction

1. Kola inhabitant, male, early thirties, reflecting on the Scandinavians.
2. The bilateral fisheries management regime for the Barents Sea is an exception, set up by Norway and the Soviet Union in 1975–1976; see Chapter 2.
3. The concept is borrowed from Brunstad et al. (2004), who discuss whether Barents Russia is destined to become either a 'big oil playground', a 'Russian bear preserve' or a 'European periphery'. See Chapter 2 for a further discussion of the prospects for an oil bonanza in north-western Russia.
4. But again unlike Meinhof, I could add, I limit my study to the population on the eastern side of the border. My investigation thus combines elements of border region analysis and the study of Russian identity (see below).
5. Among the areas of Russian politics and society I have been studying – all covering the federal level and the regional level in north-western Russia – are civil–military relations (Hønneland and Jørgensen, 1999), environmental politics (Hønneland, 2003; Hønneland and Jørgensen, 2003), fisheries management (Hønneland, 2004a), international health initiatives (Hønneland and Rowe, 2004) and centre–periphery relations (Hønneland and Blakkisrud, 2001; Blakkisrud and Hønneland, 2006b). I have also analysed the BEAR regional collaboration (Stokke and Hønneland, 2007) and published a few papers on north-west Russian identity (Hønneland, 1995, 1996, 1998, 1999).
6. The relationship between the two will become clear in the following. I am, in particular, alluding to the title of Nancy Ries's exquisite book *Russian Talk* from 1997, in which she argues that Russian identity is constructed and reproduced through everyday talk.
7. A detailed introduction to the concepts is provided by Konrad and Nikol (2008, pp. 23ff.). My own brief summary is based on their definitions. Other comprehensive discussions of these terms are found in Paasi (1996), Eskelinen et al. (1999), Pavlakovich-Kochi et al. (2004) and Brunet-Jailly (2007).
8. The argument is made by McKinsey and Konrad (1989, p. 2), cited by Konrad and Nicol (2008, p. 31).
9. The concept of borderland could be said to involve some sort of integration of the border regions (or frontiers) of either side of the boundary: 'Borderlands appear to be a matter of degree, that is, borderlands may be seen on a continuum from border regions with little evidence of integration to fully developed, interactive zones which show substantial linkage in trade, cross-border policy integration, institutional alignment and cultural belonging' (Konrad and Nicol, 2008, p. 33). That the Kola Peninsula is indeed part of a Nordic–Russian borderland with some degree of cross-border interaction is taken for granted in this book (see, in particular, the presentation of the BEAR collaboration in Chapter 2);

hence, I venture to use the concept 'borderland Russians'. Strictly speaking, a more correct a priori term would be 'border region Russians'. We have not yet concluded whether the inhabitants of the Kola Peninsula identify themselves as borderland people, and it is beyond the scope of this book to investigate whether the Norwegians and Finns on the other side of the border feel the same. Apart from the obvious linguistic temptation to call the book 'Borderland Russians', I would argue that the extensive political and cultural collaboration taking place within the BEAR alone permits the use of 'borderland'. The *extent* to which north-west Russians feel different from non-borderland Russians while entertaining a sense of community with northerners across the border is a matter of empirical investigation in the chapters to come. Viken et al. (2008) have studied the narrative identities in Kirkenes on the Norwegian side of the border and conclude this town has been 'Russianized' since the end of the Cold War, and that being a border town and centre in the Barents region has become the hegemonic narrative of the day there.

10. Kolossov (2005) gives an overview of contemporary theory in border studies, with an emphasis on postmodern approaches and the interplay between human geography and other disciplines, in particular political science and international relations. For instance, he shows how the main theoretical traditions in international relations view borders differently: While realists understand borders as strict dividing lines protecting state sovereignty and national security, liberalists tend to perceive the main role of state boundaries as to connect neighbours and to enable transnational interaction. Finally, the global paradigm claims that through the development of international networks state boundaries are gradually transformed into virtual lines and being replaced by economic, cultural and other boundaries (ibid., p. 612).

11. Commenting more generally on the development, Paasi (2005, p. 665) notes, '[...] the major difference between traditional and more recent boundary studies is that the former aimed mainly at empirical analyses of concrete border cases or the application of the perspectives used to problem solving, while the latter more often than not aim at scrutinising or theorising upon boundaries empirically within the context of key social and political categories such as state, nation, nationalism, territoriality, identity and ethnicity.'

12. Typically, recent commentators on identity tend to start with a declaration such as, 'Culture and identity are staging a dramatic comeback in social theory and practice at the end of the twentieth century' (Lapid, 1996, p. 3); 'Identity [...] has become a major watchword since the 1980s' (Paasi, 2003, p. 475); 'Identity is back. The concept of identity has made a remarkable comeback in the social sciences and humanities' (Goff and Dunn, 2004a, p. 1); and 'Research on language and identity has experienced an unprecedented growth in the last ten years' (de Fina et al., 2006a, p. 1).

13. Different standards have been put forth according to which identity is thought to be shaped at a deeper level. As pointed out by Neumann (1992), the IR literature on identity distinguishes between those who attribute

identity formation primarily to factors internal to the individual, and those who prefer group membership and relations between groups. Among the former, Bloom (1990) hinges on behavioural and psychoanalytical psychology in asserting that humans continuously seek to protect a common identity with others. States accordingly avail themselves of this psychological need to mobilize support for the polity. While Bloom infers his social and political implications from an essentially biological argument, scholars of the latter category (e.g. Hogg and Abrams, 1988) emphasize the inseparability of identity formation and the relations *between* groups. If a human collective is to nurture some kind of common identity, it has to contrast that identity to something different, the argument goes. For a discussion of identity's place in the broader schools of thought within IR, see Lapid and Kratochwil (1996). The relevance of globalization, new social movements and transnationalism in shaping identities is discussed by Krause and Renwick (1996). The linkage between boundary dynamics and the construction of identity is analysed in Petersson and Clark (2003), while Herb and Kaplan (1999) discuss the relationship between territory and space on the one hand and nationalism and identity on the other. An overview of post-Cold War identity politics in northern Europe, with an emphasis on the Baltic region, is found in Lehti and Smith (2003). See Chapter 2 for a more specific discussion of the role of identity in Nordic attempts to include Russia in transnational regional collaboration after the Cold War.

14. Czarniawska (2004, p. 17) defines a narrative as 'a spoken or written text giving an account of an event/action or series of events/actions, chronologically connected'. Gergen (2001, p. 248) uses the term self-narrative to refer to 'an individual's account of the relationship among self-relevant events across time'.

15. Czarniawska (2004, p. 19) views stories as a sub-category of narratives, distinguished by the existence of a plot, understood as 'the basic means by which specific events, otherwise represented as lists or chronicles, *are brought into one meaningful whole*' (ibid., p. 7; my emphasis). More specifically, she refers to Todorov's (1977, p. 111) definition of a 'minimal plot': '[It] consists of the passage from one equilibrium to another. An "ideal" narrative begins with a stable situation which is disturbed by some power or force. There results a state of disequilibrium; by the action of a force directed in the opposite direction, the equilibrium is re-established; the second equilibrium is similar to the first, but the two are never identical.' In turn, narrative can be viewed as a subcategory of the term 'discourse', defined by the linguist Deborah Cameron as 'language above the sentence' or 'language in use' (Cameron, 2001, pp. 10ff). The term is widely used throughout humanities and the social sciences and its meaning varies with academic discipline and epistemological stance. See de Fina et al. (2006b) for a thorough discussion of discourse and identity.

16. For a detailed account of 'the stories we live by', see McAdams (1997). The book discusses the meaning of stories and 'personal myths' in identity formation from early age to adulthood. The relationship between talk, culture and action is discussed in Swidler (2001). She suggests that 'we think of cultures as "tool kits" or repertoires of meanings upon which people draw in constructing lines of action. Cultures inculcate diverse skills and capacities,

shaping people as social actors, to be sure – by providing them tools for constructing lines of action, not by molding them to a uniform cultural type' (ibid., pp. 6–7).

17. In line with this, Gergen (2001, pp. 254–5) claims that in order to maintain intelligibility in the culture, the story one tells about oneself must employ the commonly accepted rules of narrative construction. As an empirical example of how life stories are constructed, he refers how American adolescents characterize their life stories according to narrative conventions – happy at an early stage, difficult during the adolescent years, but now on an upward swing – that do not reflect actual events in their lives, or their perception of them: 'In these accounts there is a sense in which narrative form largely dictates memory. Life events don't seem to influence the selection of the story form; to a large degree it is the narrative form that sets the grounds for which events count as important' (ibid., p. 255).

18. That narratives constitute a reservoir from which people construct their identities is largely accepted in discourse analysis. 'Discourse analysis can be seen as a method for investigating the 'social voices' available to the people whose talk analysts collect. Many social researchers today would argue that people's understandings of the world are not merely expressed in their discourse but actually shaped by the ways of using language which people have available to them. Another way of putting this is to say that reality is 'discursively constructed', made and remade as people talk about things using the 'discourses' they have access to' (Cameron, 2001, p. 15). However, to advocates of some variants of discourse analysis individuals are not necessarily caught up in webs of language practices; conversation analysts are one example, situated in the wider school of ethnomethodology. As noted by Cameron (2001, p. 48), 'The central idea of ethnomethodology is that social actors are not just 'dopes' following externally imposed rules, but are always actively creating order through their own behaviour. Some researchers became particularly interested in conversation as an example of the kind of mundane, everyday behaviour in which participants jointly create order.' In CA, researchers are not supposed to appeal to any evidence that comes from outside the talk itself, but simply note the patterns of orderliness created by conversationalists (ibid., pp. 87ff).

19. March and Olsen (1989, pp. 160–1) contrast a logic of appropriateness to a logic of consequentiality: 'In a logic of consequentiality, behaviors are driven by preferences and expectations about consequences. Behavior is willful, reflecting an attempt to make outcomes fulfill subjective desires, to the extent possible. Within such a logic, a sane person is one who is 'in touch with reality' in the sense of maintaining consistency between behaviour and realistic expectations of its consequences. The sacred texts are Bentham and classical decision theory. In a logic of appropriateness, on the other hand, behaviors (beliefs as well as actions) are intentional but not willful. They involve fulfilling the obligations of a role in a situation, and so of trying to determine the imperatives of holding a position. Action stems from a conception of necessity, rather than preference.

Within a logic of appropriateness, a sane person is one who is 'in touch with identity' in the sense of maintaining consistency between behaviour and a conception of self in a social role. Ambiguity or conflict in rules is typically resolved not by shifting to a logic of consequentiality and rational calculation, but by trying to clarify the rules, make distinctions, determine what the situation is and what definition "fits". The sacred texts are Homer and classical jurisprudence.' Pouliot (2008, p. 257) argues for yet another variant, the logic of practicality, '[...] the premise that most of what people do, in world politics as in any other social field, does not derive from conscious deliberation or thoughtful reflection—instrumental, rule-based, communicative, or otherwise. Instead, practices are the result of inarticulate, practical knowledge that makes what is to be done appear 'self-evident' or commonsensical. This is the logic of practicality, a fundamental feature of social life that is often overlooked by social scientists.'

20. As noted by Müller (2008, p. 4), 'Russia's inconsistent foreign policy and the imputed 'identity crisis' after the collapse of the Soviet Union almost invited the application of identity research. Societal dislocation in post-Soviet Russia has opened an identificatory gap which needs to be filled by new imaginations of Russia's role and place in international politics and by a new sense of belonging – in short, by a new identity.'

21. Admittedly, the authors allude to the same question being posed by British MP Henry Norman in the introduction to his 1902 *All the Russias...?* (Franklin and Widdis, 2004b, p. 1).

22. See, for instance, Waage (1990), Likhachev (1991), Zviglyanich (1993) and Bodin (2006). The following paragraphs are a summary of some of their main arguments. Brief accounts of Russian history, focusing on the events recounted here, are Franklin (2004) and Neumann (1996, pp. 5–12). Johnson et al. (2005) present a variety of views on the impact of Orthodoxy and Islam on post-Soviet Russian identity.

23. That is, if we understand slavery to mean Manorialism. From the early 1400s, the Catholic Church actively encouraged slavery of non-Christian Africans.

24. Neumann (1996, p. 1) notes: 'Debate about Europe is a traditional staple of Russian intellectual life. [...] Indeed, the idea of Europe is the main "Other" in relation to which the idea of Russia is defined. [...] Russians, when they set out to discuss Europe, also discuss themselves.'

25. See Riasanovsky (2005) for a detailed historical survey of Russian identities. A best-selling book about Russian cultural history is Figes' *Natasha's Dance* (2002). The title is from a scene in Lev Tolstoy's *War and Peace* where Natasha Rostov, an urban upper-class girl, while visiting a relative in the countryside, instinctively picks up the steps of a peasant dance she has never learnt. The author sees this scene as a metaphor for Russia's cultural see-sawing between the European cultural ideals of the French-speaking aristocracy in St Petersburg and the 'authentic' Russianness as embodied in the uneducated Russian peasant.

26. Very briefly, Communism was a 'Western' experiment that, during the Stalin era, became increasingly like Russian Romantic nationalism. Westernizers

gained influence during thaws in the Cold War under Nikita Khrushchev and Mikhail Gorbachev and, in particular, Boris Yel'tsin's presidency in the Russian Federation's first years. Vladimir Putin's reign after the turn of the millennium can perhaps be characterized as a restoration of 'official nationality', or what Medvedev (1999, pp. 44ff) calls 'vertical culture' (hardening, structuring and fixation), which tends to alternate with periods of 'horizontal culture' (spread and spill-over) in Russian history.

27. In her comprehensive discussion of 'the symbolic world of Russianness', Hellberg-Hirn (1998, p. 168) speaks of 'Russian pride in the sensitivity of the Russian soul and in the unfathomable depth of Russian feelings' and the conception that 'every Russian is moulded into a romantic shape where the Soil and the Soul of Russia harmoniously merge into their nature'.

28. Old Believers were religious dissidents who refused to accept the liturgical reforms introduced by Patriarch Nikon in the mid-17th century. Numbering millions, they were oppressed and at times prosecuted, until Tsar Nicholas II introduced an act of religious freedom in Russia in 1905.

29. A few references (in brackets) to specific authors and literary concepts have been removed from this citation.

30. Boele (1996, p. 256) for the Soviet period distinguishes between the official version of the North (the setting for explorers and resource extraction), the unofficial accounts of camp life in the North, and the semi-official 'countryside literature', which portraits the North as an icon of the 'real', indigenous Russia. In his attempt to explain Soviet Arctic politics through cultural variables, Griffiths (1990) notes how the North looms large with famous representatives of the two latter groups: '[Aleksandr] Solzhenitsyn's idea of North is one of salvation. In the Northeast he sees an undefiled space in which a Russia purged of Soviet error can once again be herself and pursue her own unique course. Living in a northern landscape, she can above all regain her culture – reknitting her ties with the past, giving true spiritual meaning to the present and greeting the future. The Northeast thus represents an opportunity to reconstitute the old ways of European Russia in a new setting with new means. It is a place to be moved to, opened up, even "conquered", albeit with benign technology and sustainable economic practices' (ibid., pp. 51–2). And speaking about the 'countryside writer' Valentin Rasputin, 'To him, Siberia is as much a notion as a place. He likens it to a bell, sounded long ago, whose echoing peal gives rise to conceptions of "something vaguely mighty and impending", of "trust and hope", of the "anxious step of man on the far land", of "relief", "renewal" and indeed "salvation"' (ibid., p. 53). This echoes with the more general 19th-century philosophical and spiritual romanticizing of the 'Arctic sublime', which presented 'an Arctic at once beautiful and terrifying, awesome and exotic, a world apart, a romantic, last frontier offering compelling opportunities and exhilarating risks' (Osherenko and Young, 1989, p. 5).

31. The Great Patriotic War is the Russian name for that part of World War II that involved the Soviet Union (1941–1945).

32. Arutiunova (2008, p. 63) makes the same point in her study of national identity among college students in Moscow: 'The findings of national surveys show that *history* of this country constitutes a key element of Russian's state identity: in 2003, in response to the question: "What is it that is associated

primarily in your mind with the thoughts of your people?", 48 percent of the respondents answered: "our past, our history" [...] It was along these same lines that the students expressed themselves: "There is a great deal in the sciences and in cultural achievements that were accomplished by our people," "a nation that won the Great War for the Fatherland. It is not even just a matter of military achievements but rather the fact that we were able to end it ... The nation did something special in this regard."'

33. Speaking of empirical orientation, Kelly (2004, p. 150) takes an amusing pot-shot at the romantic view of kitchen table talk in Russia, presumably relished by Western ethnologists and anthropologists: 'Pubs may well be reckoned typically British, but few, on reflection, would argue seriously that a visit to a pub gives access to the essence of British identity, or indeed that putting on lederhosen and going for a walk in the Bavarian Alps will make you understand the rise of the Third Reich. But books and articles suggesting that a few hours at a Russian kitchen table or inside a Russian bathhouse will let you comprehend the innermost recesses of the Russian mind seem far more respectable.' The cover of Ries's (1997) book about Russian talk (see below) wittily shows tea being poured from a teapot.

34. Boym (1994) has an intriguing discussion of everyday life in Russia as well, though not explicitly linked to identity. We shall return to her observations several times later in the book.

35. On a similar note, Waage (1990) argues that the inwardness and mysticism of the Orthodox Church, its refutation of trivial everyday life, and its contention that contemplation may give us a glimpse of heavenly glory already in this life, are constitutive of Russian identity. The religious mentality of Russians is reflected, for example, in the Soviet version of Marxism. When, in 1961, Khrushchev located the Communist paradise 'just below the horizon' – and due to materialize in the early 1980s – he was echoing ancient Orthodox prophecies. It helps us understand the paradox between the Soviet Union's ability to conquer outer space and its inability to make television sets that worked. Grandiose projects like space programmes and redirecting the course of the Siberian rivers were the stuff of dreams, as were achievements in sports and arts, all of which contributed to 'life without daily life'. Boym (1994, p. 2) states that, 'in Russian intellectual tradition as well as in Soviet official ideology, a preoccupation with everyday life for its own sake was considered unpatriotic, subversive, un-Russian, or even anti-Soviet.'

36. Explaining this approach in more detail: 'The existential question that inspires my own work is the same question I heard a thousand times in Moscow: Why is Russian experience so full of suffering and misfortune? Taking one of many conceivable approaches to grappling with that profound (and probably unanswerable) question, this book examines the possibility that the regular posing of such key rhetorical questions helps sustain the kinds of social and cultural institutions which perpetuate that "suffering". This, then, is an interpretation of cultural texts that keeps one eye on other things: social structures, power relations, models of resistance and reproduction, the difficulties of democratization, and the paradoxes of and potential for societal transformation' (Ries, 1997, p. 5).

37. In Scandinavia, we often hear people say things like 'the border [to Russia] was opened' when the Iron Curtain fell. This is, of course, not very precise.

For one thing, the Russian borders with Norway and Finland are by no means 'open', but strictly controlled. People are only allowed to cross the border with a visa. On the other hand, the borders were not completely closed during the Cold War either; at least people on the western side were able to enter Russia more or less as easily as they are today. What has changed is the sharp rise in the number of people who actually *do* cross the border (see Chapter 2). Also, border patrols are less extensive than they were during the Cold War.

38. I do not pretend to say anything about what goes on in people's heads. When I write someone *thinks* this or that, it is only to avoid writing *he or she says that he or she thinks* this or that too often. Likewise, when I speak about change or continuity in people's sense of Russianness, I do not claim this as an objective reality; I speculate on the basis of what my interviewees say. The central thing in my investigation is not what someone *thinks*, but what they *say*. This is a study of Russian talk, not of Russian thought. But linguistic variation and simplicity call for a certain flexibility in presentation. See Krebs and Jackson (2007) for the argument that researchers should avoid focusing on unanswerable questions about actors' motives and examine instead what actors say. We will return briefly to this in Chapter 6.

39. 'Nordic' and 'Scandinavian' are used intermittently in this book. Neither fits completely with the substance of my discussion. Scandinavia strictly speaking covers just Norway and Sweden (i.e. the Scandinavian Peninsula), but the term normally also includes Denmark. The Scandinavian (!) word 'Norden', from which we have the adjective Nordic, covers in addition Finland and Iceland. Only Norway and Finland have a common border with the Kola Peninsula, but Sweden is also part of the regional cooperation scheme under the BEAR and maintains a significant bilateral collaboration with north-western Russia. Denmark and Iceland, for their part, are participants in the *national* tier of the BEAR collaboration, the Barents Euro-Arctic Council (BEAC) (cf. Chapter 2).

40. That the borders between Russia and the Nordic countries have become more permeable since the end of the Cold War is for now taken for a fact. See the presentation of the BEAR partnership in Chapter 2.

41. I deliberately chose this assumed aspect of identity among those discussed by Goff and Dunn (2004b) (see above) as it is presumably easiest to distinguish and also most relevant for further discussions about international relations in the European North. My investigation is not longitudinal, so it is not possible to examine whether identity is fluid (as opposed to static). I will probably also be able to reflect on whether identity is constructed, although this is harder to 'prove'. That identity is relational, is taken for granted, but it will probably also follow from my empirical data.

42. The reliability of the interview schedule and the representativeness of the sample are central methodological issues in quantitative interview research, but downplayed in qualitative research that emphasizes reaching an authentic understanding of people's experiences. Open-ended questions are believed to be the most suitable technique for this purpose, and rather than claiming representativeness, qualitative researchers continue interviewing until saturation point is reached, that is, until new interviews do

not produce any new information. There is a burgeoning literature on qualitative research methods. See Silverman (2001) for a general overview, Kvale (1996), Wengraf (2001) and Rubin and Rubin (2005) for introductions to qualitative interview techniques. Klotz and Prakash (2008) discuss qualitative methods in IR studies, among them discourse analysis, historical representations, ethnographic research and process tracking.

43. The geographical region of Kola Peninsula corresponds to the political and administrative entity of Murmansk Oblast; see Chapter 2.

44. The environment was selected as a specific thematic issue since it is particularly relevant to international relations in the area; cf. Chapter 2. Also, I had previously studied environmental discourse in the European North, including in Russia (Hønneland, 2003), and saw comparative advantages in including the environment also in this investigation.

45. For pros and cons of using a tape recorder in qualitative interviews, see Rubin and Rubin (2005, pp. 110–12). Admittedly, most qualitatively oriented analysts seem to view the use of a tape recorder as a requirement. Among students of life and politics in Russia, however, there is a firm tradition of not using a tape recorder for fear of intimidating interviewees. As noted by Ries (1997, p. 6), describing how she treated data from informal conversations in Russia: 'While I sometimes had the audacity to pull out my tape recorder or note pad on these occasions, usually I did not, because they so inhibited conversation. Immediately after leaving someone's company, if at all possible, I jotted down notes to myself about the talk that I had heard.'

46. Translations from Russian into Norwegian are carried out by my co-interviewer Anne-Kristin Jørgensen, from Norwegian into English by my English language consultant Chris Saunders.

47. As noted by Cameron (2001, p. 51), different variants of discourse analysis emphasize the usual components of this approach differently: 'What distinguishes the approaches from each other is the balance of differing concerns, and the analytic procedures that follow from taking any particular concern as central. For example, if your main concern is with what participants in a conversation are doing to produce the orderliness of their talk (a typical question in CA), you will focus on the talk itself and be less concerned to describe the whole social or cultural milieu in which that talk is taking place. If, by contrast, you are mainly concerned with the way a certain speech event fits into a whole network of cultural beliefs and practices (a typical concern for ethnographers of speaking), you will spend more time describing things that are external to the talk itself: who the speakers are, where they are, what beliefs and customs are important in their lives.'

48. See references to my previous work above. Only books are mentioned, but they give a good impression of my interests. In addition to academic research, I have conducted a number of evaluations and consultancies in the region. I have also commentated extensively in Norwegian newspapers about life on the Kola Peninsula; some of these pieces can be found in *Vårt bilde av russerne* ('How We View the Russians') (Hønneland and Jørgensen, 2002) and *Russlandsbilder* ('Pictures of Russia') (Rowe and Hønneland, 2007a).

2   The Kola Peninsula: Politics, Society, International Networks

1. Nicknames for Ivan and Maria, the most popular forenames in Russia; also used to personify Russians.
2. Resident of Kola, female, around forty, reflecting on the state of the roads in Murmansk, indicating – as many before her – that Russia is rich and bountiful, but has no order. According to the Nestor Chronicle, the Varangian chieftain Rurik was invited to become prince of Novgorod in 862 AD, with the words: 'Our land is great and rich, but there is no order in it. Come and rule over us.'
3. This and the following section build on Blakkisrud and Hønneland (2001, pp. 8ff) and Brunstad et al. (2004, pp. 11ff.). Recent population figures are taken from Norwegian Barents Secretariat (2009).
4. For thorough, although no longer quite up-to-date, discussions of civil–military relations on the Kola Peninsula, see Hønneland and Jørgensen (1999) and Jørgensen (2001). Åtland's (2009) study is more updated, but limited to the relationship between the Northern Fleet and the petroleum industry in the region.
5. The ten so-called 'nuclear cities', located mainly in the Ural and Volga regions, were subordinate to the Ministry of Atomic Energy (Minatom) until the 2004 reorganization of Russian federal bureaucracy (under the Ministry of Industry and Energy since then).
6. For further presentations of the ZATO regime, see Rowland (1996) and Brock (1998, 2000).
7. The closed cities of Murmansk Oblast are further presented in Hønneland and Jørgensen (1998).
8. For a further discussion of this topic, see Jørgensen (2001).
9. On one occasion, the governor of Murmansk Oblast promised the Norwegian Minister of Foreign Affairs access to the storage site in Andreeva Bay. However, the Norwegians soon realized that the governor was in no position to influence this decision, which was the remit of federal authorities.
10. It is generally assumed that the Northern Fleet uses applications for such joint cruises as an opportunity to legitimize its own existence within the Russian bureaucracy, that is, to contribute to maintaining the Cold War image of East–West antagonism in the Barents Sea.
11. This section builds mainly on Brunstad et al. (2004, pp. 16–17 and pp. 39ff). Information on the Shtokman project is taken from Moe (2006) and Øverland (2008).
12. The Russian oil company Rosneft increased its re-loading capacity in Murmansk significantly in 2004 by mooring a leased 360,000 tonne Norwegian super tanker in the Kola Fjord to serve as semi permanent off-shore storage vessel. Norwegian environmental organizations criticized the move, calling the over-20-year old, single-hulled tanker a major environmental risk.
13. The scenarios are meant to be plausible, but thought-provoking. Scenarios are not meant to predict the future, but show possible outcomes enabling governments and businesses to make the necessary adjustments to policy, planning and strategy.

14. A discussion of the BEAR cooperation at the time it was established is found in Stokke and Tunander (1994). Stokke and Hønneland (2007) discuss the achievements of the collaboration a decade later.

15. BEAR is surrounded by, and partly integrated with, similar international initiatives in the Arctic. In 1991, Finland proposed setting up a an intergovernmental vehicle to promote the protection of the Arctic environment. The result was the Arctic Environmental Protection Strategy (AEPS), which includes a string of permanent working groups tasked with environmental monitoring, mapping and harmonization of national and international conservation measures, and developing projects for the protection of the marine environment. In 1998, the AEPS was incorporated into the Arctic Council, created two years earlier following a Canadian initiative. In addition to environmental protection, the Arctic Council addresses social, cultural and economic matters of particular concern to northern communities. See Tennberg (2000), Keskitalo (2003) and Stokke and Hønneland (2007) for discussions about how the Arctic Council works. Alongside developments at circumpolar level, two regional cooperative arrangements emerged in the European North, BEAR and Council of Baltic Sea States (CBSS). The latter was set up in 1992 following a Danish–German initiative to coordinate policy in the Baltic Sea states (and Iceland and Norway as well) as an aid to economic and democratic progress in the former Eastern Bloc countries. It has mainly addressed civil security, the fight against organized crime, communicable disease control, environment, labour issues, nuclear safety and transport. See Joenniemi (1993) for a presentation of the CBSS. The idea of a Northern Dimension to the EU was presented by Finland in 1997 and adopted by the EU as policy one year later. Political declarations and lists of projects in action plans largely failed to translate into tangible, practically implemented and financed projects, and in 2007 the new Northern Dimension was launched, now with Iceland, Norway and Russia as equal partners. Partnerships are established in environment, health and transport, with energy and culture possibly underway. See Aalto et al. (2008) for a discussion of the old and new EU Northern Dimension. The work of these international Arctic institutions have to some extent overlapped; see Stokke and Hønneland (2007). For instance, health projects under the CBSS have been implemented in north-western Russia (including the Kola Peninsula), although this is 'core BEAR territory'. The reason is that project finance largely came from Norway, which gives priority to its neighbouring 'Barents Russia' (Rowe and Hønneland, 2007b). Similarly, the environmental working groups under the BEAR have at times been dependent on EU funding (Stokke et al., 2007).

16. This bilateral arrangement dates back to the mid-1970s. Three cooperation agreements between Norway and the Soviet Union were signed in the period 1975–1978, and the Joint Norwegian–Soviet Fisheries Commission had its first session in January 1976. The fisheries management regime of the Barents Sea is not discussed as such in this book, but is mentioned when matters to do with the fisheries sector have wider political bearing on relations between Russia and its neighbours. See Hønneland (2000, 2004b, 2006), Nakken (1998), Stokke (2001) and Stokke et al. (1999) for more elaborate presentations.

17. *St.meld. nr. 15 (2008–2009) Interesser, ansvar og muligheter: Hovedlinjer i norsk utenrikspolitikk*, p. 49.
18. See Hønneland (2005) for examples.
19. For further discussions of BEAR achievements, see Hønneland (2003, 2005) and Stokke and Hønneland (2007). A thorough discussion of health cooperation between Russia and the Nordic states in the European North is found in Hønneland and Rowe (2004).
20. Åtland (2008) analyses the substance of Gorbachev's Murmansk initiative, the context in which it was launched and its subsequent achievements.
21. An evaluation of the Plan of Action's first years of work is found in Hønneland and Moe (2000). See also Hønneland and Jørgensen (2003).
22. Sawhill (2000) discusses the achievements of the first phase of AMEC cooperation. See also Hønneland and Jørgensen (2003).
23. The NDEP is discussed by Tykkynen (2008).
24. A comprehensive presentation (in Norwegian) of Norwegian–Russian cooperation on environmental protection is found in Hønneland and Rowe (2008).
25. The BEAR's founding father on the Russian side was the country's Minister of Foreign Affairs, Andrey Kozyrev, who in December 1993 was elected to represent Murmansk Oblast at the State Duma.
26. Less than a decade after the establishment of the new federation, the environmental bureaucracy built up in the final years of Soviet rule had been effectively dismantled. The first blow came in 1996, when the Ministry of Ecology and Natural Resources was downgraded to a State Committee for Environmental Protection. The second came in 2000, when the State Committee for Environmental Protection, along with the State Committee for Forestry, was abolished, and its remnants incorporated into the Ministry of Natural Resources.
27. Interview with Russian civil servant, Murmansk, February 2000.
28. Interview with Russian civil servant, Moscow, April 2000.
29. *Nordlys*, 12 June 2001, p. 3.
30. *Rybatskie novosti*, No. 3–4, 2001, p. 1.
31. Interview with Russian fisheries scientist, Murmansk, February 2000.
32. A Western critique of the reforms inspired by the West is found in Cohen (2000), who refers to the events as a 'failed crusade'. Cohen coined the term 'Cold Peace' in an article first published in 1992. In a postscript to the article printed in Cohen (2000, p. 104), he says: 'I do not claim a patent on the term *cold peace*, and am not even certain I was the first to use it in this context, but it subsequently began to appear frequently in the U.S. and Russian press – and remarkably even in a statement by Boris Yeltsin. (My article was published in Moscow, in Russian, under a similar title.)'
33. *Polyarnaya pravda*, 10 March 1999, p. 2. See Hønneland and Jørgensen (1999, pp. 167–8) for a discussion of the revival of patriotic values in Murmansk Oblast at the end of the 1990s.
34. He was held in custody for ten months and was finally acquitted only in April 2000.
35. Interview with Russian medical worker, St Petersburg, June 2003.
36. Others have observed similar Russian reactions. Aalto et al. (2003, p. 12), commenting on EU–Russian relations in the north, say, 'Russian commentators

[...] have occasionally expressed criticism of what they perceive to be a pure aim to gain access to and make use of the vast natural resources (e.g. oil and gas) in northwest Russia by developing infrastructure in these mostly remote and in some places permafrost locations, but without any real willingness to develop the overall industrial potential of the Russian north or genuinely deepen Russian–EU relations.' Browning (2003, p. 62) notes, 'Indeed, rather than seeing the solutions to Russia's problems as lying in the West, it is precisely the West and its universalising civilising discourse of individualism, liberalism, democracy, the separation of the church and state, and so forth, that is seen as the major cause of Russia's malaise and in particular of undermining its unique cultural heritage. This thinking underlies the suspicions that some Russians have that the regional co-operation promoted by the West and accompanied by the rhetoric of globalisation, debordering and overlapping spaces, is little more than a surreptitious attempt to unsettle the Russian Federation's territorial integrity once and for all.' A leading Russian specialist on northern affairs, for his part, attacks the ' "creeping invasion" of foreigners into the Russian North' in an article in a Western geographical journal: 'Especially alarming is the situation in the Arctic, where a network of international organizations and agreements has spun a web around an extremely weakened Russia' (Agranat, 1998, pp. 277–8). Finally, a comment related to the myth of Siberia (see Chapter 1), 'And yet the myth of Siberia will, in all probability, continue. Like the American West, the region may never totally outlive its Romantic past of exciting new frontiers, legendary outlaws, and exotic "barbarians." Throughout the centuries Siberian patriots, like many other nationalists all over the world, have always blamed the "outsiders" for destroying the innocence, purity, and beauty of their native land. Their complaints will probably go on, with the list of culprits already expanding to include Western entrepreneurs who are descending on Siberia in search of cheaper timber, gas, oil, and minerals. In the ever-present mythical struggle between the corruptive "materialistic" values of the West and Russian "spirituality," Siberia will probably be seen again and again as the last bastion of moral decency – this time not only in Russia but also in the whole world' (Diment, 1993, p. 10).

37. According to *BarentsObserver* (1 April 2009), senator from Murmansk Oblast Vyacheslav Popov called for Yevdokimov to leave his post because he stood in the way for others with commercial interests in the Shtokman project. The official reason for Yevdokimov's resignation was misuse of state funds; see, e.g., *BarentsObserver*, 8 April 2009.

38. For a broader discussion about region building in the Arctic, see Keskitalo (2003).

3   How to Be a Northerner: Distinguishing North from South

1. The interviews are presented largely uncut apart from certain sections dealing with themes addressed in the next two chapters.

2. References to interviews other than those conducted for this study, and to other literature, are given mainly in notes in order not to disturb the flow

of the text more than necessary. Although my study is not comparative, I do compare narratives on topics common to both Russia and neighbouring northern Norway when the occasion arises, based on personal familiarity with the latter region as a Norwegian citizen.

3. That narratives not only reflect but also shape identity (see Chapter 1) is for now taken for granted. It is difficult to test this hypothesis empirically, at least within the scope of the present study. But I will revert to a brief discussion on this in the concluding chapter.

4. Later in the interview, however, he tells the story of a visit to the hairdresser's in Ukraine. Admittedly, Ukraine is not Russia, but Marina always speaks about Ukraine when referring to the south. Implicitly, she equates the south with the southern post-Soviet states. This supports an interpretation of Ivan's interpolation at this point as seeking to underscore his Scandinavian experience (availing himself of the opportunity to make the remark that he has been 'all over the place in Norway') to his dinner companions.

5. We return to this later in the chapter.

6. I discuss this section later in the chapter.

7. There were eighty-nine federal subjects in the Russian Federation at the time when the interviews were conducted. Since then, several federal subjects have merged. At the time of writing, the number is eighty-three.

8. Ries (1997, p. 37) lists 'shopping tales' as a typical Russian female speech genre. She also describes the expected behaviour of shop attendants in a way that explains Nastya's surprise, 'The oft-remarked brusqueness of Russian saleswomen was, in fact, a genre of this scolding variety. Foreigners encountering it for the first time usually interpreted it as pure rudeness stemming from the fact that there is no incentive to be polite in the absence of free market competition. In fact, the saleswomen's way of speaking to customers was a mark of social class and category, an expressive genre which in many ways was an essential part of the entire sport of shopping' (ibid., p. 72).

9. In traditional Russian shops, customers pick up their goods from different counters (standing in line for each of them) before they go to the cashier to pay.

10. We will hear more laments about Russian authorities in Chapter 5.

11. Many interviewees were not concerned with trying to define 'the south' in political or geographical terms. Of those who did raise the question, most seemed above all curious to know whether the former Soviet republics that are now independent states should be included, such as Ukraine and the South Caucasus. The Russian 'middle belt' also seemed to be perceived as the south by the interviewees – Smolensk, Penza and Samara were referred to as southern cities, among others. For one interviewee, south meant 'at least south of Piter'.

12. Elements of the story recall what Ries (1997, pp. 51ff) identifies as tales of female sacrifice and heroism in Russia. The sex of the victim – female – appears to add weight to the story. Would Sergey have bothered to tell the story if it had been a man who had helped them? In any event, by reiterating the gender of the person who came to their aid, he obviously wants to attract attention to what he considers an important detail.

13. Some point to the flow of people in the other direction today (still with the same perception of northern attributes), 'I've noticed a tendency here. I may

be wrong, but I get the impression that the people who move from the north to the capital are leaders, people in advertising, programmers, doctors, etc. And from the south waiters, bartenders and secretaries. But I couldn't say why' (female, early twenties).

14. Interestingly, the alleged openness and sociability of southerners goes together with stinginess, while northerners are characterized as extravagant and generous, albeit calm and cultured. In neighbouring Norway, the northerner is generally believed to be open, sociable and generous, while the stereotype of a southerner is calm and cultured (at least more cultured than the northerner), but stingy.

15. As we will see in Chapter 4, similar ways of talk as these women use to describe themselves as Russian northerners, are also used by my interviewees to portray Scandinavians. 'Incubator' seems to be a rather popular word.

16. These are the main positive attributes of the northern character according to my interviewees. Razumova (2007, p. 145) offers a slightly different, though related, explanation. Claiming that Kirovsk is more civilized than its immediate neighbour Apatity (both belong to the same conurbation), one of her interviewees argues that people are more cultured in the towns that were built by political prisoners (like Kirovsk in the 1930s) than by volunteers (which Apatity was in the 1960s). The political prisoners of the early Communist period were people of principle, hardy from the ordeals of life, while the volunteers moving up north after World War II were simply people who 'could not find anywhere else to settle down' [my translation]. Interestingly, also Razumova's discussion revolves around the *kul'turnost'* of Russian northerners.

17. See also the interview with Ashot from Yerevan in the next chapter.

18. One wonders why she does not simply state that she suffered a depression, which happens to many people from time to time, but so eagerly connects it to the 'large phenomena' of the outer environment: temperature and pressure. In one of the interviews that is rendered in more or less full length in the next chapter, our interviewees – two psychologists – claim that until recently you did not speak openly about depression in Russia. One of them did a study fifteen years earlier about the impacts of living in the north, showing a high degree of sickliness, especially among children, but was not allowed to publish the results. His colleague claims that the constant whiteness (*belizna*) makes northerners depressed, 'It's a scientific fact, though you would not hear it officially. It's been a virtual state secret since Soviet times' (female, early forties). If Nastya has not heard about the whiteness problem, changes in temperature and atmospheric pressures are part of the vocabulary available to her when she is trying to understand the changes in her state of mind. In neighbouring Norway, there is some focus in the media about so-called winter depression among northerners. The main scientific explanation given is lack of light during the polar night, and strong lamps are provided for both prophylaxis and treatment. Neither whiteness, temperature changes or atmospheric pressures are part of the public discourse on winter depression in Norway.

19. We also remember how Marina linked the kindness of northerners to climatic conditions without explicating the causal connection. Another interviewee explains, 'Southerners are different from us temperamentally,

they are more active, emotional. We are compelled by the climate to be more conservative, even-tempered. Because of the weather we've learned to put up with the way things are, so we're more patient than southerners' (female, mid-forties). Her conversation partner adds, after being asked by the interviewer how these differences can be ascribed to natural conditions, 'It's not very hot up here, so people try to spread a bit of warmth in their personal relations' (male, mid-forties). As an exception, one young woman relates the good manners of northerners to other things than climate and money, 'Broad-minded, that's my impression of northerners. Because ALL sorts came from ALL OVER, and they had little choice but to find a modus vivendi' (female, early twenties).

20. It is also an argument I have heard countless times during other research projects on the Kola Peninsula, and from simply talking to people there. For instance, during a study of public child care in the region in the late 1990s, I often heard child welfare officials express dismay at the idea of letting children grow up under Arctic conditions. It isn't natural, they protested. But there wasn't the money to let children in care spend the summer months from May to September in sunnier climates, something they used to do. Many officials at residential care homes cited the 'unnatural' climatic conditions as a main cause of illness among children. (Industrial pollution and its probable effect on the children's health were not mentioned once, a point we shall discuss in Chapter 5.) At one institution (notably for healthy, rather than ill or disabled children), the director told us that close to half of her wards were officially designated 'sickly'. Asked which diseases predominated, she replied 'Arctic sight', that is, reduced vision as a result of the long polar night. It was mentioned by both Anton and Sergey in first and second interview extracts – and by many others in my sample – and seems to be well known to Kola inhabitants. In Finnmark, on the Norwegian side of the border, I doubt if many people have ever heard of it. In any event, it is not part of public discourse there.

21. This combination of negative attitudes to life in the north and eagerness to be considered a northerner strengthens my assumption of a close connection between being a northerner and certain acquirable attributes (the four Cs) rather than a matter of geographical location alone. Viktor, I believe, would continue to think of himself as a northerner even if he returned to his native Crimea. Switching back and forth between seemingly positive and negative opinions on the subject of discussion (be it the north, southerners or Scandinavians) is another striking feature of many interviews – a point I will also discuss further. Viktor, who believes it was a crime to build a city of half a million people north of the Polar Circle and *in-hu-mane* to let people stay there, also commends Murmansk as 'the best city in Russia'. He is reminded by his fellow interviewees of what he had said a few days earlier. To which he responds: 'I take it all back. Best in Russia, maybe, but it's just that I want to live abroad – it's better there.' There follows a heated discussion about problems with life in the north, leading to the 'crime conclusion'. More inconsistencies – or is he just picking selectively among the various narrative resources available to him, all constituent parts of Russian northern identity? We return to this in the conclusion.

22. As mentioned in Chapter 1, my study is not longitudinal, so it is not possible for me to say much about how things were before the border was opened. I can only show how people comment on the established cross-border relations and relate this to their assumed feeling of northernness and Russianness.

23. More about this in the next chapter.

24. More about this, too, in the next chapter.

25. Ries (1997, p. 87) understands litanies as 'ritual elevations' of Russian speech that create 'generalized social bonds' between members of a moral community, or a community of shared suffering. (See Chapter 1 for definition.) Unlike Ries's respondents, who generally complained about the fate of Russia at a time of social upheaval, Marina's litany creates a 'community of shared Russianness' at a time when the significance of national borders is receding. Although she moaned about southerners earlier in the interview, she only reaches the elevated state of litany speech (raised voice, in turn looking all her conversation partners in the eye after each rhetorical exclamation) at this point. Interestingly, Ivan does not object to Marina's sarcastic comments about Norwegian education and health care, as one might have expected since he is so keen to demonstrate his Norwegian experience. Instead he joins in with a comment about the prerogatives of the Russian school. The trio agree about the hopelessness of the Russian south, but also seem to agree – perhaps with some moral purpose in mind – about protecting their sense of Russianness despite cross-border contacts.

26. I am not surprised by their criticism of the Norwegian education system, which is obviously less centred on facts and skills, and more on helping students develop a critical, reflective faculty and become active citizens. The criticism of Norwegian health care is more unexpected and not immediately comprehensible to me. Having visited a number of Russian health care institutions (and a few Norwegian), it seems absurd for a Russian to say she would not trust the medical service in Norway for anything in the world. Did Marina get carried away by her own litany, or has she really heard criticism of Norway's health care? Is there a general scepticism towards things from the other side of the border? Hopefully we will be able to flesh these issues out in the next chapter. For now, the most interesting thing is perhaps the combination of enthusiasm for cross-border collaboration and disdain about what the other side has to offer.

27. Strictly speaking, whether she has become 'more' conscious is difficult for me to state as a fact since I did not interview her before the border was opened (and, of course, since I can only report what she says, not what she thinks), and even if I had interviewed her then (and had access to her thoughts), there would have been the problem of proving causalities between the opening of the border and her sense of Russianness. I can, however, point to the fact that she uses descriptions of post-opening-border phenomena (cross-border marriages) to fervently defend features of Russian society and criticize those same features in Scandinavia. In any case, she is not overly positive to how things are done on the other side of the border, open or not.

28. St Petersburg was built by Peter the Great in the early eighteenth century as a gateway to the more advanced societies of Western Europe. 'White

nights' and other northern specialities are often ascribed to St Petersburg. As Ivan's narrative shows, the city also cultivates an 'intellectual' image. Another interviewee said, emphasizing both northernness and intellectualism, 'Many say northerners are better than southerners. It follows logically then [sic], people in Leningrad [using the Soviet name for the city] are better than Muscovites' (female, late thirties).

29. As Ivan noted, the Kola Peninsula had been mostly 'built by people from Piter'. The region was administered as an okrug ('district') of Leningrad Oblast from 1927 to 1938, the year Murmansk Oblast was established. It was part of Arkhangelsk Gubernia for more than two centuries (see Chapter 2) before becoming a gubernia in its own right for a brief period, 1920–1927.

30. A few of my other interviewees mention the relationship between St Petersburg, the Kola Peninsula and Scandinavia, 'Northern Russia looks more to St Petersburg, while the south looks to Moscow. With regards to other countries, northerners look to Scandinavia and other European countries, while the south, I believe, look more to the Baltic countries' (female, early twenties). According to most interviewees, St Petersburg and the Kola community are linked by mutual bonds of affection, 'The young up here in the north all can't wait to get out. You don't need to go far to find examples. More than half of our fellow students live in Piter today. They've set up home, have a job and are very content with their life. And they try to tempt the rest of us to join the "Piter diaspora"' (female, early twenties). 'There's a demand for our students in our capital cities. As long as you're not without talent completely, you've got an 80 per cent chance of getting a good job. My husband asked recently about our students at the head office of a Petersburg-based business. It's like this in Piter. If you have a choice between a southerner and a northerner, you'll choose the northerner. On the one hand, it's got to do with better education opportunities here, on the other on capacity for work. Northerners are usually honest, and ready to work for wages which newly qualified students from Moscow would turn down' (female, early twenties).

4   How to Be a Russian: Distinguishing East from West

1. I found it less important to provide the context in the third interview. Notably, there were palpable breaks in the first two interviews when the conversation turned to the interviewees' impressions of Scandinavians, which were not found in the third one.

2. As in the previous chapter, I provide sporadic comments in notes about how things are perceived in the Scandinavian countries (based on personal experience as a Norwegian), although my investigation is not explicitly comparative.

3. Henrik Ibsen (1828–1906), Norwegian playwright; Roald Amundsen (1872–1928), Norwegian Polar explorer.

4. This seems to be the case whether the interviewer was Norwegian or Russian, and whether questions about Scandinavians came early or late in the interview.

5. Judging on the basis of my interviews and wider experience of life in the Kola
   Peninsula, Murmansk folk tend to notice the appearance of Scandinavians,
   their clothing, how they walk etc. Like Larisa above, many are struck by
   foreigners' gaze, expressing curiosity and interest (as opposed to Russians
   who stare at a fixed point in front of them). Foreigners seem to walk slowly
   and apparently aimlessly (as opposed to Russians needing to get from point
   A to point B without dawdling). Foreigners are helpless when it comes to
   dressing. They dress inappropriately for the weather (go without a fur hat in
   winter, for instance) and for the occasion (they don't wear suit and tie when
   it is expected of them). They seem incapable of observing even the simplest
   rules of proper dress, like buttoning up your jacket ('jackets undone', as several of my interviewees observe). Recall what Boym (1994, p. 289) noted
   in the epigraph at the beginning of this chapter, that eating ice cream on
   the underground is something you simply do not do in Russia. Driving
   through a red traffic light is, conversely, considered acceptable behaviour
   (we will return to this). A female colleague of mine was once scolded by
   a Russian scientist for breaching the dress codes. She had bought a winter
   coat at the inexpensive, but rather modish Swedish chain store *Hennes &
   Mauritz*. She was sauntering around downtown Murmansk (probably with
   her 'eyes wide open' and no particular aim in mind) when a Russian scientist of her acquaintance rushed up to her exclaiming: '[Name], is that
   you?! When I saw a woman from afar wearing an awful, cheap winter coat
   I assumed she was one of our *bomzhy* (bag ladies). But what do I discover on
   closer inspection? It was you! [Name], you just can't dress like that in Russia.
   That coat's only fit for *bomzhy*! Go and get yourself a respectable fur coat!'
   The subject of Scandinavian women's dress would fill a chapter; according
   to many Russians they do not even look like women. A Kola-based female
   scientist – a declared feminist – once told me: 'When I'm at the University
   of Tromsø [northern Norway], the way the women dress is simply unbearable: big sweaters, shapeless shoes, no make up – not the slightest trace of
   femininity!'
6. In my experience, 'boring' is arguably how most north-west Russians think
   about life in the Nordic countries. I have heard it said countless times, by
   friends, taxi drivers, newspaper articles and lectures (on how the Russian
   diaspora in Norway perceive life there). It also looms large in my interviews;
   cf., for example, Marina's opinion quoted in Chapter 3, 'We've heard it's
   quiet, clean but, you know, a bit boring perhaps [*skuchnovato*]. Well, that's
   what they say, that Norway's boring [*skuchno*]'.
7. The Russians' liberal attitude to compliance with the law is key to their
   self-perception, according to Boym (1994, p. 289) (see quote again at the
   start of this chapter). Eating ice cream on the underground is not approved
   of, but driving through red lights is (though the latter is proscribed in law,
   not the former). Boym tells a story about the Russian critic Mikhail Epstein
   who joined a march in the US against the first Gulf War. He was astounded
   to see the protesters after the rally – still beating drums and shouting slogans and insults about President Bush – stop at a red light even when there
   were no cars at the crossing! 'For an American, the protest and the stopping
   at the red light were both part of the democratic ritual; in fact both his
   protest and his everyday behaviour were lawful. For a Russian accustomed

to routine violations of everyday prohibitions and cynical about the laws because they were part and parcel of the official order, this combination of simultaneously protesting and observing the rules is nearly inconceivable' (ibid., p. 289). The Russian inclination to violate everyday regulations whenever they have the opportunity, is infamous. For instance, many Russians don't attach their safety belts when driving because it would be doing what the authorities tell them to do. To avoid fines, however, they hold the seat belts in place, but without fastening them! I once took the bus in Murmansk together with a political science lecturer at one of the city's universities. Smiling, he told me he always took the bus without paying. His mother had lost all her savings in the inflation that followed the economic reforms of the early 1990s, and this was his silent way of protesting, not paying the state for riding on the bus.

8. The usual Russian word for Norwegian is *norvezhets*. *Norg* (plural *norgi*) and *nord* (plural *nordy*) are slang for Norwegians, slightly derogatory but very common in north-western Russia in recent years.

9. This interview may be a variant of what Ries (1997, pp. 65ff) refers to as the 'mischief tale', which she identifies as a typical male speech genre in Russia. Shocking comments, bragging and exaggeration are typical features of mischief tales. 'If shopping tales were a predominant genre of stories told by and about Russian women (and used to define Russian women), mischief tales were the outstanding genre through which the identity and nature of the Russian male was exposed, explored, and enjoyed' (ibid., p. 65). Further, she speaks about mischief as 'a symbolic tale of resistance, autonomy, and transcendence of the social order' (ibid., p. 70). Tolik, Kolya and Genya – all male – were obviously vying with each other to tell the most alarming stories about Scandinavians. Would they have expressed themselves differently if they had been interviewed with a wife or girl friend? Are their comments about deformed Scandinavians meant to facilitate male bonding while expressing resistance to changes in the social order (e.g. the opening of the border)? The interesting thing is that statements about disproportionately large or small heads and obvious lack of intelligence among Scandinavians are part of the narrative repertoire of north-west Russians, though they are only activated in certain situations. I doubt if you would hear Scandinavians express similar opinions about Russians; the closest would probably be comment on the lack of personal hygiene and a disposition towards criminal activity.

10. Line from the late 1990s' international hit *Barbie Girl* by the Scandinavian (i.e. Danish–Norwegian) pop group Aqua.

11. One of my interviewees (female, around forty) in fact likened Scandinavia to the classic American soap opera *Santa Barbara*, notorious for its glamorous but empty characters and the 'slow motion' of its plot.

12. Scandinavians, one of my interviewees (male, around forty) says, find no pleasure in picking and eating wild mushrooms. They prefer to stuff themselves [*davit'sya*, indicating lack of pleasure] with mushrooms bought in the shop. Russians tend to have a low opinion of the Norwegian kitchen, in my experience. Those dry open sandwiches can't be compared with the vast riches of the Russian table.

13. This is a slightly paraphrased version of a statement by Hellberg-Hirn (1999, p. 56). A poignant description of the Russian perception of soul is given by

one of Ries's (1997, p. 30) interviewees, a Russian philosopher, 'The Russian people think they have soul and they doubt that anyone else has. Russians have *dusha* [soul] because they are moral. Being moral – it is not just to be kind, generous, it is basically some kind of connection between individual and community and nature. So there is a feeling that you yourself are not that important, but you are important through the community of which you are a part, and through nature, and this always made Russian soldiers so good, because they thought nothing of sacrificing themselves for their motherland. So even though the feeling of individual value is weakened, the feeling of community is completely strengthened ... so that is *dusha*, which is the mechanism of this. *Dusha* is basically a mechanism of involvement, maybe not direct involvement, but a mechanism of association of oneself with a broader set – *narod* [the people].'

14. There are a few possible exceptions. Viktor has no reservations in his admiration for Scandinavian orderliness and dismay over Russia's lack of the same; Sveta wants a future for her disabled child abroad. Neither of them suggest, however, that Russia should learn from the Nordic countries. Of course, this might have to do with assumptions that Russia is unlikely to change in their lifetime.

15. Again (see Chapters 1 and 3), I can only speculate about what the opening of the border has implied since I have only interviewed people – and talked to people in Murmansk more generally – after the border was opened.

16. See discussion in Chapter 1 of the term 'opened'. My point there was that the border was not completely 'closed' prior to the fall of Communism, nor is it completely 'open' subsequent to it.

17. The largest cities in northern Norway, Sweden and Finland, respectively.

18. They may simultaneously lament Scandinavian dullness, lack of spirituality or taste – but that is another story.

19. It is my general impression that many people in Murmansk have seen the Norwegian tourists and attach little good to them. An artist I know in Murmansk once told me, 'Geir, it has been such an eye-opener for me to get to know you. Before, the only Norgs I had seen were the tourists, and I honestly did not believe there were *kul'turnye* people in Norway at all. I don't want to sound prejudiced, but that's what we've had to judge from.'

20. This reminds me of a story an experienced Russian–Norwegian interpreter (a Russian native living in Norway) once told me. She was used to accompanying Norwegian delegations to Murmansk. On the flight over, Norwegians often moaned, she said, about 'all that vodka we'll have to drink over the next days!' And when she was with the Russian delegation, they would sigh, 'Oh, those Norwegians! Now we have to drink for days on end again!' Norwegians and Russians seem caught up in myths about each other's drinking habits.

21. Admittedly, there is an addendum: 'there might be something there, though, worth considering'. By and large, however, no one speaks of reconstructing Kola on a Scandinavian model, for example, a Scandinavian-type welfare state. On the contrary, of the interviewees with an opinion, most are highly opposed to the welfare state because it cripples personal initiative. A notable exception is when interviewees talk about Russia's poor treatment of its pensioners (see Chapter 3).

22. Apart from implementation problems, training may have unintended consequences. As noted by Sergey from Chapter 3, 'Norwegians are increasingly "Russianized", they can't be trusted, they've learned from us, like. Unfortunately, that's what's happening. Norwegians always want something from us; wasn't like that in the beginning, but having been conned by Russians, they've picked up a thing or two. In the beginning, the "crooks", it was always the Russians. We didn't have much experience of international justice, so we ended up losing every time [in the courts].'

23. She continues, 'In more prosaic contexts, of course, my Russian friends were far more expert than I could ever be at devising intricate and ingenious solutions to the problems of everyday existence. In a sense, their lamentation of structural challenges allowed them simultaneously to celebrate their own highly developed but impromptu coping skills' (Ries, 1997, p. 36). This is reflected in my own material as well. There are few, if any, suggestions in my interviews as to how the structures and practices of Russian society could be improved. But as far as the practical challenges of everyday life are concerned, Russians pride themselves on their coping skills, cf. Elena's story about the helicopter mechanic who constructed a cheese knife for the snooty foreigners on the tundra.

5   Living in the Northern Environment

1. Viktor Chernomyrdin, prime minister of Russia 1992–1998.
2. It is an over-simplification to state that environmental concerns had no place in Soviet policy. While increasing production was the first priority, the government took steps to protect large swathes of land and wildlife. The first nature reserves, *zapovedniki*, were created as early as 1921 to preserve a certain landscape or habitat, preserve or re-establish rare or endangered species of flora and fauna, and to enable scientific research. By the early 1970s, semi-open national parks were created: preserved land but open to the public for recreational use. See Ziegler (1987), Pryde (1991) and Weiner (1999) for overviews of Soviet environmental management and nature protection.
3. The expression and gesture are supposed to prevent bad luck ensuing after commenting on a spate of good – or at least neutral – luck.
4. Refers to the following riddle: Question: What do you do if an atom bomb goes off? Answer: Wrap yourself in a sheet [i.e. winding sheet or shroud] and creep towards the church yard.
5. That is, according to 'the good life in the north' narrative.
6. The dictionary translation is 'perhaps', but it is not the usual Russian translation of this word. *Na avos'* is translated as 'at random', but again this is not the customary Russian expression.
7. Slang for 'Norwegian'; see Chapter 4.
8. The reference is to an old Murmansk anecdote about the building of the Hotel Arktika, placed at the very heart of Murmansk facing the Five Corner Square, which progressed incredibly slowly. There was this group of tourists from abroad who, on seeing the building in progress, asked their guide, 'What's that going to be over there?' 'Ah, a hotel – they've been building it for the past century,' said the guide, who later was given an official

reprimand by the Communist Party for levity. So the next time tourists asked him about the building work, he said 'Haven't a clue. It wasn't there yesterday!'

9. A lively debate was in train in Murmansk about depositing radioactive waste underground at the time of my interviews, that is, mid-2000s.

10. As we saw in Chapter 3, though, many people say that living in the north doesn't affect the young as much as the old.

11. This play with words sounds more elegant in Russian than in English. The Russian word for 'safety' is *bezopasnost'*, which literally means 'without danger'.

12. As one of the scientists at the federal Russian institute for fisheries research and oceanography said, 'Of course, there are some "eco-pessimists" out there who doom and gloom whatever action you take, so you can't extract oil and gas on an industrial scale, the fish will disappear etc. And naturally, they're an irritant. But as far as I can see, it is an emotional reaction, because even scientists are divided and express different opinions. Studies in the US show how far emotions affect opinions, and how little objective information counts when issues like this are on the table. [...] There's a lot of room for speculation. It's an admirable stand to take, not to let anyone near [the shelf]. Obviously there are risks, but it's important in this matter to achieve a compromise. Of course, there will be oil spills, deliberate and accidental; of course it will affect the environment, but how strong the effect will be is extremely difficult to predict. It's an empirical question. [...] If we go by the experience of others, things will go well. In Siberia about 1–2 per cent of treated oil leaks into the ground because of the ancient technology, leaking pipelines etc., but not more than one part per thousand is lost in the North Sea. [...] And it's difficult to avoid accidents altogether. But the experience of other countries show these problems can be solved.' A marine biologist at one of the Murmansk-based research institutes says: 'As a specialist, I don't think there is any danger to the fish stocks in the Barents Sea which can't be dealt with. Modern technology and governmental requirements should ensure that everything goes well. If, contrary to expectations, they do not, the mistake will be the engineers', not because too little attention has been paid to the environment.'

13. The precautionary principle has been a leading device in international environmental law since the UN Rio Conference on Environment and Development in 1992. The principle demands that states take regulatory action even in the absence of incontrovertible scientific evidence of environmental degradation.

14. The Norwegian discourse on oil and gas production in the Barents Sea is very different. There environmental NGOs have dominated public debate with precautionary arguments – although they did not succeed in halting the offshore gas production at the Snow White field, which opened in 2007. See Jensen (2007) for an overview of the Norwegian discourse.

15. Reference to the country's vast size is a very common justification in Russia for many of its problems. 'You know, Russia is an enormous country...', many start their explanation of why it is so difficult to govern Russia.

16. Colloquial form of *chto* ('what') or *zachem* ('why').

17. Colloquial form of *otsyuda* ('from here').

18. While the interviews were being recorded, workers were constructing houses on a private estate on the outskirts of Murmansk with a dedicated security service and infrastructure.

19. Dima uses the word *narod*, that is, 'the people'. Ries (1997, p. 27) calls this word 'the key "key word" ' of Russian talk. 'There was a certain Russian word which I could bring myself to pronounce only with difficulty in my conversations with friends and informants. This was odd, as the word was one of the most common in Russian talk, a key word, important and useful. But I always felt sheepish trying to use this word; it was like borrowing someone else's slang, or, more accurately, like saying someone else's prayer. The word was *narod*, people, populace, folk. In Russian, the word *narod* is employed in a variety of ways; it can mean "people" as connoting "the citizens of a nation"; "ethnic group", as in "the Soviet Union is made up of many different peoples"; and simply "people" as in "there are many people here" ("it's crowded"). But its most significant usage, perhaps its most common – yet often most sacred – use is to mean "the Russian people". While it can be modified as *"russkii narod"*, the *"russkii"* is not really necessary in most contexts. To say *"narod"* is to pronounce a metaphor; *narod* in this usage is a word which refers not to any literal demographic entity as much as to a mythical conceptual one, with a wide range of implications and metaphoric ramifications' (ibid., pp. 27–8).

20. Cf. the statement of former prime minister Viktor Chernomyrdin cited in the epigraph at the beginning of this chapter.

21. I sometimes receive chain emails depicting Russian absurdity. One example, a selection of absurd photos titled 'Russia as it is' (*Rossia kak ona est'*) can be found at http://www.wrecker.newmail.ru/www/russia.htm. It shows a door fitted into a wall with a drop of about two feet to floor level, a couple of new windows fitted askew the original framing (and a sign saying that the building houses Russian building authorities!), bricked-up windows with the pane still in place, outside steps leading to a window instead of a door, somebody sunbathing on what looks like a combination of beach and rubbish tip, a peasant who has hitched his wife to the plough like a draught animal, policemen drinking beer on duty and all kinds of crazy improvisations for getting things done (see discussion in Chapter 4). I can imagine many Russians smiling proudly (see discussion below) at these pictures, 'yeah, that's our Russia!'.

22. Even Russian environmentalists embrace this view. An official at the Murmansk office of the Norwegian environmental group Bellona once told me about his first experience with the organization: 'When they first came to Murmansk in 1991–92, with offensive slogans on large banners displayed on their ship, as a Russian citizen I experienced this extremely offensive. It was such 'maximization' (*maksimalizm*).' A regional government official in Murmansk said during an interview on the joint Russian–Norwegian scientific expeditions to the Barents and Kara Seas to investigate radiation levels around dumped nuclear waste sites, 'The project was necessary for the Norwegians. Our experts knew that the ocean was clean, that the sites had been carefully selected for dumping, and that the surrounding ocean area was monitored. But that was not enough for the Norwegians.'

6 Narrative, Identity and International Relations

1. A young professor at one of the universities in Murmansk recently spoke to me of the Nordic countries' obvious territorial ambitions in north-western Russia: 'Norway has behaved very wisely to secure its long-term interests in the Kola Peninsula. You have occupied all the important positions in Murmansk [referring to the political partnerships in various functional fields established at Norwegian initiative], so when the Russian Federation falls apart in thirty years' time – yes, I am convinced it will happen within thirty years – you can quietly add the Kola Peninsula to the Norwegian territory.' See reference in Chapter 2 to Russian perceptions that 'a network of international organizations and agreements has spun a web around an extremely weakened Russia [in the Arctic]' (Agranat, 1998, p. 278), and that 'Western entrepreneurs [...] are descending on Siberia in search of cheaper timber, gas, oil, and minerals' (Diment, 1993, p. 10). Browning (2003, p. 62) speaks about 'the suspicions that some Russians have that the regional co-operation promoted by the West and accompanied by the rhetoric of globalisation, debordering and overlapping spaces, is little more than a surreptitious attempt to unsettle the Russian Federation's territorial integrity once and for all.'

2. Whether this limits the political options is another question, beyond the scope of this book.

3. I repeat my methodological remark from Chapter 1: I do not pretend to say anything about what goes on in people's heads. When I write someone *thinks* this or that, it is only to avoid writing *he or she says that he or she thinks* this or that too often.

4. Ringmar (1996, p. 71) speaks of the usefulness of circling in the key metaphors used in a society: 'Perhaps we could image gathering all the reverberations which a certain society attaches to its words, and in this way to compile enormous lists of all possible metaphors and all their potential uses. Such lists would constitute a dictionary which tells us, not what things "are", but instead what things *may mean* to a certain set of people in a certain time and place. Perhaps we could talk about the total collection of all such meanings as the "culture" of a particular society.' See also Swidler (2001) for a discussion of talk, culture and action.

5. These labels are shorthand for more elaborate accounts of events and actions, which constitute real narratives (see Chapter 1). For instance, 'the good life in the north' can comprise stories of how people moved to the north because experts were needed there and salaries high, how they spent their time in the north acquiring even more qualifications since there was little else to do, and the like. 'The good life in the West' comprises stories of how Scandinavians do not have to labour, but relax while the state supports them, or while technology or servants (or Russians) do the job for them.

6. The picture is not quite clear, though, as my interviewees also talk about Scandinavians as naïve.

7. There are a few alternative voices in my interview material. We remember Elena and Nikolay who in Chapter 3 said northerners might not be better than southerners after all; 'if they took away all the perks we northerners enjoy, and cut off our [heating oil], you'd soon see how kind and honest we

are.' They also warn northerners to be careful about becoming too cocky, like Muscovites.

8. There is an overweight in my interview sample of people with personal experience of working with Scandinavians. A randomized sample would almost certainly have included a larger ratio of people without such experience.

9. Needless to say, not all north-west Russians feel like this; this conclusion summarizes the general trend in my interview sample. I know people from Murmansk – most of them now living abroad – who *do* think it would be worth the price to reform Russia as a Western-style liberal democracy, and who do *not* miss Russian unpredictability, inventiveness and 'fun'.

10. It is generally assumed by many qualitatively oriented social scientists that people express different opinions in different contexts. In his introduction to ethnographic research in IR studies, Gusterson (2008, p. 105) writes, 'Researchers who subscribe to more positivist understandings of the world than I do assume that research subjects have stable "values," "preferences," "beliefs," "ideologies," or "cultures" and that it is the researcher's job to find out what they are as clearly as possible [...]. But I soon noticed that subjects I interviewed more than once might contradict themselves in interesting ways, or that some interviewees presented themselves quite differently to journalists and to me. Positivists would see such fluctuations as "noise" to be eliminated in order to ascertain what the informant "really" thinks. I came, instead, to see these instabilities of discourse as themselves part of informants' cultural identities.'

11. Yes, there is a contradiction here. However, she may dislike Norwegian schools, but approve of the more general insight Russian students get about life in Norway while attending them.

12. He was named Commander of the Royal Norwegian Order of Merit in September 2007 for work to promote good relations between Norway and Russia.

13. *Polyarnaya Pravda*, 23 September 1998 (my translation). See Hønneland and Jørgensen (1999, pp. 113–16) for a further discussion of these events.

14. People use familiar ways of talking even if what they say does not correspond to the observed reality; see, for instance, Gergen (2001, pp. 254–5).

15. Again, I have only interviewed Russians for this investigation, but use my background as Norwegian myself to at least give a preliminary sketch of how northerners are presented on the western side of the border.

16. This picture is presented by the media and followed up through political action in the form of various support programmes for Russia.

17. See Browning's (2003) discussion, referred in Chapter 2, of how the West since the end of the Cold War has taken the role of a guide and teacher of wisdom to Russia, and how this has served to re-inscribe Russia's difference from the West in negative terms.

References

P. Aalto, S. Dalby and V. Harle (2003) 'The Critical Geopolitics of Northern Europe: Identity Politics Unlimited', *Geopolitics*, 8, 1–19.

P. Aalto, H. Blakkisrud and H. Smith (eds) (2008) *The New Northern Dimension of the European Neighbourhood* (Brussels: Centre for European Policy Studies).

G. A. Agranat (1998) 'The Russian North at a Dangerous Crossroads', *Polar Geography*, 22, 268–82.

B. Anderson (1983) *Imagined Communities: Reflections on the Origin and Spread of Nationalism* (London: Verso).

H. Armbruster and U. H. Meinhof (2002) 'Working Identities: Key Narratives in a Former Border Region in Germany' in U. H. Meinhof (ed.) *Living (with) Borders: Identity Discourses on East–West Borders in Europe* (Aldershot and Burlington, VT: Ashgate Publishing), pp. 15–32.

E. Arutiunova (2008) 'Russian Identity as Perceived by College Students in Moscow', *Russian Education and Society*, 50, 53–70.

K. Åtland (2008) 'Mikhail Gorbachev, the Murmansk Initiative, and the Desecuritization of Interstate Relations in the Arctic', *Cooperation and Conflict*, 43, 289–311.

K. Åtland (2009) 'Russia's Northern Fleet and the Oil Industry – Rivals or Partners? Petroleum, Security, and Civil–Military Relations in the Post-Cold War European Arctic', *Armed Forces and Society*, 35, 262–84.

S. Benhabib (1999) 'Sexual Difference and Collective Identities: The New Global Constellation', *Signs*, 24, 335–61.

R. Bergman and A. Baklanov (1998) *Radioactive Sources of Main Radiological Concern* (Stockholm: Swedish Council for Planning and Coordination of Research/Swedish Defence Research Establishment).

H. Blakkisrud and G. Hønneland (2001) 'Introduction' in G. Hønneland and H. Blakkisrud (eds) *Centre–Periphery Relations in Russia: The Case of the Northwestern Regions* (Aldershot and Burlington, VT: Ashgate Publishing).

H. Blakkisrud and G. Hønneland (2006a) 'The Russian North – An Introduction' in H. Blakkisrud and G. Hønneland (eds) *Tackling Space: Federal Politics and the Russian North* (Lanham, MD and Oxford: University Press of America), pp. 1–24.

H. Blakkisrud and G. Hønneland (eds) (2006b) *Tackling Space: Federal Politics and the Russian North* (Lanham, MD and Oxford: University Press of America).

W. Bloom (1990) *Personal Identity, National Identity and International Relations* (Cambridge and New York: Cambridge University Press).

P-A. Bodin (2006) *Ryssland och Europa: En kulturhistorisk studie* (Stockholm: Natur och kultur).

O. Boele (1996) *The North in Russian Romantic Literature* (Amsterdam and Atlanta, GA: Rodopi).

S. Boym (1994) *Common Places: Mythologies of Everyday Life in Russia* (Cambridge, MA and London: Harvard University Press).

G. Brock (1998) 'Public Finance in the ZATO Archipelago', *Europe–Asia Studies*, 50, 1065–81.

G. Brock (2000), 'The ZATO Archipelago Revisited: Is the Federal Government Losing its Grip?', *Europe–Asia Studies*, 52, 1349–60.

C. S. Browning (2003) 'The Region-Building Approach Revisited: The Continued Othering of Russia in Discourses of Region-Building in the European North', *Geopolitics*, 8, 45–71.

E. Brunet-Jailly (ed.) (2007) *Borderlands: Comparing Border Security in North America and Europe* (Ottawa: University of Ottawa Press).

B. Brunstad, E. Magnus, P. Swanson, G. Hønneland and I. Øverland (2004) *Big Oil Playground, Russian Bear Preserve or European Periphery? The Russian Barents Sea Region towards 2015* (Delft: Eburon Academic Publishers).

D. Cameron (2001) *Working with Spoken Discourse* (Thousand Oaks, CA and London: SAGE Publications).

B. Czarniawska (2004) *Narratives in Social Science Research* (London and Thousand Oaks, CA: SAGE Publications).

S. F. Cohen (2000) *Failed Crusade: America and the Tragedy of Post-Communist Russia* (New York and London: W.W. Norton and Company).

A. de Fina, D. Schiffrin and M. Bamberg (2006a) 'Introduction' in A. de Fina, D. Schiffrin and M. Bamberg (eds) *Discourse and Identity* (Cambridge and New York: Cambridge University Press), pp. 1–23.

A. de Fina, D. Schiffrin and M. Bamberg (eds) (2006b) *Discourse and Identity* (Cambridge and New York: Cambridge University Press).

G. Diment (1993) 'Introduction: Siberia as Literature' in G. Diment and Y. Slezkine (eds) *Between Heaven and Hell: The Myth of Siberia in Russian Culture* (New York: St. Martin's Press), pp. 7–10.

G. Diment and Y. Slezkine (eds) (1993) *Between Heaven and Hell: The Myth of Siberia in Russian Culture* (New York: St. Martin's Press).

H. Eskelinen, I. Liikanen and J. Oksa (eds) (1999) *Curtains of Iron and Gold: Reconstructing Borders and Scales of Interaction* (Aldershot and Burlington, VT: Ashgate Publishing).

O. Figes (2002) *Natasha's Dance: A Cultural History of Russia* (London and New York: Allen Lane).

S. Franklin (2004) 'Russia in Time' in S. Franklin and E. Widdis (eds) *National Identity in Russian Culture: An Introduction* (Cambridge and New York: Cambridge University Press), pp. 11–29.

S. Franklin and E. Widdis (eds) (2004a) *National Identity in Russian Culture: An Introduction* (Cambridge and New York: Cambridge University Press).

S. Franklin and E. Widdis (2004b) 'All the Russias ... ?' in S. Franklin and E. Widdis (eds) *National Identity in Russian Culture: An Introduction* (Cambridge and New York: Cambridge University Press), pp. 1–8.

K. Gergen (2001), 'Self-Narration in Social Life' in M. Wetherell, S. Taylor and S. J. Yates (eds) *Discourse Theory and Practice: A Reader* (Thousand Oaks, CA and London: SAGE Publications), pp. 247–60.

J. R. Gibson (1993) 'Paradoxical Perceptions of Siberia: Patrician and Plebeian Images up to the Mid-1880s' in G. Diment and Y. Slezkine (eds) *Between Heaven and Hell: The Myth of Siberia in Russian Culture* (New York: St. Martin's Press), pp. 67–93.

P. M. Goff and K. C. Dunn (2004a) 'Introduction: In Defence of Identity' in P. M. Goff and K. C. Dunn (eds) *Identity and Global Politics: Empirical and Theoretical Elaborations* (New York and Basingstoke: Palgrave Macmillan), pp. 1–8.

P. M. Goff and K. C. Dunn (eds) (2004b) *Identity and Global Politics: Empirical and Theoretical Elaborations* (New York and Basingstoke: Palgrave Macmillan).

P. M. Goff and K. C. Dunn (2004c) 'Conclusion: Revisiting the Four Dimensions of Identity' in P. M. Goff and K. C. Dunn (eds) *Identity and Global Politics: Empirical and Theoretical Elaborations* (New York and Basingstoke: Palgrave Macmillan), pp. 237–47.

F. Griffiths (1990) *Arctic and North in the Russian Identity* (Toronto: Centre for Russian and East European Studies, University of Toronto).

H. Gusterson (2008) 'Ethnographic Research' in A. Klotz and D. Prakash (eds) *Qualitative Methods in International Relations: A Pluralist Guide* (Basingstoke and New York: Palgrave Macmillan), pp. 93–113.

E. Hellberg-Hirn (1998) *Soil and Soul: The Symbolic World of Russianness* (Aldershot and Brookfield, VT: Ashgate Publishing).

E. Hellberg-Hirn (1999) 'Ambivalent Space: Expressions of Russian Identity' in J. Smith (ed.) *Beyond the Limits: The Concept of Space in Russian History and Culture* (Helsinki: Finnish Historical Society), pp. 49–69.

G. H. Herb and D. H. Kaplan (eds) (1999) *Nested Identities: Nationalism, Territory, and Scale* (Lanham, MD and Oxford: Rowman & Littlefield Publishers).

M. A. Hogg and D. Abrams (1988) *Social Identifications: A Social Psychology of Intergroup Relations and Group Processes* (London and New York: Routledge).

G. Hønneland (1995) 'Northerners: Common Identity or Worlds Apart?' in M. Dahlström, H. Eskelinen and U. Wiberg (eds) *The East–West Interface in the European North* (Uppsala: Nordisk Samhällsgeografisk Tidskrift), pp. 29–44.

G. Hønneland (1996) 'Identitet og funksjonalitet i Barentsregionen', *Internasjonal Politikk*, 54, 3–32.

G. Hønneland (1998) 'Identity Formation in the Barents Euro-Arctic Region', *Cooperation and Conflict*, 33, 277–97.

G. Hønneland (1999) 'Orders, Borders and Identities in the New European North' in L. Hedegaard and B. Lindström (eds) *The NEBI Yearbook 1999: North European and Baltic Sea Integration* (Berlin: Springer), pp. 333–47.

G. Hønneland (2000) *Coercive and Discursive Compliance Mechanisms in the Management of Natural Resources: A Case Study from the Barents Sea Fisheries* (Dordrecht and Boston, MA: Springer).

G. Hønneland (2003) *Russia and the West: Environmental Co-operation and Conflict* (London and New York: Routledge).

G. Hønneland (2004a) *Russian Fisheries Management: The Precautionary Approach in Theory and Practice* (Leiden and Boston, MA: Martinus Nijhoff Publishers/ Brill Academic Publishers).

G. Hønneland (2004b) 'Fish Discourse: Norway, Russia and the Northeast Arctic Cod', *Human Organization*, 63, 68–77.

G. Hønneland (2005) *Barentsbrytninger: Norsk nordområdepolitikk etter den kalde krigen* (Kristiansand: Høyskoleforlaget).

G. Hønneland (2006) *Kvotekamp og kyststatssolidaritet: Norsk-russisk fiskeriforvaltning gjennom 30 år* (Bergen: Fagbokforlaget).

G. Hønneland and H. Blakkisrud (eds) (2001) *Centre–Periphery Relations in Russia: The Case of the Northwestern Regions* (Aldershot and Burlington, VT: Ashgate Publishing).

G. Hønneland and A-K. Jørgensen (1998) 'Closed Cities on the Kola Peninsula: From Autonomy to Integration?', *Polar Geography*, 22, 231–48.

G. Hønneland and A-K. Jørgensen (1999) *Integration vs. Autonomy: Civil–Military Relations on the Kola Peninsula* (Aldershot and Brookfield, VT: Ashgate Publishing).

G. Hønneland and A-K. Jørgensen (2002) *Vårt bilde av russerne: 25 debattinnlegg om samarbeidet i nord* (Kristiansand: Høyskoleforlaget).

G. Hønneland and A-K. Jørgensen (2003) *Implementing International Environmental Agreements in Russia* (Manchester and New York: Manchester University Press).

G. Hønneland and J. H. Jørgensen (2005) 'Federal Environmental Governance and the Russian North', *Polar Geography*, 29, 27–42.

G. Hønneland, J. H. Jørgensen and A. Moe (2007) 'Miljøpersepsjoner i Nordvest-Russland: Problemoppfatninger knyttet til petroleumsutbygging i Barentshavet', *Internasjonal Politikk*, 65, 7–22.

G. Hønneland and A. Moe (2000) *Evaluation of the Norwegian Plan of Action for Nuclear Safety: Priorities, Organisation, Implementation*, Evaluation Report 7/2000 (Oslo: the Norwegian Ministry of Foreign Affairs).

G. Hønneland and L. Rowe (2004) *Health as International Politics: Combating Communicable Diseases in the Baltic Sea Region* (Aldershot and Burlington, VT: Ashgate Publishing).

G. Hønneland and L. Rowe (2008) *Fra svarte skyer til helleristninger: Norsk-russisk miljøvernsamarbeid gjennom 20 år* (Trondheim: Tapir akademisk forlag).

H. van Houtum, O. Kramsch and W. Zierhofer (2005) 'Prologue' in H. van Houtum, O. Kramsch and W. Zierhofer (eds) *B/ordering Space* (Aldershot and Burlington, VT: Ashgate Publishing), pp. 1–13.

L. C. Jensen (2007) 'Petroleum Discourse in the European Arctic: The Norwegian Case', *Polar Record*, 43, 247–54.

P. Joenniemi (ed.) (1993) *Cooperation in the Baltic Sea Region* (London and New York: Taylor & Francis).

P. Joenniemi (2008) 'Introduction by Guest Editor: Russia's Narrative Resources', *Journal of International Relations and Development*, 11, 121–7.

J. Johnson, M. Stepaniants and B. Forest (eds) (2005) *Religion and Identity in Russia: The Revival of Orthodoxy and Islam* (Aldershot and Burlington, VT: Ashgate Publishing).

A-K. Jørgensen (2001) 'The Military Sector: Federal Responsibility – Regional Concern' in G. Hønneland and H. Blakkisrud (eds) *Centre–Periphery Relations in Russia: The Case of the Northwestern Regions* (Aldershot and Burlington, VT: Ashgate Publishing).

C. Kelly (2004) '*Byt*: Identity and Everyday Life' in S. Franklin and E. Widdis (eds) *National Identity in Russian Culture: An Introduction* (Cambridge and New York: Cambridge University Press), pp. 149–67.

E. C. H. Keskitalo (2003) *Negotiating the Arctic: The Construction of an International Region* (London and New York: Routledge).

A. Klotz and D. Prakash (eds) (2008) *Qualitative Methods in International Relations: A Pluralist Guide* (Basingstoke and New York: Palgrave Macmillan).

V. Kolossov (2005) 'Border Studies: Changing Perspectives and Theoretical Approaches', *Geopolitics*, 10, 606–32.

V. Konrad and H. N. Nicol (2008) *Beyond Walls: Re-inventing the Canada–United States Borderlands* (Aldershot and Burlington, VT: Ashgate Publishing).

J. Krause and N. Renwick (eds) (1996) *Identities in International Relations* (Basingstoke and New York: Macmillan Press).

R. R. Krebs and P. T. Jackson (2007) 'Twisting Tongues and Twisting Arms: The Power of Political Rhetoric', *European Journal of International Relations*, 13, 35–66.

S. Kvale (1996) *InterViews: An Introduction to Qualitative Research Interviewing* (Thousand Oaks, CA and London: SAGE Publications).

Y. Lapid (1996) 'Culture's Ship: Returns and Departures in International Relations Theory' in Y. Lapid and F. Kratochwil (eds) *The Return of Culture and Identity in IR Theory* (Boulder, CO and London: Lynne Rienner Publishers), pp. 3–20.

Y. Lapid and F. Kratochwil (eds) (1996) *The Return of Culture and Identity in IR Theory* (Boulder, CO and London: Lynne Rienner Publishers).

B. Latour (1993) *La Clef de Berlin et Autres Leçons d'un Amateur de Sciences* (Paris: La Decouverte).

M. Lehti and D. J. Smith (eds) (2003) *Post-Cold War Identity Politics: Northern and Baltic Experiences* (London and Portland, OR: Frank Cass Publishers).

D. Likhachev (1991) *Reflections on Russia* (Boulder, CO: Westview Press).

V. Losskiy (1972) 'Ocherk misticheskogo bogosloviya Vostochnoy Tserkvi', *Bogoslovskie trudy*, 8, 7–128.

J. G. March and J. P. Olsen (1989) *Rediscovering Institutions: The Organizational Basis of Politics* (New York: The Free Press).

D. P. McAdams (1997) *The Stories We Live By: Personal Myths and the Making of the Self* (New York and London: The Guildford Press).

J. McCannon (1998) *Red Arctic: Polar Exploration and the Myth of the North in the Soviet Union 1932–1939* (New York and Oxford: Oxford University Press).

L. McKinsey and V. Konrad (1989) *Borderlands Reflections: The United States and Canada* (Orono, Maine: University of Maine Press).

S. Medvedev (1999) 'A General Theory of Russian Space: A Gay Science and a Rigorous Science' in J. Smith (ed.) *Beyond the Limits: The Concept of Space in Russian History and Culture* (Helsinki: Finnish Historical Society), pp. 15–48.

S. Medvedev (2001) '[the_blank_space] Glenn Gould, Finland, Russia and the North', *International Politics*, 38, 91–102.

U. H. Meinhof (ed.) (2002) *Living (with) Borders: Identity Discourses on East–West Borders in Europe* (Aldershot and Burlington, VT: Ashgate Publishing).

U. H. Meinhof, H. Armbruster and C. Rollo (2002) 'Identity Discourse on East–West Borders in Europe: An Introduction' in U. H. Meinhof (ed.) *Living (with) Borders: Identity Discourses on East–West Borders in Europe* (Aldershot and Burlington, VT: Ashgate Publishing), pp. 1–14.

A. Moe (2006) 'Sjtokman-beslutningen: Forklaringer og implikasjoner', *Nordisk Østforum*, 20, 389–403.

M. Müller (2008) 'Situating Identities: Enacting and Studying Europe at a Russian Elite University', *Millennium: Journal of International Studies*, 37, 3–25.

O. Nakken (1998) 'Past, Present and Future Exploitation and Management of Marine Resources in the Barents Sea and Adjacent Areas', *Fisheries Research*, 37, 25–35.

I. B. Neumann (1992) 'Identity and Security', *Journal of Peace Research*, 29, 221–6.

I. B. Neumann (1994) 'A Region-Building Approach to Northern Europe', *Review of International Studies*, 20, 53–74.

I. B. Neumann (1996) *Russia and the Idea of Europe: A Study in Identity and International Relations* (London and New York: Routledge).

Norwegian Barents Secretariat (2009) *Barents Monitoring Murmansk Oblast 2008: The Social-Economic Development of Murmansk Oblast in 2008* (Kirkenes: Norwegian Barents Secretariat).

G. Osherenko and O. R. Young (1989) *The Age of the Arctic: Hot Conflicts and Cold Realities* (Cambridge and New York: Cambridge University Press).

I. Øverland (2008) 'Natural Gas Projects in the Russian North: Implications for Northern European Cooperation' in P. Aalto, H. Blakkisrud and H. Smith (eds) *The New Northern Dimension of the European Neighbourhood* (Brussels: Centre for European Policy Studies), pp. 131–44.

A. Paasi (1996) *Territories, Boundaries and Consciousness: The Changing Geographies of the Finnish–Russian Border* (Chichester and New York: John Wiley & Sons).

A. Paasi (2003) 'Region and Place: Regional Identity in Question', *Progress in Human Geography*, 27, 475–85.

A. Paasi (2005) 'Generations and the "Development" of Border Studies', *Geopolitics*, 10, 663–71.

V. Pavlakovich-Kochi, B. J. Morehouse and D. Wastl-Walter (eds) (2004) *Challenged Borderlands: Transcending Political and Cultural Boundaries* (Aldershot and Burlington, VT: Ashgate Publishing).

B. Petersson (2001) *National Self-Images and Regional Identities in Russia* (Aldershot and Burlington, VT: Ashgate Publishing).

B. Petersson and E. Clark (eds) (2003) *Identity Dynamics and the Construction of Boundaries* (Lund: Nordic Academic Press).

V. Pouliot (2008) 'The Logic of Practicality: A Theory of Practice of Security Communities', *International Organization*, 62, 257–88.

P. R. Pryde (1991) *Environmental Management in the Soviet Union* (Cambridge and New York: Cambridge University Press).

I. Razumova (2007) 'Sotsialisticheskiy gorod v pamyati zhiteley' in N. Baschmakoff, P. Fryer and M. Ristolainen (eds) *Texts and Communities: Soviet and Post-Soviet Life in Discourse and Practice*, Aleksanteri Series 4/2007 (Helsinki: Aleksanteri Institute), pp. 145–58.

N. Riasanovsky (2005) *Russian Identities: A Historical Survey* (Oxford and New York: Oxford University Press).

N. Ries (1997) *Russian Talk: Culture and Conversation during Perestroika* (Ithaca, NY and London: Cornell University Press).

E. Ringmar (1996) *Identity, Interest and Action: A Cultural Explanation of Sweden's Intervention in the Thirty Years War* (Cambridge and New York: Cambridge University Press).

L. Rowe (2007) 'Den russiske pendelen svinger', *Aftenposten*, 24 May 2007.

L. Rowe and G. Hønneland (2007a) *Russlandsbilder: Nye debattinnlegg om naboskap i nordområdene* (Bergen: Fagbokforlaget).

L. Rowe and G. Hønneland (2007b) 'Communicable Disease Control' in O. S. Stokke and G. Hønneland (eds) *International Cooperation and Arctic Governance: Regime Effectiveness and Northern Region Building* (London and New York: Routledge), pp. 50–77.

R. H. Rowland (1996) 'Russia's Secret Cities', *Post-Soviet Geography and Economics*, 37, 426–62.

H. J. Rubin and I. S. Rubin (2005) *Qualitative Interviewing: The Art of Hearing Data* (Thousand Oaks, CA and London: SAGE Publications).

S. Sawhill (2000) 'Cleaning-up the Arctic's Cold War Legacy: Nuclear Waste and Arctic Military Environmental Cooperation', *Cooperation and Conflict*, 35, 5–36.

D. Silverman (2001) *Interpreting Qualitative Data: Methods for Analysing Talk, Text and Interaction* (Thousand Oaks, CA and London: SAGE Publications).

Y. Slezkine (1993) 'Introduction: Siberia as History' in G. Diment and Y. Slezkine (eds) *Between Heaven and Hell: The Myth of Siberia in Russian Culture* (New York: St. Martin's Press), pp. 1–6.

J. Smith (1999) 'Introduction' in J. Smith (ed.) *Beyond the Limits: The Concept of Space in Russian History and Culture* (Helsinki: Finnish Historical Society), pp. 7–14.

M. R. Somers (1994) 'The Narrative Constitution of Identity: A Relational and Network Approach', *Theory and Society*, 23, 605–49.

O. S. Stokke (2001) 'Managing Fisheries in the Barents Sea Loophole: Interplay with the UN Fish Stocks Agreement', *Ocean Development and International Law*, 32, 241–62.

O. S. Stokke, L. G. Anderson and N. Mirovitskaya (1999) 'The Barents Sea Fisheries' in O. R. Young (ed.) *The Effectiveness of International Environmental Agreements: Causal Connections and Behavioral Mechanisms* (Cambride, MA and London: MIT Press).

O. S. Stokke and G. Hønneland (eds) (2007) *International Cooperation and Arctic Governance: Regime Effectiveness and Northern Region Building* (London and New York: Routledge).

O. S. Stokke, G. Hønneland and P. J. Schei (2007) 'Pollution and Conservation' in O. S. Stokke and G. Hønneland (eds) *International Cooperation and Arctic Governance: Regime Effectiveness and Northern Region Building* (London and New York: Routledge), pp. 78–111.

O. S. Stokke and O. Tunander (eds) (1994) *The Barents Region: Cooperation in Arctic Europe* (London and Thousand Oaks, CA: SAGE Publications).

H. Suganami (2008) 'Narrative Explanation and International Relations: Back to Basics', *Millennium: Journal of International Studies*, 37, 327–56.

A. Swidler (2001) *Talk of Love: How Culture Matters* (Chicago and London: The University of Chicago Press).

C. Taylor (1989) *Sources of the Self: The Making of Modern Identity* (Cambridge and New York: Cambridge University Press).

M. Tennberg (2000) *Arctic Environmental Cooperation: A Study in Governmentality* (Aldershot and Burlington, VT: Ashgate Publishing).

T. Todorov (1977) *The Poetics of Prose* (Oxford: Blackwell).

N. Tykkynen (2008) 'Experiences of Environmental Cooperation between the Nordic Countries and Russia: Lessons Learned and the Way Forward' in P. Aalto, H. Blakkisrud and H. Smith (eds) *The New Northern Dimension of the European Neighbourhood* (Brussels: Centre for European Policy Studies), pp. 71–90.

A. Viken, B. Granås and T. Nyseth (2008) 'Kirkenes: An Industrial Site Reinvented as a Border Town', *Acta Borealia*, 25, 22–44.

P. N. Waage (1990) *Russland er et annet sted: En kulturhistorisk bruksanvisning* (Oslo: Aventura).

D. R. Weiner (1999) *A Little Corner of Freedom: Russian Nature Protection from Stalin to Gorbachëv* (Berkeley, CA and London: University of California Press).

T. Wengraf (2001) *Qualitative Research Interviewing* (London and Thousand Oaks, CA: SAGE Publications).

A. White (2004) *Small-Town Russia: Postcommunist Livelihoods and Identities* (London and New York: RoutledgeCurzon).

E. Widdis (2004) 'Russia as Space' in S. Franklin and E. Widdis (eds) *National Identity in Russian Culture: An Introduction* (Cambridge and New York: Cambridge University Press), pp. 30–49.

M. C. Williams and I. B. Neumann (2000) 'From Alliance to Security Community: NATO, Russia, and the Power of Identity', *Millennium: Journal of International Studies*, 29, 357–87.

C. E. Ziegler (1987) *Environmental Policy in the USSR* (Amherst, MA: University of Massachusetts Press).

V. Zviglyanich (1993) *The Morphology of Russian Mentality* (Lewiston, NY: The Edwin Mellon Press).

Index